Loaded Fictions

Loaded Fictions
Social Critique in the Twentieth-Century Western

Scott Emmert

University of Idaho Press
Moscow, Idaho
1996

Copyright © The University of Idaho Press
Published by the University of Idaho Press
Moscow, Idaho 83844-1107
Printed in the United States of America

00 99 98 97 96 5 4 3 2 1

Library of Congress Cataloging-in-Publication Data

Emmert, Scott, 1962–
     Loaded fictions : social critique in the twentieth-century western
/ Scott Emmert.
          p.   cm.
     Includes bibliographical references and index.
     ISBN 0–89301–194–0 (alk. paper)
     1. Western stories—History and criticism.   2. American
fiction—20th century—History and criticsm.   3. American fiction—
West (U.S.)—History and criticism.   4. Literature and society—
West (U.S.)   5. Social problems in literature.   I. Title.
PS374.W4E44   1996
813'.087409—dc20
                                                                96–18607
                                                                CIP

C O N T E N T S

ACKNOWLEDGMENTS

Many people have contributed to this work. While the book's defects belong to me alone, I must share the credit for any of its virtues. I would like, then, to thank the following people: Professor Harry Targ of Purdue University for his comments on an early draft; Jeff Miller for the unselfish loan of a big-screen TV; Mark Emmert for his keen editorial skills; the taxpayers of Minnesota for funding excellent libraries; the staff of the University of Idaho Press for believing in the work and for greatly improving the text. I am indebted to you all.

Finally, this work is dedicated to the memory of my grandfathers who, though different in so many ways, shared a love for reading.

ONE
Introduction

WHEN, IN 1950, CRITIC Henry Nash Smith labeled the entire Western genre "near-juvenile,"[1] such a judgment may have accurately described the bulk of Western novels and films produced up to that time. Unfortunately, Smith's critical assessment of the Western has been echoed through the years, seemingly shared by other critics such as John G. Cawelti, who see Westerns as formula-driven escapism.[2] Today, however, after the release of films like *Dances With Wolves* (1990) and *Unforgiven* (1992), critics and the general public seem more willing to grant Westerns higher status— status that is derived from the genre's ability to evoke insights into contemporary problems like racism and violence.[3]

One need not look only at the most recent Westerns to discover such apparent social criticism. Even before 1950, and more so since then, there have been Western novels and films that depict complicated issues and mature themes and that do not merely pander to simple-minded readers in search of escape. An examination of twentieth-century Westerns reveals dozens of works which offer the kind of social criticism most often associated with more "literary" films and novels.

Still, it remains to be explained why much criticism of the Western, while not as harsh as Smith's, tends to trivialize the genre as a whole, even as it may take seriously some of the cultural ideologies[4] embedded in the various "formulas" of the Western novel. Cawelti, who helped legitimize the scholarly study of the Western, characterizes the genre as an audience-driven set of formulas which help readers and viewers escape the ambiguity of their everyday lives by supplying simple stories in which plot and characterization follow clear-cut, Manichaean lines: good characters versus bad characters, with good usually winning. The fact is many

Westerns can indeed be categorized along these lines, but only those novels and films which recycle established formulas to supply their plots. Since there are also a substantial number of Western novels and films which deliberately subvert these formulas, it's a mistake to lump all Westerns into the same stewpot.

Nevertheless, too often critics are tempted to read popular genres as mere "formula" fiction. Such readings ignore those works that bear enough resemblance to the conventions of the genre to be properly categorized within it, but that also attempt something new. Genre is a category which is made distinctive by virtue of its iconography—costume and setting, for example—or by its tone—seen perhaps most clearly in the Gothic or the hard-boiled detective novel. The designation "formula fiction" describes a mode of production and a predictable result. Predictable plots appear in most genres, and frequently separate genres employ the same basic plot devices—for example, the Western and the thriller, both of which often conclude with a cathartic act of violence. Confusing genre with formula blurs the distinction among genres while it refuses to grant to producers of genre fiction and film the ability to offer anything new in terms of story and theme.

Individual works within genres should not be viewed as all the same, or even as so similar that unique differences are less important than alleged universals. To view them so cheapens both criticism and the works of individual authors. The fact is that genre fiction is perhaps one of the few available vehicles left today for serious authors. Screenwriters are also frequently required to produce dramas that can be clearly categorized. In a society in which book sales and box office draw take precedence over aesthetic criteria (however subjective and nebulous those may be), writers must look to satisfy the marketplace as well as concern themselves with providing thematically rich stories. The result is authors like Sara Paretsky, who consciously created a feminist detective in her V. I. Warshawski series,[5] and Tony Hillerman, who offers rich and subtle characterizations of Native Americans in his mystery novels set on the Navajo reservation.

Some Westerns have been less formulaic and more sophisticated than many critics have imagined; moreover, certain Western novels and films deliberately alter established formulas in order to supply a social critique.

These critiques are sometimes conservative, offering a lament about ideas and modes of behavior that are being lost—and by implication, should be conserved—and sometimes more radical, presenting ideas and issues that challenge the status quo—and, by implication, call for change.

These critiques occur within six general areas: commentary on politics, repudiation of violence, presentation of a feminist vision, explosion of racial stereotypes, critical examination of a commercial culture, and critique of the intellectual paradigms upon which much of American culture is based. These categories represent, in what could be called a canon of socially conscious Westerns, the types of social critique that are most often advanced, and they are connected by a common rationale: Each represents a critique of dominant ideologies.

The first category, commentary on politics, is important in this regard because Westerns frequently offer implicit support for governing political ideologies. As critic Richard Slotkin demonstrates in *Gunfighter Nation*, Westerns often reflect ideological positions. Slotkin argues, for example, that Owen Wister's 1902 novel *The Virginian* is anti-populist in theme, supporting social Darwinism and the belief that America is best run by a ruling elite—both dominant ideas in the age of robber barons and U.S. senators not elected by popular vote.[6] In another example, Slotkin reads John Ford's film *Rio Grande* (1950) as ideologically akin to "the rationales and procedures of 'covert action' and 'secret war,' which would be typical features of American Cold War tactics in the ensuing forty years."[7] Slotkin demonstrates that as a genre Westerns have been flexible, able to adapt to ideological shifts. Therefore, it is enlightening to examine Westerns that offer critique of specific political positions and that do not merely reflect dominant ideologies.

The second and third categories, repudiation of violence and presentation of a feminist vision, are important because in their presentation of violence and their marginalization of women most Westerns reinforce prevalent ideologies; therefore, any individual work in the genre which refuses to accept violence or stereotype women deserves attention.

In addition, since over the years many Westerns have correctly been identified as reinforcing pernicious stereotypes in connection with Native Americans and as ignoring the significant place of African-Americans in the West, it is meaningful to examine Westerns that attempt to overturn racial stereotypes and present more positive portrayals of non-whites.

In chapter six my interest extends to the economic realm. Because the Western has developed mainly as a commodified popular fiction designed to sell itself to large audiences, those Westerns which critique the very commercial culture which spawned them become, in a curious way, patricidally subversive.

And finally, though the last category, critique of intellectual paradigms, is in large part stylistic, the use of parody and metafiction to satirize the Western genre becomes in essence an attempt to expose the cultural ideologies that the stereotypical Western subtly reinforces.

What Westerns within each of these categories represent, then, is a concerted effort to undermine certain ideas and values which appear without critique in the majority of Western fiction.

I employ a certain definition of "Western." In a time when critics have seen *Midnight Cowboy* (1969) as a Western,[8] read the hard-boiled detective as an extension of the alienated cowboy hero,[9] and interpreted the film trilogy *Star Wars* as an outer-space horse opera, it helps to define one's view of the genre.[10] For this study, any story written or filmed in the twentieth century which uses North American frontier settings and/or characters is considered a Western. Thus I define the genre more by its iconography than by its use of standardized plots.

Readers will undoubtedly note, however, that the last chapter violates this definition of the Western by examining certain novels and films set in the post-World War II West. This chapter demonstrates how certain themes found in tales of the Old West are updated in stories about the modern West. While not Westerns as I have defined them, these novels and films do offer social critique and reveal both how attitudes toward the Old West have changed and how they have remained surprisingly close to ideas exhibited in even the most formulaic Westerns.

To place my study in relationship with previous criticism on the Western, and to help familiarize readers with the various directions such criticism has taken, I have relied on many sources. The critical work on Western novels and films is rich and extensive, and most often critics choose to examine either Western films or novels. Many, and rightly so, argue that movie Westerns have a greater hold on the American consciousness. For that reason, particularly if they wish to generalize about the functions served by Western stories or the cultural value or harm to be found in such stories, certain critics confine their primary sources to films. Nevertheless, it is frequently possible to apply specific critical insights on the Western to both the novelistic and cinematic forms. John G. Cawelti, for example, offers formulations which can apply equally to both written and filmed Westerns.

Critical approaches to the Western have generally followed one of two directions: examinations of individual authors and works, be they novels or films; and attempts to examine the genre as a whole and account for some kind of common thematic concern among most, if not all, Westerns. The first critical approach is more traditionally literary in that critics examine the thematic concerns of particular authors or directors. The second kind of criticism tends to be psychological or cultural in nature, as critics explore the societal conditions under which the Western is produced as well as the collective fantasies such fiction satisfies. My method, however, is a hybrid of these two approaches. While my study examines individual authors and directors and their subversion of formulas for the sake of social critique, it also shows that social critique itself has frequently been a common activity among a number of Western authors and filmmakers.

That scholarship which examines the genre as a whole can be summarized to reveal that, in such criticism, discussion of separate artists is often sacrificed for the sake of establishing generalizations which presumably apply to all Western fiction. I certainly do not wish to suggest that all of this criticism is invalid. Students of popular culture naturally wonder why well-liked novels and films are so appealing to wide numbers of people, and criticism which views the Western genre as a whole frequently seeks to answer that curiosity. For my purposes, moreover, such scholarship is valuable in delineating the formulas which may seem to dominate, although I would argue not to the point of exclusion, the Western genre.

In their examination of the Western as a whole, critics frequently try to explain the attraction of a genre which often offers, particularly in its cinematic form, a number of formulaic plots. This functional approach first identifies the formulas to be found in Westerns; then it theorizes on the various reasons for the widespread attraction to such formulaic tales. In *The Six-Gun Mystique* and *Adventure, Mystery, and Romance: Formula Stories as Art and Popular Culture*, Cawelti locates in these formulaic stories a particular psychological attraction.

Cawelti is arguably the most important critic of Western formulas. First, to be fair to him, it must be noted that he has made the connection between the Western and social critique, but only in passing and without apparent enthusiasm.[11] Mainly, however, Cawelti's criticism concerns itself with examination of Western formulas and how they work to satisfy collective psychological needs on the part of readers. In short, Cawelti sees production of Western stories as audience-driven, as authors and filmmakers try to answer the reader's or viewer's need for escapist entertainment. Indeed, he argues that escape from ambiguity and fear is the most powerful attraction of all formula fiction. Cawelti writes that consumers of popular fiction "seek escape from [their] consciousness of the ultimate insecurities and ambiguities that afflict even the most secure sort of life: death, the failure of love, [the] inability to accomplish all that [they] had hoped for."[12] Cawelti argues that formulas in fiction, like those found in so many Westerns, offer escape from ambiguity. These are essentially "safe" stories in that readers or viewers can easily recognize the conventions of the genre and can successfully predict the outcome of stories within that genre: the lawman will save the day, the detective will catch the murderer, etc. As a critical tool, there is much to be said for this general account of the widespread interest in popular narrative. The desire to escape reality on the part of readers of popular stories can lead us to fruitful examinations of the connection between literature and culture. By exploring the specific fears a certain audience may seek to avoid, it is possible to apprehend more fully the most influential ideologies of certain cultures: in other words, those ideas which support the status quo. In "escapist literature" both the social conditions which threaten the stabilizing philosophies of a particular culture as well as the dominant ideologies of that culture are often revealed.

The nineteenth-century dime novel has also been read as largely escapist in nature. In his work, *The Dime Novel Western*, Daryl Jones connects the popularity of these mass-produced and highly formulaic tales to the desire for readers to escape the harsh realities of industrial society:

"But though totally subject to these [economic and social] forces, power-less to effect any real change in his life, the common man could yet find needed diversion in popular fiction. Here, at least, there existed a world where the grim realities of everyday life did not intrude."[13] Jones notes that, although the audience for such fiction was mainly working class, "[d]ime novels provided a source of entertainment and diversion for any individual of any social class who sought relief from the anxieties of the age."[14]

The primary cause of this anxiety seems to have been the collision of the belief in progress—which continues to pervade much of American thinking—with a reality which belied such optimism. Additionally, Jones identifies relief from this anxiety as a factor in the continuing popularity of Westerns: "Altered, inverted, even parodied, the popular Western formula nonetheless survives. And it will continue to survive as long as it extends to humanity some glimmer of hope that a golden age still lies ahead."[15] Here a critic supplies a connection between an ongoing fear—that industrial and technological development robs one of personal con-trol over one's destiny—and the long-term success of a brand of for-mula fiction which assuages this fear. Once again, a set of fears which is relieved by a particular kind of narrative identifies a dominant concern which arguably possesses an entire culture.

Since the offering of escapist fantasies has been read as the most im-portant function of Westerns—Cawelti, for example, believes all popu-lar fiction must offer "temporary escape from the serious restrictions and limitations of human life"[16]—Westerns must, according to that read-ing, conform to certain recognizable patterns in order to fulfill their function. Form does follow function in this case, and—the argument runs—since the function is omnipresent, so must certain forms be. To allow the audience an escape from a complicated and uncertain world, the Western, in Cawelti's theory, must stick to a clear black and white pattern which simplifies conflict.

To describe how the formulas in Westerns work, Cawelti uses a game analogy to illustrate his notion that the Western novel or film "must have clearly opposing players" as well as "a set of rules indicating which ac-tions are legitimate and which are not."[17] Every Western plot, then, must simplify its action and characters; ambiguity must never be allowed to leak in. Cawelti notes one result of such simplification when he writes that "[i]n the case of the Western, one of the most important rules is that the hero cannot use violence without certain justifications."[18]

Some critics object to Cawelti's argument that formulaic stories like those which make up the bulk of Western fiction serve primarily psychological functions. Theorist Will Wright, for example, believes that the formulas found in Western films provide cultural myths which serve the ends of social institutions. In *Six Guns and Society: A Structural Study of the Western*, Wright contends:

> Through their stories and characters, and their uncon-
> scious, structural significance, myths [i.e., Western sto-
> ries] organize and model experience. Familiar situations
> and conflicts are presented and resolved. Human experi-
> ence is always social and cultural, and the models of
> experience offered by a myth therefore contain in their
> deepest meanings the classifications, interpretations, and
> inconsistencies that a particular society imposes on the
> individual's understanding of the world."[19]

Wright is still interested in the formulas found in Westerns, but he believes that these formulas achieve mythic status and come to serve social and cultural ends rather than purely psychological ones. Western movies, he argues, become ways in which audiences can connect with the dominant social mores—mores, he implies, which serve the status quo. To help make his case, Wright deliberately chooses only the most popular Western movies of certain eras. In this way, he seeks to strengthen the causal connection between audience appreciation as a matter of satisfaction and the social messages transmitted through these Western "myths." The popularity of these Westerns, he argues, is determined "by the presence of the expected social symbolism."[20] Though different from Cawelti's psychological explanation for the popularity of Westerns, Wright's theories are still functional in approach. That is, he addresses the audience needs that Westerns satisfy.

Another critic who examines the formulaic nature of Westerns to determine their appeal is Jane Tompkins. In *West of Everything: The Inner Life of Westerns*, Tompkins argues that Westerns function primarily by serving male fantasies. They are, she writes, "about men's fear of losing their mastery, and hence their identity, both of which the Western tirelessly reinvents."[21] For Tompkins, then, Westerns have static themes that reflect and complement a rigid view of masculinity. She asserts: "Westerns believe that reality is material, not spiritual; they are obsessed with pain and celebrate the suppression of feeling; their taciturn heroes want to dominate the land, and sometimes to merge with it completely—they are trying to get away from people and themselves."[22]

While Tompkins's view of the genre is circumscribed—she insists, for example, that there is no difference between Western novels and movies[23]—she raises intriguing critical considerations. Working within the idea that popular fictions encode and reinforce gender identities, Tompkins examines such issues as the Western's apparent love of death and the connection between the language used in Westerns and an exclusive masculine image.

Other critics, eschewing the functional approach, examine the genre as a whole to reveal how Westerns have reflected the political and social ideas of particular eras in American history. These critics include John H. Lenihan and Richard Slotkin. In *Showdown: Confronting Modern America in the Western Film*, Lenihan tries to

> demonstrate the Western's relevance to changing contemporary issues and outlooks in America since World War II. A thematic analysis . . . will clearly illustrate implications pertinent to commonly recognized topics of historical interest: the Cold War, racial equality, and the problem . . . of individual identity and freedom in an increasingly regulated but uncertain society.[24]

In his belief that Westerns can deliberately offer social commentary, Lenihan comes closest to my position. However, he treats Westerns as cultural artifacts worthy of examination by historians for their clues to the relevant social issues of a particular historical era. In this, he finds Westerns to be mainly mirrors of society, rather than advocates of social positions: "The western movie is one of the mechanisms a democratic society used to give form and meaning to its worries about its own destiny at a time when its position seemed more central and its values less secure than ever before."[25]

Like Lenihan, Richard Slotkin also takes a cultural-historical approach to Westerns to explain how stories within the genre have operated as mythic encodings of American political and cultural ideologies. Of his critical purpose, Slotkin writes: "By giving a historical account of the use and periodic revision of the symbolic language of the Myth [of the frontier] I hope to explain the broad appeal and persuasive power of a set of symbols that is apparently simple yet capable of varied and complex uses."[26]

For Slotkin, ongoing social and cultural changes feed into tales of the Old West, and these tales come to operate as myths that lend an unquestionable air to ideologies currently popular in the public arena. Such myth making can have a calcifying effect in that the themes of these mythic stories tend to be accepted as givens. Slotkin writes that "[a]lthough myths are the product of human thought and labor, their identification with venerable tradition makes them appear to be products of 'nature' rather than history—expressions of a trans-historical consciousness or of some form of 'natural law.'"[27] If the ideologies embedded in these myths are accepted as inviolable cultural truths, it is difficult to argue with the public policies supported by reference to Old West myths. For example, Slotkin argues that Ronald Reagan's supply-side economic policy was boosted by frequent references to an economic "frontier" which echoed an Old West prosperity based on self-reliance and a lack of government regulation.[28]

Like Lenihan, then, Slotkin critiques Westerns for their political and cultural messages. However, Slotkin examines Westerns in the aggregate in order to trace thematic changes which bear on an evolving social and political scene. For the most part, he argues that while Westerns reflect and adapt to changing ideological debates, they have largely failed to "envision the nation as polyglot, multicultural, and egalitarian."[29] Indeed, Slotkin calls for deliberate myth-making that will offer such a multicultural vision and that will resist the tendency of "powerful corporate and political institutions . . . [to] 'imagine the nation' *for* us."[30] Slotkin calls for a kind of proactive storytelling which will challenge America to be more inclusive and intellectually subtle. But certain writers and directors of Westerns have already told such provocative stories.

Westerns can offer, and have, something more than a reflection of dominant ideologies. In fact, it should be recognized that popular fictions in any genre can offer more than escapist entertainment and can provoke thought on relevant social issues.

Canadian author Margaret Atwood, for one, noted the potential of popular fiction to reach mass audiences with political messages. In the novel *Lady Oracle*, protagonist Joan Foster writes "Gothic Romances" in secret and imagines the influence her paperback novels could have if she used them to support the leftist ideologies her husband disseminates in a radical magazine, a magazine read only by other radicals devoted more to philosophical quibbling than to social action.[31] Though Atwood's novel is largely satirical, her point is valid: How can one influence large numbers of people except through an already popular medium?

As a popular genre, Westerns seem ideally suited to the communication of under-represented points of view. Historian Richard White acknowledges the continuing validity of Westerns in this regard when he notes that "stories we tell about the West matter. They not only reveal how we think about ourselves but also help to determine how we choose to act toward each other."[32] And Slotkin says that Westerns in particular offer a unique opportunity for advocates of social change: "Because it is so closely identified with American history, the western provides superb opportunities for artists to reexamine our past and reimagine our myths."[33]

There is significant potential for Westerns with social messages to reach audiences. While the audience for Westerns has shrunk relative to that for other popular kinds of fiction,[34] the genre itself periodically enjoys revival. Veteran Western writer Don Coldsmith, quoted in 1994, notes the enduring appeal of the genre: "I've seen the Western declared dead three times during my writing career, but it always seems to come back."[35] An article in *Publishers Weekly* attests to the most recent revival of reader interest in Westerns, noting that "almost 225 million copies of Louis L'Amour's novels have been published world wide, and as yet there are no signs of reader boredom."[36] The article also details the efforts of publishers to meet and create demand for Westerns, and quotes an editor of historical romances as saying that "[t]he vast majority of our reader mail is from people demanding more westerns."[37] The article further reports that as Westerns have become more realistic and less dependent on formulaic plots featuring white, male protagonists, publishers have seen an increase in female readers. An official with Avon books is quoted estimating that as much as 20 percent of the readership for Westerns is female.[38]

Indeed, the demographic appeal of Westerns is startlingly diverse. As quoted in Jeff Strickler's article "Why Are Westerns Popular?," Yardena Rand, a Brown University researcher who is conducting a survey on the popularity of Westerns, says she has heard from people

> *who, regardless of age, gender, race, sexual orientation, occupation and political beliefs, love movie westerns. I have heard from African Americans in Mississippi, Native Americans in Montana, Latino Americans in Texas, Asian Americans in California, as well as many whites, men and women, liberal and conservative. They represent as many diverse beliefs, lifestyles and views as you can possibly imagine, and they all love westerns for different and unique reasons.* [39]

The enduring appeal of Westerns makes the genre a productive vehicle for authors and directors who wish to explore contemporary issues in an already accepted format. In a nation continually struggling to define national goals and identities, Western stories can give voice and form to the desires of a diverse people who share an imaginative kinship with a place and time still able to speak to our personal and national values. But the genre is flexible enough that stories within it need not merely reflect prevailing cultural beliefs. Western novels and films are not condemned to simply reworking a given set of themes; rather, they can help to shape cultural faiths. The question of who Americans are as a people will in all likelihood never be resolved, but the effort to understand ourselves can be seen even in our popular fictions, especially those fictions that challenge us to confront new questions in our most crucial national debates.

TWO
The Western and Politics

WESTERNS CAN BE POLITICAL. One small but suggestive example of the connection between political ideology and tales of the Old West can be found on the Signet edition of Glendon Swarthout's *The Shootist*. At the top of its paperback cover *The Shootist* is billed as "The classic Western novel that President Ronald Reagan calls 'a treasure.'" Further, on the back cover appears a facsimile of a letter signed by Reagan which asserts that the novel is a "treasured addition to [his] library," in part because he and Swarthout "concur on the description of a Westerner."[1]

At first glance, such support may be passed off merely as clever marketing; however, it is not surprising that *The Shootist*'s plot features an aging and misunderstood gunfighter who represents the kill-or-be-killed ethics of the stereotyped Old West. Such a simplistic view is wholly in keeping with a Reaganesque vision of America's world position: Recall the cowboy President saddling up to do battle with the Evil Empire.

While that quip may seem to trivialize the connection between the formulaic Western and political ideology, the Cold War mind-set— which sees world events in terms of good Americans versus bad Communists or Middle Eastern dictators— is reflected in the standard Western plot, which features a hero winning a clear-cut victory over a menacing evil.[2] Indeed, an apt metaphor for American military intervention in foreign countries in the post-World War II era can be found in the figure of the mysterious gunfighter—a Shane for example—who rides into town, guns down the evil characters, then rides out, leaving behind the belief that civilization has been preserved.

Whether one believes that the myths and symbols of a culture have a power of their own or that they exist merely as tools employed by elites to control public opinion, one should heed Richard Slotkin when he writes:

> It is by now a commonplace that our adherence to the *"myth of the frontier"*—the conception of America as a wide-open land of unlimited opportunity for the strong, ambitious, self-reliant individual to thrust his way to the top—has blinded us to the consequences of the industrial and urban revolutions and to the need for social reform and a new concept of individual and communal welfare.[3]

The perpetuation of certain myths, then, can be seen to support the status quo in politics and society.[4]

Without suggesting a strictly causal connection between cultural myth and political practice, the extent to which the vision of the active, justice-loving cowboy (arguably the most American of symbols) has been internalized by Americans reflects the degree to which such a vision accommodates a worldview that, if nothing else, makes it easier for politicians to justify military intervention in foreign countries. In writing about the American myth in which captives are saved by noble hunters, Slotkin underscores the relationship between a worldview fed in part on cultural mythologies and the political/military practices of the Lyndon Johnson administration:

> Thus President Johnson went on to emphasize that the *[Vietnam]* war was undertaken not for worldly gain but for the rescue of the helpless and to offer a super-TVA-type development of the Mekong delta as a vision of the regeneration that might follow peace on American terms. It is clear that this widely (if never universally) persuasive invocation of myths obscured both the nature of the conflict and the character of our participation in it, with grave military and social consequences. One officer aptly (and without irony) remarked at the time of the Tet offensive in 1968, "We destroyed the city in order to save it."[5]

A cultural myth, one articulated frequently in popular fiction, becomes a justification for real violence and destruction.

In fact, the novel which is widely credited with giving birth to many of the Western's formulas has been interpreted as the "Gentlemen's [or large ranchers'] apologia"[6] for the murder committed under their auspices during the Johnson County War in 1890s Wyoming. Of Owen Wister's *The Virginian*, critic Bernard DeVoto writes that it "created Western fiction—created the cowboy story, the horse-opera novel, the conventions, the clichés, the values, and the sun god."[7] More interestingly, however, DeVoto reads *The Virginian* in political terms, as apology for the "commercial hegemony" the large ranchers held over the region.[8] As hero, the Virginian helps the ranchers maintain their economic position by helping to track down and hang Steve, a rustler who has also been the Virginian's friend. As DeVoto tells it:

> It turns out that in one part of the Old West, or Cibola, small property owners have taken the mechanisms of government away from the Gentlemen. The Gentlemen have no choice but to replace them with murder. [In the novel] Judge Henry tells Miss Wood that murder is all right, it is in accordance with the strictest principles of our republican forms and with the evolution of law in society, when it is done—or in this instance hired—by Gentlemen of a certain economic station. Miss Wood has little difficulty believing him . . . but The Hero must grapple with an inner conflict. . . . There was no getting away from the fact that Steve, the hanged baddie, had been his partner; it is a bitter thing that property must transcend not only law but friendship too. Still there is an alleviation: Steve dies game.[9]

This Western novel, which may have created a modern formula, conveys, ultimately, a message that might is right, and that the wealthy may dictate social action. Such an ideology is not hard to find in the history of American foreign policy, from the Spanish-American War to the Persian Gulf War.

Over the years, however, there have been Western novels and films which have sought to challenge readers and viewers to form a specific stance on specific contemporary political issues. Perhaps the most well-known "political" Westerns are the so-called countercultural films of the late 1960s and early 1970s. Films like *Little Big Man* (1971) and *Soldier Blue* (1970), for example, have been read as critiques of the Vietnam War. A centerpiece in each of these films is a massacre of Indians by United States Cavalry. A portrayal of the cavalry as a genocidal, colonizing force out to destroy the Native's ancient, harmonious existence was taken as a parallel to contemporary events in Vietnam.

Indeed, the Soviet newspaper *Pravda* praised *Little Big Man* for its supposedly anti-capitalist views. In July of 1971, this headline appeared in the *New York Times*: "Pravda Finds 'Little Big Man' Exposes 'Crimes of Capitalism.'" According to the article, Arthur Penn's film had been screened in Moscow, where it was lauded for revealing "'the enormous crimes against mankind that have marked the path of capitalism from the beginning to our days.'" Specifically, the article noted that *Pravda* found that "the main scene of violence in the film—when General Custer's men ravage an Indian village—reminded people of 'what was done by the Hitler barbarians and in our day is carried out by the American military in Indochina.'"[10]

Directors and writers of certain Vietnam-era Westerns also spoke publicly about the anti-war intentions of their films. Ralph Nelson, the director of *Soldier Blue*, intimated that he had based his cinematic cavalry/Cheyenne massacre on the very real My Lai slaughter.[11] And Pete Hamill, who in the screenplay for *Doc* (1971) subverted the legend of Wyatt Earp by making him a vicious thug, claimed to be attacking the violence of Vietnam. As quoted in *Past Imperfect: History According to the Movies*, Hamill asserted that in Southeast Asia, Americans "'were continuing to fight because of some peculiar notions of national macho pride. Indochina was Dodge City, and the Americans were some collective version of Wyatt Earp.'"[12]

However, significant as these films were to many Vietnam-era viewers, allusions to contemporary social and political issues had appeared in previous Westerns. Take the work of John Ford, for instance. As a filmmaker and a person, John Ford has been called everything from conservative to racist, and it is rare when his films come under discussion as offering much more than romanticized portrayals of the Old West. Critics frequently deplore Ford's themes, even as many of them praise his films' unique visual power. One recent criticism of John Ford's oeuvre calls it "a series of flag-waving, down-home, contradictory signals designed to make a very un-American message seem American."[13] The critic here is Max Westbrook and his immediate objection is with *Fort Apache* (1948). Westbrook argues that the ending of this film, which sees stalwart cavalry captain Kirby Yorke refusing to challenge the heroic status of a commanding officer who stupidly led his command into a massacre, is designed to "sell a policy of cop-out and cover-up as necessary ingredients of the American dream."[14] For Westbrook such cover-up and preoccupation with image can be seen in real-life American politics; he cites Watergate as an example.

Nevertheless, even if one accepts the predominant critical view of Ford's work, many of his films do supply suggestions, however muted and brief, of social criticism. Go back to the ending of *Fort Apache*, for example. While it is true that this ending evades the "truth" about the reckless Lieutenant Colonel Owen Thursday, the phony image it posits is obvious to anyone who has seen the entire film. Indeed, the film makes it apparent that history is frequently romanticized to sustain in the popular imagination "heroes" who in actuality were anything but "heroic." So when Yorke protects Thursday's good name, the viewers are aware of what the film has shown them: that Thursday was a glory-seeking, promotion-conscious martinet.

Curiously, Ford has shown us an act of deliberate myth-building. A similar depiction occurs in his *The Man Who Shot Liberty Valance* (1962). Here the public image of the main character is based on a deliberate lie: he did not kill Liberty Valance, yet he is credited with the act, accepts the heroic status accorded him, and reaps the reward of a successful political career. One character in this film acknowledges that many of America's cultural heroes are really fabrications when he says, "When the legend becomes fact, print the legend."[15] In both *Fort Apache* and *Liberty Valance*, then, John Ford subtly debunks certain Old West myths. Some Westerns accept these myths at face value, but Ford is aware of their untruthful basis.

While Ford does not attack these myths (indeed, he seems to claim for himself, as an artist, the responsibility to make them in the first place), by exposing the lie behind the myth he opens an avenue to a kind of social critique. Cultural observers like Slotkin believe that society is governed by the myths it embraces. Slotkin writes, "A people unaware of its myths is likely to continue living by them, though the world around that people may change and demand changes in their psychology, their worldview, their ethics, and their institutions."[16] The first step to freedom from the social constraints of a particular myth is to recognize it as a myth. John Ford's artistic choices in *Fort Apache* and *The Man Who Shot Liberty Valance* help to offer this kind of recognition. These films arguably make a tentative first step toward the postmodern notion that metanarratives—those overarching constructs such as the notion that progress is inevitable or that civilization proceeds out of struggle between good and evil—are essentially fictions.

Other Ford films also offer hints of social criticism. For example, an obvious political message bearing on Franklin Delano Roosevelt's banking reform policies can be found in *Stagecoach* (1939) which features a group of outcasts traveling through Apache country. Among them is a banker named Gatewood who has skipped town with a payroll deposited in his bank. Despite his pious plea that "what's good for the banks is good for the nation," Gatewood rails against government interference in banking, complaining that there is talk of hiring federal bank examiners.[17] Ironically, and probably obvious to many viewers of this Depression-era film, examiners are needed precisely because of men like Gatewood. A populist vision, certainly, but also a scene which implicitly supports reforms like the 1933 creation of the Federal Deposit Insurance Corporation. Ten years later, Ford's *She Wore A Yellow Ribbon* (1949) offered a pacifistic message when a cavalry officer played by John Wayne tells an Indian chief that it is up to old men to prevent war—and later the Native's horses are run off to forestall a violent confrontation. In addition, his *The Searchers* (1956) can be seen to reflect the psychological costs of racism as the John Wayne character Ethan Edwards allows hate to drive him in his relentless pursuit of Comanches who have captured his nieces. Even if the film ultimately reinforces anti-miscegenational beliefs, *The Searchers* does show, however suddenly and perhaps unrealistically, the softening of Edward's prejudices.

For the most part, however, Ford's Westerns seem conservative in that they are largely odes to a noble American past. And it may be open to debate whether Ford was a deliberately "political" filmmaker, though this does not preclude, of course, a political reading of his films.[18] Other producers of Westerns, however, saw the genre as ideally suited to political commentary. In 1943, for example, author Sinclair Lewis and playwright and filmmaker Dore Schary collaborated on a screenplay which would transport the rise and (hoped-for) fall of fascism in Europe to the American Old West. Although, according to Lewis's biographer Mark Schorer, the finished script was never produced—presumably because of MGM's "political timidity"[19]—the story did presciently end the lives of the characters who stood in for Mussolini and Hitler, "the film representative of the first hung by his boots (from stirrups, to be sure), of the second, consumed in a burning village."[20]

A movie Western that was produced and that is often considered to be overtly political is *High Noon* (1952) directed by Fred Zinnemann. It is commonplace in film studies to view this classic Western about a small-town lawman who must stand up alone against revenge-seeking killers as an "allegory on McCarthyism."[21] Critics are tempted to read *High Noon* in such political terms because both producer Stanley Kramer and screenwriter Carl Foreman were politically left-wing. Moreover, after the film was released, Foreman was blacklisted by Joseph McCarthy's House Un-American Activities Committee.

While it may never be known how many of the original viewers of *High Noon* were aware of the supposed political undertones of the film, some contemporary reviewers suggest a tantalizing connection between the film's plot and events unfolding in 1952. Bosley Crowther, for example, reviewed the film in the *New York Times* this way:

> [T]his tale of a brave and stubborn sheriff in a town full
> of do-nothings and cowards has the rhythm and roll of a
> ballad spun in pictorial terms. And, over all, it has a
> stunning comprehension of that thing we call courage in
> a man and the thorniness of being courageous in a world
> of bullies and poltroons.[22]

In this passage and in his insistence that the film is "meaningful in its implications," Crowther perhaps alludes to the political importance of *High Noon*.

Later critics are more pointed in their political analysis of the film. In its plot, *High Noon* features sheriff Will Kane (played by Gary Cooper in his second Oscar-winning performance) waiting for a showdown with three gunmen. Newly married to a Quaker woman, Kane must confront his own fears and the townsfolks' refusal to help him in his confrontation with the killers. The townspeople refuse to aid Kane, in part, because investors are thinking of building businesses in town, and gunplay in the streets is bad for business. When high noon comes, Kane faces the killers and shoots them, although he is helped by his wife who has renounced her nonviolent views. In the end, however, he scorns the adulation of the citizens who had so cravenly abandoned him. In a symbolic conclusion, Kane throws his badge into the dirt and leaves town.

It is this story line and Foreman's later comment that "[w]hat [*High Noon*] was about at the time was Hollywood and no other place but Hollywood and about what was happening in Hollywood and nothing else but that,"[23] that lead critic Terry Christian to conclude that *High Noon* is an explicit comment on "the filmmakers' abandonment of their colleagues who were under attack by HUAC [House Un-American Activities Committee]."[24]

However, at least one other critic is not so sure that *High Noon* was intended to be anything other than a well-told story. Jon Tuska believes that Foreman did not see his script as "a parable of the Cold War or a statement about social decay in the United States." Rather, Tuska insists, "[i]t was [Foreman's] objective to make a picture that narrated the events of an hour and forty minutes and which took exactly an hour and forty minutes to narrate."[25]

It is interesting that critics who believe *High Noon* is an anti-McCarthy film and those who do not cite as supporting evidence Foreman's comment that the movie was "about Hollywood." Ultimately, then, Foreman's intentions may not be clear.[26] It is clear, however, that the film was accepted as worthy of imitation. One *High Noon* knockoff, *Silver Lode* directed by Allan Dwan, has been called a Western "with a political dimension, as the frenzy of . . . a lynch mob is made to recall that of Senator McCarthy's witch hunts."[27] *High Noon* had detractors as well, notably John Wayne, who disliked the portrayal of cowardly pioneers and who starred in *Rio Bravo* (1959), a conservative answer to *High Noon*.[28]

Taken as a political film, *High Noon* yields a multifaceted analysis. One rich interpretation comes from Peter Biskind, who argues convincingly that the film "attacks both centrist models of community: the federally focused, top-down model favored by corporate liberals and the more bottom-up, populist model favored by conservatives."[29] Neither the established government (lead killer Frank Miller is released from prison by government officials) nor the town's citizens help Will Kane. In Biskind's formulation, Kane stands alone as symbol of the embittered 1950s liberal:

> *Producer Robert Warshow took producer Stanley Kramer to task for what he called* High Noon*'s 'vulgar anti-populism,' but the film was made by leftists on the receiving end of the blacklist, who felt betrayed and embattled for the same reasons conservatives felt secure and comfortable. In the fifties, many leftists felt let down by the 'people,' whom they had courted throughout the thirties and forties. Hence, for all* High Noon*'s contempt for the bourgeoisie, the lowlife (formerly the salt of the earth) . . . were little better. . . . In* High Noon *. . . Kane asks for help but doesn't get it. He must depend on himself alone if he hopes to survive. Hadleyville is a bad town, not just corrupt at the bottom or top, but through and through, from top to bottom.*[30]

Since it offers no solutions, only a thorough critique of the corruption of society, in the final analysis, *High Noon* may lose its political force. After all, what is the political ideology of the message: "We all stand alone"? Biskind admits to this diffusion of political critique when he writes that "aside from its disdain for business values, it would be difficult to tell *High Noon* apart from a right-wing film. Once stripped of its historical context, it becomes indistinguishable from, say *Dirty Harry* (1971), which also ends with a lawman throwing down his badge in disgust."[31]

While the political charge of *High Noon* may not resonate as much today, one Western novel written over forty years ago still delivers a potent political message. The novelist in this instance, rather than use his work to serve the status quo, seems to have deliberately sought to shape a specific political response on the part of his readers. Certainly, Walter Van Tilburg Clark's *The Ox-Bow Incident* is more than political propaganda; it is literature rich in psychological depth and subtle characterization.

But it is also an anti-fascist work which cleverly uses that most recognizable American icon, the cowboy, to explode America's complacency over the rise of Mussolini and Hitler. Clark's goal, however, is not just to encourage U.S. intervention to halt the spread of European fascism, but to warn Americans that fascism is as much an American phenomenon as a European one, and that is the message that carries force today.

At this point two ideas must be underscored. First, Clark deliberately chose to write in the Western genre. As he wrote nineteen years after publication of *The Ox-Bow Incident*:

> Like everyone else who has ever wanted to use western materials, especially from the past (and it seems to me we have to establish contact with the past, literally, before we can handle the present with any depth), I had repeatedly found the stereotypes, both the people and the situations, of the standard 'horse oprey' in my way. . . . So, in part, I set about writing The Ox-Bow Incident as a kind of deliberate technical exercise. It was an effort to set myself free in that western past by taking all the ingredients of the standard western (which were real enough after all) and seeing if, with a theme that concerned me, and that had more than dated and local implications, and a realistic treatment, I could bring both the people and the situations alive again.[32]

Clark used the genre to explode, from the inside out, the Western formula as well as a stereotyped view of the Old West as a place where justice reigned by virtue of the noble cowboy or lawman. By putting his reader in "contact with the past, literally" Clark de-mythologized the ideal of the Old West as a place where natural-born heroes intervened to ensure that justice would triumph over lawlessness.

Second, it must be noted that Clark knew from the outset that he was writing an anti-fascist work.[33] As he told Walter Prescott Webb:

> The book was written in 1937 and '38, when the whole world was getting increasingly worried about Hitler and the Nazis, and emotionally it stemmed from my part of this worrying. A number of the reviewers commented on the parallel when the book came out in 1940, saw it as

something approaching an allegory of the unscrupulous and brutal Nazi methods, and as a warning against the dangers of temporizing and of hoping to oppose such a force with reason, argument, and the democratic approach. They did not see, however, or at least I don't remember that any of them mentioned it (and that did scare me), although it was certainly obvious, the whole substance and surface of the story, that it was a kind of American Naziism [sic] that I was talking about. I had the parallel in mind, all right, but what I was most afraid of was not the German Nazis, or even the Bund, but that ever-present element in any society which can always be led to act the same way, to use authoritarian methods to oppose authoritarian methods.

What I wanted to say was, "It can happen here. It has happened here, in minor but sufficiently indicative ways, a great many times."[34]

In great measure, then, *The Ox-Bow Incident* explores American totalitarianism, and by setting his story in the pre-1890s West—when the frontier was still officially "open"—Clark debunks the notion of a purer past, one inhabited by a more democratic people. He does this while embracing the notion that individual conscience and action are necessary to preserve democracy.

Specifically, *The Ox-Bow Incident* is set in and near the town of Bridger's Wells, Nevada, in 1885. The story is focalized through a cowboy named Art Croft who, along with his sidekick Gil Carter, has come to town after a long winter to get drunk. The opening chapter follows a recognizable Western formula: Both men drink in the saloon, Gil more than Art; Gil wins a large sum at poker and is accused of cheating; and ultimately a fight ensues in which Gil is knocked unconscious by a bottle-wielding bartender. One can easily picture these events unfolding in a black-and-white movie.

This conventional opening serves Clark's purpose well, for by employing a plot line familiar to readers, he invites them into his novel—lulls them into thinking he will fulfill standard expectations, only to supply something radically different and disturbing. Mark Twain uses a similar tactic in *Adventures of Huckleberry Finn*. The slave Jim starts out as the stereotypical "darky," an object of ridicule. Later, of course, Twain develops Jim into a rich character, a man of depth and nobility. Twain must appeal to the stereotypes first in order to hook his readers; only then can he begin to subvert their prejudices.

Similarly, after chapter one, *The Ox-Bow Incident* develops in ways unique to Western fiction in that action—in the form of pursuit and cathartic gun play—does not supply the novel's plot. It is clear early on that the men in the saloon are uneasy over some recent cattle rustling, more so than usual because it is obvious that someone known to all must be doing the stealing. So when, at the end of chapter one, a boy rushes into the saloon to announce that rustlers have shot and killed a man named Kinkaid, the stage is set for Clark's exploration of mob psychology. Over the protests of the shopkeeper Davies, 27 men and one woman form a vigilante group to hunt down the alleged killers. Eventually this group locates three men, uses circumstantial evidence to accuse them of murder and rustling, and hangs them. However, in the end it is revealed that Kinkaid is still alive and that the three hanged men were innocent.

Among the novel's many themes, one that is central to exploring the American brand of fascism is the conflict between upholding justice as an ideal and understanding an individual's quest for power. Davies is the spokesman for justice. In his zeal to stop the vigilantes, he elevates law and justice to a pinnacle higher than any other:

> Law is more than the words that put it on the books; law
> is more than any decisions that may be made from it; law
> is more than the particular code of it stated at any one
> time or in any one place or nation; more than any man,
> lawyer or judge, sheriff or jailer, who may represent it.
> True law, the code of justice, the essence or our sensations
> of right and wrong, is the conscience of society. It has
> taken thousands of years to develop, and it is the great-
> est, the most distinguishing quality which has evolved
> with mankind. None of man's temples, none of his reli-
> gions, none of his weapons, his tools, his arts, his sciences,
> nothing else he has grown to, is so great a thing as his
> justice, his sense of justice. The true law is something in

itself; it is the spirit of the moral nature of man; it is an
existence apart, like God, and as worthy of worship as
God. If we can touch God at all, where do we touch him
save in the conscience? And what is the conscience of any
man save his little fragment of the conscience of all men
in all time?[35]

Countering Davies' idealism is the figure of Major Tetley, the driving force of the vigilantes. Tetley is a Hitler-like character[36] who represents power and self-aggrandizement for its own sake. Indeed, he joins the group wearing his Confederate officer's uniform, a neat parallel to the love of uniforms displayed by the Nazis. His son, Gerald—who is not megalomaniacal like his father—speaks of the drive for power that exists in all people, the Tetleys of the world especially:

[A]ll we use it [human intelligence] for is power. Yes
we've got them [wild animals] scared all right, all of
them, except the tame things we've taken the souls out of.
We're the cocks of the dungheap, all right; the bullies of
the globe. . . . All any of us really want any more is
power. We'd buck the pack if we dared. We don't, so we
use it; we trick it to help us in our own little killings.
We've mastered the horses and the cattle. Now we want
to master each other, make cattle of men. Kill them to
feed ourselves. The smaller the pack the more we get.[37]

Clearly, Gerald is expressing the fascists' psychology: the desire to use the collective will to gain individual power.

Art Croft, the narrator, finds himself torn between Davies' and Gerald's respective positions:

I realized that queerly, weak and bad-tempered as it was,
there had been something in the kid's raving which had
made the canyon seem to swell out and become immate-
rial until you could think the whole world, the universe,
into the half-darkness around you: millions of souls
swarming like fierce, tiny, pale stars, shining hard, wink-
ing about cores of minute, mean feelings, thoughts and
deeds. To me his idea appeared just the opposite of Davies'.
To the kid, what everybody thought was low and wicked,

*and their hanging together was a mere disguise of their
evil. To Davies, what everybody thought became, just because everybody thought it, just and fine, and to act up
to what they thought was to elevate oneself. And yet both
of them gave you the feeling of thinking outside yourself,
in a big place; the kid gave me that feeling even more, if
anything, though he was disgusting. You could feel what
he meant; you could only think what Davies meant.*[38]

What the younger Tetley describes is the anti-democratic desire for
power sanctioned by the collective will. What Davies describes is a democratic society built on belief in abstract principles. Ultimately, Art Croft
feels the former more than the latter operating in his world. Surely, Croft
must be one of the most self-reflective cowboys in the history of the Western, but his dilemma as a man divided between accepting either power
or ideas as the engine of society represents America's dilemma not only in
deciding how to confront Hitler, but also in how to interpret its own past.

For it is clear that the notion of a democratic people ensuring the
cause of justice in the American Old West, that most venerated of places
and epochs, is hollow. In the end, three innocent men are hanged. Only
five men vote not to hang the three, and Art Croft and Gil Carter are
not among them. All along Gil has told Art that they do not have to
follow the mob, but in the end they do. Despite Gil's famous line—one
that was given to Henry Fonda playing Art in the film version of the
novel—that "[h]anging is any man's business that's around,"[39] the two
cowboy protagonists do nothing to ensure that justice will triumph. The
mob mentality—which after all is precisely the basis of fascism—proves
to be too strong. The strength of ideals cannot contend with the brute
exercise of power.

Immediately after it is revealed that the hanged men were innocent,
blame is fixed on Tetley. The members of the mob search for a scapegoat
to erase their individual culpability. Art knows that such evasion is wrong,
but he keeps silent. Davies, however, underscores the novel's theme of
individual weakness:

*I've thought of all the excuses [for not acting]. I told
myself I was the emissary of peace and truth, and that I
must go as such; that I couldn't even wear the symbol of*

> *violence. [Davies has been blaming himself for not bring-*
> *ing along a gun to shoot Tetley.] I was righteous and*
> *heroic and calm and reasonable. . . . All a great cow-*
> *ardly lie. . . . All pose; empty gutless pretense. All the*
> *time the truth was I didn't take a gun because I didn't*
> *want it to come to a showdown. The weakness that was*
> *in me all the time set up my sniveling little defense. I*
> *didn't even expect to save those men. The most I hoped*
> *was that something would do it for me.*[40]

At the end of *The Ox-Bow Incident*, Clark emphasizes the need for action, both individual and national, to ensure justice. While the myth of the innately just Western hero is exploded in the novel, Clark reveals his belief that individual responsibility is the foundation of democracy and freedom, implying that as a nation which privileges such ideals, America has a responsibility to intervene to prevent fascism. Moreover, concerned about home-grown fascism—anxious about "that ever-present element in society which can always be led to act the same way, to use authoritarian methods to oppose authoritarian methods"[41]—Clark uses his novel to urge both the adherence to ideals, albeit with some skepticism, and the willingness to act on those ideals, but independent of the mob. Governments, he implies, act like the Tetleys of the world: They build collective psychologies to give base to their power. So to believe, as Davies does, that what the collective thinks is somehow automatically sacred is to play into the hands of those who would use ideals to serve their own ends. Safety from authoritarianism requires not only autonomy of action but also collective belief in the higher principle that justice is not the result of haste or hate.

It is a delicate balance between individual action and collective belief, one that is easily tipped in favor of those who would bend collective ideologies to advance their own ends. One of the more important lessons of *The Ox-Bow Incident* is that such abuses of power have happened in America, in incidents as disparate as the Salem witch trials, Southern lynch mobs, hysteria in the Sacco and Vanzetti case, and the imprisonment of Japanese-Americans in World War II. Preserving democracy, Clark demonstrates, is no easy task, either within the United States or abroad. Nor are Americans inalienably endowed with the qualities that make them natural protectors of democracy. In the figure of the passive cowboy, Clark provides a warning that freedom is not possible without eternal recognition of its fragility.

Clark's political critique can be considered both liberal and conservative. It is liberal given its urgent call to refuse the status quo of neutrality and to intervene in Europe; it is also daring in its rejection of an ideology which leads to complacency. On the other hand, *The Ox-Bow Incident* can be considered conservative in that it accepts democracy as an ideal and does not posit some other political system.

More generally, by challenging the ideological status quo, Clark enters the political arena. In fact, it could be argued that any Western novel which calls for the rethinking of old attitudes and the consideration of new ones could be considered political, if only in the sense that maintaining an open political process requires that more than one voice be heard. In that sense, then, all of the works considered on the following pages have political edge, even if some of them raise conservative responses while others are more liberal in their themes.

T H R E E
Repudiation of Violence

ONE OF THE MORE widely deplored aspects of American society is its violence, and more than one critic has made a causal link between real violence and the glamorized mayhem which appears on the nation's television and movie screens. While it is oversimplification to argue that murder and assault are perpetrated by people mainly because they have seen such violence on TV, the symbolic representation of violent acts seems to involve the satisfaction of a curious psychological need. In his study of American psychology and cultural myth, Richard Slotkin traces how real violence, that which was used by European settlers to subdue native populations and exploit natural resources, becomes transformed into an excusatory mythology embodied in such cultural icons as Daniel Boone. Slotkin argues that tales like the Indian war narrative helped to accommodate a European sensibility to the dictates of an unfamiliar and harsh environment.[1] In effect, stories of violence help to justify real violence, and the "regeneration" Slotkin writes of is the belief that somehow destruction of people and natural resources lends to the destroyer a moral and spiritual superiority. Americans were able to connect to an authentic experience because they had the power to destroy, and the exercise of that power in real life is encoded and justified in the nation's fictional representations of a whole lineage of Western heroes, from the hunter to the cowboy.

In the formulaic Western, the use of violence by the hero is usually justified because it serves higher ends. Cawelti believes that the "savage" in the Western, cast either as Indian or outlaw, is more violent than the hero.[2] By implication, the hero is justified in killing the savage in order to preserve peace in the community. In justified killing, violence becomes the vehicle not only for conflict resolution, but for protection of higher values: peace, law, and domestic harmony. Furthermore, Cawelti demonstrates that in some Westerns, violence is used to "reaffirm [the hero's] individual code," to maintain his isolation from both the savage world and the civilized milieu evolving in the town which he is usually called upon to save.[3]

Nevertheless, not all Western novels and films treat violence in the same way. In presentation, for example, Western movies can easily be seen to have become more graphic in the depiction of violence. In their earliest variety, movie Westerns featured heroes so adept with a pistol that they could bloodlessly shoot six guns out of outlaws' hands. Even when, in later films, heroes had to kill bad guys, little blood was shown whenever a character was shot, and usually one clean bullet did the job. However, in terms of body count, later Westerns seem to have taken to heart the classic Walter Brennan line from *My Darling Clementine*: "When you pull a gun, kill a man."[4] Further, beginning mostly in the 1960s, certain Western directors let the blood flow, often lingering on shots of multiple, gore-spilling bullet wounds. The most famous of these bloodier Westerns is Sam Peckinpah's *The Wild Bunch* (1969).

Graphically, then, Westerns, like films in other genres, can be said to have become more violent. Thematically, however, even the earliest Westerns implicitly condoned violence by depicting gun battles as proper ways to resolve conflicts, as long as the good guys won, of course. In fact, one plausible, if partial, explanation for the popularity of Westerns in the 1950s is that so many of them reassured Americans that we were the good guys in the Cold War. Symbolically, the characters who won showdowns represented the United States' use of force to check Communist aggression. (See Chapter Two.) Significantly, however, there were hints of uneasiness in this symbolic role. Both Shane and Will Kane must leave the communities they have violently defended. Nonetheless, despite the occasional Western hero who exhibits misgivings over the use of force, so many Westerns are built around the unequivocal righteousness of taking a dispute into a deserted street and settling it with a quick-draw that the Western as a genre is rightly labeled violent.

Still, over the years there have been Westerns which have critiqued the use of violence. Even as Westerns tended to become more graphic, thematically—and often in curious contradiction to the action—some of them attempted anti-violence messages.

For the sake of convenience, three categories of the thematic depiction of violence in Westerns can be established to demonstrate the level of the acceptance of violence in the genre. Into the first category can be placed all of the Westerns which present violence as an unambiguous way to resolve conflict. In works within this category, there is little real critique of violence because, even though the brutality perpetrated by bad characters—outlaws, cattle barons, Indians—is deplored, the use of violence by good characters is justified. In these Westerns, heroes restore order through violent acts. Often these heroes are lent moral superiority because they are forced to respond to the results of violence begun by the evil characters. Furthermore, in many Westerns there is something tacitly weak about characters who cannot act violently to protect themselves and so have to hire gunmen to act for them. This is the case in *Shane*, for example, which features the title character restoring order in a conflict between farmers and cattle ranchers. Shane protects the helpless farmers by gunning down the cattle ranchers' hired killer. However, in a typical aspect of many formulaic Westerns, the hero cannot remain in the community he has just saved: He is a "civilizing" influence that cannot be civilized, so he must ride on.[5]

Other Westerns also tend to justify violence. However "political" in its implications, the conflict in *High Noon* is resolved through a shoot-out; indeed, sheriff Will Kane's Quaker wife comes off as an unrealistic pacifist, and significantly she changes her nonviolent beliefs. In addition, most of John Wayne's Westerns have the Duke dealing brutally, albeit justifiably within the context of the plot, with outlaws and desperadoes. Even the anti-heroic Western characters Clint Eastwood has often portrayed are frequently shown to be warranted in their use of violence. In *High Plains Drifter* (1972), for example, Eastwood plays an apparitional character who takes revenge on an entire town for its citizens' cowardice in allowing his brother to be killed. In this case, a "proper" interceding act of violence would have saved the townspeople the revenge visited upon them by Eastwood's character.

Certainly, in American popular entertainment, selected Westerns are not alone in justifying violent reprisals as a response to violent aggression.

Popular novels and films, particularly of the "action" variety, frequently rely on the stale plot of an embattled hero ridding the world of evil by wiping out bad guys with superior violent skill and force. Rarely is the hero's right to use violence questioned in such films. The message is clear: In a violent world, only a more skillful purveyor of violence can keep the peace.

A second category of depiction presents a more ambiguous thematic approach to violence. In the Western novels and films which fit this category, violence becomes pure spectacle rather than a means to a supposedly noble end. In these Westerns the violence does not resolve conflict; often, in fact, it destroys all of the characters. Because, however, the violence is often graphically depicted and because the characters frequently become attracted to violence as a high-energy solution to boredom and inaction, the amount of social critique in these Westerns is open to question.

Cawelti's response to certain Westerns of the late 1960s and early 1970s illustrates the problematic nature of Westerns which feature violent anti-heroes who are far more skillful with their fists or a gun than the other characters. Cawelti believes that films, like those directed by Italian Sergio Leone, reflect ambiguity toward violence in society. These are not anti-violent films, Cawelti argues; rather, they merely attempt to elicit a new protective response to real violence:

> [T]hese films perhaps appeal as much to a sense of passivity as to violence. Their grotesque humor may well be more an invitation to laugh at our own sense of helplessness and victimization than an incitement to strike out against it. Their moral ambiguity, their rejection of clear distinctions between the hero and villain, and their grotesque horror might just as well be interpreted as an attempt to transform our sense of moral paralysis and impotence in the face of worldwide violence into mockery and bitter comedy.[6]

Clearly, Cawelti is shocked by such films, and since the moral justification of violence disappears in these more violent, anti-heroic Westerns, one's response to them is left open. Cawelti can only say that "perhaps" his formulation is the expected response. Thus, those Western novels and films which graphically depict violence and create anti-heroes offer, at best, a disturbing ambiguity. Critics and viewers must ultimately decide what the authorial stance toward violence is in these Westerns.

Two works illustrate this category well. The first is a novel, *Bloody Season*, by Loren D. Estleman. While *Bloody Season* does repudiate the belief that violence can be used to effect higher ends, to protect a personal code or set of communal values, its graphic presentation of violent acts by anti-heroic characters mutes whatever social commentary may be found in its theme. Estleman creates a violent world without heroes, and his novel often blends elements from urban crime fiction set in the later twentieth century to refashion a West in which life was indeed "nasty, brutish, and short."[7]

Estleman's novel retells the story of the gunfight at the O.K. Corral between the Earp brothers, with Doc Holliday and the Clanton gang. Estleman describes the battle, as more of a massacre and at the end of chapter one, emphasizes that the Earps and Holliday were not instantly considered heroes after the skirmish because they were all four arrested for murder. Thus Estleman challenges the notion that the Earps were well-loved lawmen who triumphed over a despicable band of outlaws to prevent a savage influence from despoiling a civilized community.[8] Indeed, there seem to be no heroes at all in *Bloody Season*, unless one counts Holliday's sometime mistress, Big Nose Kate, who is ennobled by having survived a harsh and brutal life while still maintaining some dignity. Reinforcing the brutality of the Earp brothers and Doc Holliday, Estleman presents their violence graphically, in contrast with the stereotypical Western novel or film which usually presents gunshot victims who either bleed very little or die in stylized ways. For example, in describing the wounds of the dead Frank McLaury, Estleman borrows the language and style of an autopsy report to create the kind of passage which often appears in urban crime fiction:

> *Robert Finley McLaury—Frank—had been shot twice in the abdomen and once in the head. The first ball had penetrated the small intestine and burrowed into the lumbar muscles in the arch of the back. The second had deflected off the ninth rib on the left side, separated into six fragments, and perforated the stomach, colon, and*

large and small intestines and nicked the pancreas. The
ball in the brain, after entering half an inch below the left
ear between the temporal and inferior maxillary bones of
the skull, had tunneled through both hemispheres, trans-
fixing the cavernous sinus and superior petrosal sinus,
and come to rest among the epithelial cells in the subdu-
ral space at the rear of the brain case on the right side.[9]

According to Cawelti, the sanitization of violence is a necessary feature of Westerns: "One major focus of the Western . . . is on the justification of acts of violent aggression. In other words, one of the major organizing principles of the Western is to so characterize the villains that the hero is both intellectually and emotionally justified in destroying them."[10] One way to justify violence is to sanitize it by not lingering on the effects of gunshot wounds; if the effects of violence, either physical or psychological, are not depicted, then it is easier to believe that "good" characters have acted properly in shooting "bad" characters. But Estleman portrays no heroes or "justified" killings, and his description of the various wounds of the three dead men is almost as long as his narration of the gunfight itself, thus placing emphasis on the insidious motivation behind and the horrible effects of shooting people and not on the supposed righteousness of such acts.

Neither are Estleman's characters involved in the kind of "shoot out" that Cawelti discovers in so many Westerns. In *The Six-Gun Mystique*, Cawelti tries to explain the thematic purpose of the pistol and its use: "We might say that the six-gun is that weapon which enables the hero to show the largest measure of objectivity and detachment while yet engaging in individual combat. This controlled and aesthetic mode of killing is particularly important as the supreme mark of differentiation between the hero and the savage."[11] In contrast, Estleman shows us the ugly side of gun fighting—its rapid, brutal effects. Violence, Estleman could be suggesting, has no redeemable value in art unless it is depicted as accurately as possible, for to represent in fiction an "aesthetic mode of killing" is to obscure the sinister motivations behind real violence. Put another way, Estleman cannot puncture the Earp legend unless he also refuses to sanitize his depiction of the violence the Earps used to exercise their power. If the motivation is ugly, so must the method be.

By refusing to sanitize the violence in *Bloody Season*, Estleman does make a social comment that violence cannot be used to gain moral superiority or to effect noble ends. But the graphic depiction of violence muddles this theme and makes it ambiguous. Moreover, because the violence in *Bloody Season* is presented "objectively" without authorial comment, it could just as easily be argued that Estleman has provided mere spectacle. Much depends on audience response, a slippery thing to measure. While one reader may read a detailed description of gunshot wounds as a critique of the results of violence, other readers may simply enjoy the depiction for its own sake. Because none of the characters in *Bloody Season* shows remorse for his violent acts, and because in the popular imagination the Earps have long been considered to be above reproach, the novel could be taken by readers to be simply a good action yarn. For this reason, *Bloody Season* illustrates the difficulty of both presenting violence and critiquing it. In a culture in which depictions of violence have become purely entertainment, it is difficult for authors and filmmakers to divorce the popular acceptance of fictional violence as titillation from any critique of real violence they may wish to offer.[12]

A film that illustrates the category of Western which graphically depicts violence while remaining ambiguous as to its legitimacy is Sam Peckinpah's *The Wild Bunch* (1969). Though contemporary critics of Peckinpah's film were divided on its merits,[13] most often the basic objection was over the movie's portrayal of violence in stylized, often slow-motion shots which featured blood spurting from gunshot and knife wounds. Peckinpah and star William Holden issued statements, however, that the mayhem in the film was purposefully designed to underscore the brutality of real violence.[14] Such statements notwithstanding, reading *The Wild Bunch* as a critique of violence remains problematic for many critics.

On the one hand there is the opinion of author Brian Garfield that Peckinpah and Holden's "defensive statements were [probably] dreamed up after the fact, since nothing in the story or the production of *The Wild Bunch* indicates that it was designed as an anti-violence movie."[15] On the other hand, critic Stanley J. Solomon argues that the film does critique the violence that is presented:

> *Everyone in the film has been tainted by violence—*
> *including children who appear from time to time as*

*participants, most memorably in the film's opening im-
ages, where they are shown torturing a scorpion. In the
final gunfight a child shoots Pike in the back. In
Peckinpah's view, cruelty and slaughter have pervaded
all facets of society, and an inevitable confrontation with
violence or its consequences awaits us all.*[16]

It seems, however, that Peckinpah wants it both ways in this film: He
wants to revel in what Garfield has termed "beautiful" shots of individual
violent acts, while simultaneously offering a plot in which violence re-
solves nothing in society. Because there is no reassertion of social order
through violence in *The Wild Bunch*, thematically Peckinpah can be said
to be conveying an anti-violent message, albeit one severely weakened
by his filmmaking technique.

The film's plot features a band of aging outlaws, throwbacks to a
nineteenth-century lawlessness but also a legendary code of ethics, who
rob a bank and flee to Mexico. The year is 1912; revolution and savagery
grip Mexico, so the setting is in keeping with the Western's use of territories which have yet to be "civilized." After escaping an ambush by a
group of railroad-financed mercenaries, the members of the Bunch discover that the money bags they have been carrying contain nothing but
steel washers—proof that they were set up by the railroad's bounty hunters. At this point, the five members of the gang left alive threaten to split
up, but their leader, Pike Bishop (played by Holden), holds them together. In his insistence that the band remain united by some kind of
implicit loyalty to one another, Pike reveals himself to be an old-fashioned man of honor. This sense of honor (at one point Pike and Dutch
Engstrom, played by Ernest Borgnine, exchange views on the importance of following through on one's word) elevates the Bunch as anachronisms in a century bereft of ethical codes. In one important way, then,
The Wild Bunch connects to older film Westerns in its insistence on delineating proper codes of behavior. Indeed, Garfield has written that "[i]t is
surely ironic that this most violent and bloody of all American Westerns
is also, in its curious and contradictory way, the most stubbornly moral
and moralistic of all post-Cooper Westerns."[17]

Eventually, the Bunch agrees to work for Mapache, a corrupt Mexican bandit, who hires them to rob a shipment of U.S. Army guns and

ammunition. When Mapache double-crosses the Bunch by refusing to pay them for the robbery, Pike threatens to blow up the munitions. Mapache is only temporarily defeated, however, and he seeks his revenge by holding hostage a member of the Bunch, Angel, who has shot one of Mapache's prostitutes. The remaining four members of the gang decide to rescue their comrade, and when Mapache cuts Angel's throat, a bloody battle ensues. This climatic scene features a seemingly endless carnage, often filmed in slow motion. The Bunch employs a Gattling gun to shoot Mapache's men, and each of the gang members is killed in turn—but only after receiving multiple wounds. Though bloody, many of the individual depictions of death in this scene are shot in almost loving slow motion. For that reason, it is easy to understand why so many critics have scoffed at Peckinpah's insistence that this was an anti-violence film.

Nevertheless, despite Peckinpah's apparent glee in filming gory confrontations, thematically *The Wild Bunch* could still be called anti-violent, for the violence in this film, like that which is portrayed in Estleman's *Bloody Season*, solves nothing. In the end of *The Wild Bunch*, the character Deke Thornton, a man who has been hunting the Bunch, joins with a band of guerrillas who have decided to fight to protect their villages. Though these guerrillas have noble cause, it is clearly implied that the killing in Mexico will continue; indeed, violence is seen to be begetting further violence. In this film, one in which most every character is killed, the sacrifice of human life has no value. The Bunch die only to protect their outmoded sense of honor; their sacrifice—unlike that of earlier Western heroes—cannot bring peace to a murderous milieu. Peckinpah's story certainly undercuts the notion that violence can bring about social stability, even as his camera isolates and stylizes individual acts of assault.

Clearly, *The Wild Bunch* and *Bloody Season* represent a category of problematic Westerns. Are the uses of violence truly critiqued in this kind of Western, or is a nihilistic milieu simply presented as spectacle to supply a jaded thrill? If nothing else, the various answers to these questions make these Westerns more thought provoking than some others in the genre.

A third category of the depiction of violence in Westerns offers more obvious critique of violence. In these Westerns, violence is not stylized or offered as spectacle. More important, the violence that is depicted cannot properly solve conflicts, primarily because the characters must live with the results of their violent acts. The violence affects all of the characters negatively; rather than an unambiguous solution, their complicity in violent acts becomes a moral burden that the characters must bear.

Such an approach to violence can be found in *The Ox-Bow Incident*, for the hanging is unjustified and those characters who carried it out must confront the moral implications of their actions. Additionally, from time to time certain films have questioned the use of violence to solve conflicts. *Red River* (1948) and *The Gunfighter* (1950) are two examples. In *Red River*, Dunson, played by John Wayne, rules by force; however, he is shown to be an anachronism in an evolving world through the character of Matt, a young man who prefers to rule by consensus and not as a rugged individualist violently enforcing his will.[18] *The Gunfighter* is a story about an aging gunslinger stalked by a young killer out to make his mark. Critic William K. Everson believes that while the audience "is asked to sympathize with a killer" (the older gunfighter), in *The Gunfighter* "violence, killing for the sake of 'glory,' and the taking of the law into one's own hands are heartily condemned."[19]

An anti-violence theme also shows up in later anti-Vietnam War Westerns. In films like *Soldier Blue* (1970) and *Little Big Man* (1971), the Indians are often peace-loving children of nature who are attacked by vicious white conquerors.[20]

In a lighter vein, the television series *Maverick* (1957-62) satirized violence by frequently portraying characters who use their wits rather than their shooting irons to extricate themselves from grave situations.

It must be kept in mind, however, that those Westerns which distinctly critique violence are clearly the minority in the genre. This minority status lends special significance to two recent Western films—Kevin Costner's *Dances With Wolves* (1990) and Clint Eastwood's *Unforgiven* (1992)—which offer overt criticism of violence.[21] While *Dances With Wolves* follows in the steps of the countercultural films of the late 1960s and early 1970s which deplore only white aggression, both of these widely popular films offer clear and compelling condemnation of violence at a time when so many of Hollywood's movies, Westerns included,[22] seem to revel in mayhem designed more as Roman-style spectacle than serious social comment.

By supplying the story of a Union officer who escapes the bloodshed of the Civil War to come to live among the Sioux in the Dakota Territories, *Dances With Wolves* criticizes a Euro-American culture which used violence to subjugate native peoples. Certainly, the simple reversal in Westerns which made the whites evil and the natives pure precedes Costner's film.[23] Nevertheless, while *Dances With Wolves* may be said to be anti-racist due to its respectful treatment of Native American culture (indeed, the film's popularity led some politicians to address, at least briefly and in publicized ways, Native American issues), its strongest message lies in its repudiation of the violence it perceives in Euro-American society. Throughout the film a clear dichotomy between white uses of violence and native uses of force is emphasized. The civilization of the whites verges on madness, while the Sioux way of life seeks the discovery of what lead character Lieutenant John J. Dunbar terms "harmony."[24]

The film opens in a Union Army field hospital in 1863. Dunbar, played by Costner, has been wounded in action, and the surgeons have decided to amputate his leg. Immediately this scene establishes the effects of war; in fact, as Dunbar looks out of the hospital tent he sees soldiers who are amputees. When the surgeons leave Dunbar, he manages with great pain to pull on his boot and make his way back to the front. Here, two lines of Union and Confederate soldiers are stalemated, sniping at one another from behind fences on opposite sides of a field. In a clear suicide attempt, Dunbar mounts a horse and rides to the Confederate line, allowing the enemy to shoot at him. Ironically, his act inspires a charge by the Union soldiers, and the skirmish is won by the Federals.

As a reward for his "bravery," Dunbar is granted the medical attentions of a general's personal surgeon, his leg is saved, and he is allowed to choose a new post. Dunbar decides to go west and serve on the Dakota Territories because—displaying a rather anachronistic sense of urgency from a character living in the mid-1860s—he wants to see the frontier "before it is gone." But as the film unfolds, it becomes clear that Dunbar is seeking some kind of psychic rejuvenation by choosing to live on the frontier. He is, in short, trying to save himself by attempting to escape the madness of a civilization which is tearing itself apart in a bloody war.

As he comes to find himself isolated from white society while serving alone at a remote outpost, Dunbar slowly becomes a part of the Sioux culture—living with them; hunting and fighting with them; and marrying a white woman, Stands With a Fist, who was captured as a child but who has become a fully accepted member of the tribe. In the end, white soldiers threaten to destroy Dunbar—who has adopted the Sioux name Dances With Wolves—and the people he has embraced, so he and his wife decide to leave the tribe in order to help save it. In this, the reversal of a stereotypical Western formula is complete: As has been noted, in many Westerns the hero, a la Shane, saves a white civilization of which he cannot be a part; Dances With Wolves tries to save a truly civilized Native American culture by leaving it behind.

The dichotomies in the film between white and Native American cultures are established in obvious ways: White civilization is at the very least crude, and at the very extreme insane. The commanding officer of the "fort" Dunbar first comes to on the Great Plains urinates in his pants before shooting himself. A wagoneer is described by Dunbar as "the foulest man I've ever met." Near the film's end, an illiterate Calvary trooper uses the pages in Dunbar's journal for toilet paper.

The white man's violence, having been established as destructive, irrational, and maddening in the opening scenes, is presented throughout the film as utterly senseless. While out with the Indians, Dunbar discovers a prairie littered with skinned bison carcasses, animals which have been killed by whites for their hides and tongues and nothing more. In a voice-over, Dunbar concludes that the slaughter was done by a people "without value." Later, after Dunbar has come to live permanently with the Sioux, he has his horse shot out from under him by soldiers who see him as an Indian. In this scene, close-ups of bullets striking the horse underscore the monstrosity of white violence. Still later, just for the sport of it, soldiers shoot the wolf Dunbar has tried to tame.

The wolf, in fact, can be seen as a symbol of a benign nature, a nature the Sioux embrace. In *Dances With Wolves*, Native American culture is the more civilized one, precisely because the Sioux live close to nature and because their actions follow the logic of taking from the land only that which is needed to survive.[25] As Dunbar comes to admire the Sioux he notes that they are "devoted to family" and that they live in "harmony." The most triumphant scene in the film features a buffalo hunt, an activity which is central to Sioux survival: in contrast to white hunters, the Sioux make use of the entire buffalo.

Moreover, there is dignity in the violence the Sioux are required to use. Certainly, warriors are needed, and it is true that glory in battle lends status to male Sioux, but this is glossed over. In the film, violence is not shown to be a way of life among the Sioux. It can be averted, as when Dunbar and a member of the tribe work out a trade for the soldier's hat instead of coming to blows. The Sioux are not merely bloodthirsty, either, something which is supported in a scene that has a Sioux boy—Smiles A Lot—show remorse after killing a soldier. Nor is war taken lightly in this culture, as we see in shot of a warrior touching foreheads with his wife before going out on a raid against the Pawnee.

When the Sioux use violent force, it is almost always justified. They fight the Pawnee, for example, only to protect themselves. After the Sioux successfully repel a Pawnee attack, a voice-over has Dunbar articulate the justifications for the fight:

> *It was hard to know how to feel. I'd never been in a battle like this one. There was no dark political objective. This was not a fight for territory or riches or to make men free. It'd been fought to preserve the food stores that would see us through the winter, to protect the lives of women and children and loved ones only a few feet away.*

Significantly, this point in the film marks Dunbar's complete acceptance of his life with the Sioux. Feeling "a pride [he'd] never felt before," Dunbar rejects the white way of life, and in doing so, he repudiates violence which is justified through abstraction, the kind of violence which soon becomes meaningless and can drive men to suicide. When Chief Ten Bears says near the very end of the film, "Our country is all we have. We will fight to keep it," such concrete reasoning helps to ennoble the Sioux as they seek to preserve their way of life.

There is no final confrontation with the army in *Dances With Wolves*; the Sioux manage to elude battle by moving their camp before the soldiers can find it. The film concludes with these words appearing on the screen: "Thirteen years later, their homes destroyed, their buffalo gone, the last band of free Sioux submitted to white authority at Fort Robinson,

Nebraska. The great horse culture of the plains was gone and the American frontier was soon to pass into history."

In essence, the film's last sentence completes the reversal of Indian stereotypes which appear in so much Western fiction. In *Dances With Wolves*, the true "American frontier" is a native one. The violence used by whites to subdue this frontier, it is suggested, effectively destroyed it. Ultimately, then, *Dances With Wolves* implies that any narrative in Western fiction which glorifies white violence ironically celebrates the death rather than the vitality of America's frontier.

Unforgiven, directed by Clint Eastwood, offers a more thorough critique of violence than does *Dances With Wolves*. In the Costner film, the Sioux are excused in their use of force; in Eastwood's film, none of the violence portrayed is excused or justified. Just as important, the adverse psychological effects of violent acts are forcefully underscored.

Unforgiven opens in Big Whiskey, Wyoming, in 1880. An enraged cowboy cuts the face of one of the town's prostitutes. When the sheriff, Little Bill Daggett, is summoned, he at first wants to punish the cowboy and his partner by whipping them. Then he relents, ordering them to pay a fine in ponies—not to the prostitute herself, but to the saloon owner and pimp. Believing that this punishment does not match the crime, an outraged Strawberry Alice, the prostitutes' leader, has the women pool their money to place a bounty on the offending cowboys. For Alice, nothing short of execution will satisfy her sense of justice. Immediately, the moral equation that violence must be answered with greater violence is established.

Learning of the $1,000 bounty, a young man shows up at the farm of William Munny to enlist his aid in carrying out the contract. Munny is a reformed killer living on an isolated farm with his two children. The wife who reformed him from a murdering drunk is dead, and Munny frequently invokes her name to remind himself of her continuing influence. So when the Schofield Kid asks for Munny's help in executing the two cowboys, the reformed killer insists, "I ain't like that anymore, Kid."[26] Nevertheless, he eventually decides to join the Kid, because he wants the money for his children, and because it occurs to him that he was a better killer in the past than he is a pig farmer in the present.

One of the issues the film raises, then, is one's ability to escape a violent past, for it soon becomes clear that Will Munny was a notorious killer who would slaughter people for no reason. So many stories of the people he killed are sprinkled throughout the film that one wonders how he managed to survive. But as he says late in the story, "I've always been lucky when it comes to killing people." By the end of the film, all of the events that have come before that statement load it with irony.

Munny has had to live with his past deeds for 11 years, and they are never far from his mind. After adding his old partner, Ned Logan, to the expedition, Munny talks about his shooting a drover for no reason, and he unhappily recalls the fear he instilled in other men. At two different times late in the film, Munny relates the details of nightmarish dreams. In the first he has dreamt of a man he killed, by the name of Hendershot: "His head was all broken open. You could see inside of it. . . . Worms was coming out." In the second dream, he sees "the angel of death . . . He's got snake eyes." Then he admits to Ned that he is afraid of dying, and, horrified, he confesses that he has had a vision of his wife: "I seen Claudia, too. Her face was covered with worms."

Munny is made sympathetic by his attempt to change and escape a violent past. In this, he is unlike most Western protagonists, many of whom gain their status by having been skillful fighters or shootists. Different, too, is the character of Little Bill, played by Gene Hackman. As a sheriff, Little Bill is unlike the stereotypical lawman of most Westerns. He is brutal, and proud of it. When English Bob, a professional killer, comes to Big Whiskey to collect on the prostitutes' contract, the sheriff, backed by a number of armed deputies, takes his guns from him. Then Bill savagely beats Bob because, he claims, he wants to send a message to other would-be assassins who may be considering fulfilling the prostitutes' contract. As sheriff Bill viciously kicks English Bob, many of the townspeople, including some of the deputies, are shown to be sickened by the sight, yet Bill seems to enjoy his power. Unlike other Westerns which would simply show violence, *Unforgiven* frequently includes reaction shots to disapprove of depicted acts of violence.

In addition to these disapproving reaction shots, the film critiques those who would fictionalize violence and offer it as a vicarious thrill. Traveling with English Bob is a sycophantic dime novelist named W. W. Beauchamp whom English Bob calls his biographer, for Beauchamp has written a book about Bob called *The Duke of Death*. Though a coward himself, Beauchamp enjoys glorifying violence. Little Bill skeptically pronounces it "The Duck of Death": he was present during one of the gun battles depicted in the book. He tells Beauchamp that in reality English Bob shot a man not to protect the honor of a lady, but out of jealousy over a prostitute. As Bill tells it, the drunken Bob would have easily been killed except that his opponent first shot himself in the foot because he tried to draw his pistol too fast, and then his defective weapon blew up in his hand. By scoffing at Beauchamp's glorified version of events, Bill ridicules the dime novels of the era, and by implication the bulk of Western fiction to follow. In this scene, the fictional glorification of violence, which arguably could be one of Western fiction's principal attractions, is undermined.

Additionally, what sets *Unforgiven* apart from stereotypical Westerns is the film's depiction of remorse. In this film, those characters who cannot kill or who cannot justify killing become the closest thing to heroes. Little Bill is not one of these characters; in fact, he seems to revel in his ability to use violence to keep the town "peaceful." Ned Logan, on the other hand, cannot bring himself to kill one of the marked cowboys. After shooting the horse upon which the cowboy was riding, Ned is unable to fire again and kill the young man. Munny then takes the rifle from Ned and shoots the cowboy, but the bullet strikes the man in the abdomen, and the trio of would-be contract killers must listen to his dying groans.

After this, Ned decides he has had enough, and he leaves the band, much to the disgust of the Kid, who fancies himself a cold-blooded killer. But the Kid is mainly bluster, lying about having killed five men, seeing the fulfillment of the contract as an adventure. However, when the Kid, who has seemed so nonchalant about killing and who has idolized Munny, does actually kill a man, he experiences intense remorse. After shooting the second cowboy to death, the Kid tries to anesthetize himself with whiskey. Shaking from grief the Kid tells Munny, "It don't seem real. He ain't never going to breathe again ever. . . . All on account of pulling a trigger." To this Munny replies, "Hell of a thing killing a man. You take away all he's got and all he's ever gonna have."

> Kid: "Guess he had it coming."
> Munny: "We all have it coming, Kid."

In this same scene the two men learn that Ned has been captured and tortured to death by Little Bill. Munny begins to drink, needing to get drunk so his buried, violent self will be raised to take revenge for Ned's murder. Partly, however, Munny is responding to his sense of culpability: "So Little Bill killed him on account of what we done." Munny borrows the Kid's pistol, and the Kid vows never to kill again. "I ain't like you, Will," he says.

In the final confrontation, Munny enters the saloon where Little Bill has gathered his posse. Munny shoots Little Bill and those deputies who do not flee. Before Munny kills the wounded Little Bill, they exchange these words:

> Bill: *"I don't deserve this, to die like this. I was building*
> *a house."*
> Munny: *"Deserves got nothing to do with it."*

These lines, coming so close to the end of the movie, emphasize the anti-violence theme of the film. Killing should not be glorified or excused by turning it into something which is justified, something which lends moral superiority to those who kill for ends they deem righteous. *Unforgiven* exposes as hollow the formulaic Western's notion that violence can be forgiven if it is committed by "heroes."

Finally, films and novels which offer exception to Cawelti's observation that Westerns tend to be organized around acts of violence which lead to the reassertion of social order can be said, at least in some measure, to be thematically anti-violent. Those Westerns which can depict violent acts while undercutting the supposed justification of violence are even stronger in their critique. The most anti-violent Westerns, then, will more than likely concentrate on the negative results of violence. It may not be an overstatement to suggest that Westerns which find ways to repudiate the connection between violence and progress, a connection which permeates American history, may serve positive societal as well as thematic ends.

FOUR

A Feminist Effort:
Moving Women to Center Stage

WHEN I BEGIN TO watch many Western films, one of the first things that strikes me is how few female actors appear in the opening credits. Often, three or more male names appear before the first woman is credited. Obviously this is more than just a matter of movie-industry sexism, for the fact is that in many Westerns, novels included, the female characters are largely superfluous: Take the token love scene out of most oaters, and the plot remains largely unchanged.[1] In *The Six-Gun Mystique* Cawelti notes the limited role women generally play in most Westerns: Women are usually typed as good girls or bad, the former being the schoolmarm type who represents a civilizing influence while the latter is cast as a seductress who symbolizes the dangers of continued allegiance to the wilderness.[2] Henry Nash Smith discovers a simple dichotomy between the lady and the Amazon in his study of the nineteenth-century dime novel. The character of Calamity Jane, for example, often appears as a woman fallen from gentility into the rough manners of the West. In a discussion of one story, Smith reveals that Jane will never be able to marry because "[h]er prospects . . . have suffered from her neglect of appearances."[3]

In the stereotypical Western, women often not only play an ancillary role to the adventure tale, but they frequently represent a threat to male independence. As Cawelti observes "The town [the sphere of the female] offers love, domesticity, and order as well as the opportunity for personal achievement and the creation of family, but it requires the repression of spontaneous passion and the curtailment of the masculine honor and camaraderies of the older wilderness life."[4]

Indeed, the Western becomes a boys' club, at least for Cawelti, because its violent milieu is based on "the sense of decaying masculine potency which has long afflicted American culture."[5] The six-gun becomes a phallic symbol, and its use represents the symbolic reclamation of a "masculine supremacy" in an industrial economy which has rendered individual effort moot:

> *[T]he American tradition has always emphasized individual masculine force; Americans love to think of themselves as pioneers, men who have conquered a continent and sired on it a new society. This radical discrepancy between the sense of eroding masculinity and the view of America as a great history of men against the wilderness has created the need for a means of symbolic expression of masculine potency in an unmistakable way. This means is the gun, particularly the six-gun.*[6]

That the Western seeks largely to serve male fantasies is the thesis of Jane Tompkins' *West of Everything: The Inner Life of Western* "[The Western] is about men's fear of losing their mastery, and hence their identity, both of which the Western tirelessly reinvents."[7] One extreme attitude toward women in many Westerns is expressed in a brief exchange in the film *These Thousand Hills* (1959). When a character finds out that a saloon full of cowboys has been discussing women, he states, "That's a limited subject." Then he asks if anyone wants to talk about horses.[8]

Since she recognizes that the genre has been historically male-dominated, critic Sandra Kay Schackel is not surprised that the roles for women in Westerns are circumscribed by male fantasies and fears. Along with Cawelti, Schackel also finds two recurring roles for women in Westerns "nurturer/civilizer" and "femme fatale/vamp,"[9] and she effectively illustrates the various forms these two basic parts have taken in twentieth-century Western movies. In addition, she sees these roles as the result of a male-centered view of history. She writes, "[B]ecause men have most often written and directed Westerns, the films view women from a male perspective that emphasizes the male hero. The lack of a female counterpart to John Wayne is a reminder that the frontier West was perceived by many as a masculine experience."[10]

However, Schackel does discover that as society's attitudes toward women have changed, so too have the depictions of women in Westerns. Citing such films as *Cat Ballou* (1964), *Soldier Blue* (1970), *The Missouri*

Breaks (1970), *McCabe and Mrs. Miller* (1971), and *Heartland* (1979), Schackel discovers a new, more flattering role for women in Westerns "[A] new stereotype has appeared in the past twenty-five years that differs from the two traditional images of women. This new image is the strong, independent woman who can take care of herself in most situations and expects to do so."[11]

Presumably, this new role for female characters marks a positive step in the portrayal of women in Westerns. Yet Schackel labels this role a "stereotype," and in the end she calls for more variety in the Western's depiction of women. Acknowledging that films "tend to reflect the changing social and cultural climate in which they are created," Schackel hopes that an ever changing view of women, in history as well as in contemporary society, will cause creation of a new female Western hero:

> *Increased public awareness of women's rights as well as changes in scholarship have finally recognized the complexity of women's roles on the frontier. As women's and men's roles change, the predominantly male Western no longer fits today's values. And as the genre moves away from roles men thought women ought to play and toward roles they actually did play, Western films will more realistically reflect women's role in the celluloid winning of the West.*[12]

Interestingly enough, aside from the limited images of women that their frequently circumscribed roles in Westerns convey, the lack of strong and complex female characters in many Western movies may be the most prominent reason the bulk of these films have been labeled "juvenile." Film critic Molly Haskell argues that numerous American movies, Westerns included, delineate immature male characters precisely because these characters are not dramatized in mature male/female relationships. Haskell contends that a number of Westerns—from *Two Rode Together* (1961) and *Ride the High Country* (1962) to *Butch Cassidy and the Sundance Kid* (1969) and *The Hired Hand* (1971)—feature a pair of central male characters in plots almost completely without female equals. Haskell labels the relationship between these central male characters "adolescent, presexual, tacit, the love of one's *semblable*, one's mirror reflection."[13] This kind of immature relationship, Haskell believes, has both thematic and societal consequences. Believing that men have not successfully negotiated "a painful transitional period,"[14] Haskell argues that men "haven't yet adjusted to a new definition of masculinity, one that would include courage and bravery in personal relationships."[15]

Moreover, those Westerns which focus on male relationships to the exclusion or detriment of male/female relationships lead to a lack of thematic texture. Haskell writes that the male characters in these Westerns have not learned that "the real risks . . . lie in rising to meet other challenges, the challenge of another human being, of someone different but equal, in a love that relishes separateness, grows stronger with resistance, and, in the maturity of admitting dependence, acknowledges its own mortality."[16]

In the search for Westerns which do not marginalize women, then, two basic criteria emerge (1) The female characters must challenge both genre and gender roles, and (2) they must be fully involved in the plot. The first criterion is significant because if the female characters are not cast in traditional genre roles, that is if they move beyond merely taming or tempting the male characters, then quite possibly they may be more fully developed characters. Secondly, if the female characters in a particular Western are allowed to interact fully with the male characters, if they play an active role in the action and the relationships depicted, then that Western may portray women as equals to men, and not as sex objects or foils in a male-dominated shoot-em-up.

In a few exceptional cases Western novels and films have allowed their female characters to become more than mere stage props, to become in effect the heroes of the story. Take, for instance, Charles Portis' novel *True Grit*. Here, the tale is told by a woman, Mattie Ross, as she looks back on her gutsy pursuit of her father's killer in 1870s Arkansas. Such a narrative device reverses the "classic" point of view found in a novel like *Shane*, that is, of a man recounting his boyhood adventure in the West. Moreover, it is clear in *True Grit* that the "grit" of the title refers not only to qualities possessed by Rooster Cogburn, the marshal Mattie hires to help her in her pursuit, but to the determination of Mattie herself. In the end of the novel, we are treated to Mattie's sense of independence as she speaks of the reaction she receives after she has moved Rooster's body to her hometown:

People here in Dardanelle and Russellville said, well,
she hardly knew the man but it is just like a cranky old
maid to do a 'stunt' like that. I know what they said
even if they would not say it to my face. People love to
talk.They love to slander you if you have any substance.
They say I love nothing but money and the Presbyterian
Church and that is why I never married. They think every-
body is dying to get married. It is true that I love my
church and my bank. What is wrong with that? I will tell
you a secret. Those same people talk mighty nice when
they come in to get a crop loan or beg a mortgage exten-
sion! I never had the time to get married but it is nobody's
business if I am married or not married. I care nothing
for what they say. I would marry an ugly baboon if I
wanted to and make him cashier. I never had the time to
fool with it. A woman with brains and a frank tongue
and one sleeve pinned up and an invalid mother to care
for is at some disadvantage, although I will say I could
have had two or three old untidy men around here who
had their eyes fastened on my bank. No, thank you![17]

Mattie is a developed character, and in her determination, independence, and financial acumen one finds a hero fit for both the demands of the Old West and the challenges of an emerging commercial society.

On film, one 1950s Western stands out as feminist critique by virtue of its attempt to explore issues of female sexuality. Director Nicholas Ray's 1953 movie *Johnny Guitar* focuses on the enmity between two women, Vienna, played by Joan Crawford, and Emma, played by Mercedes McCambridge. At its heart this film is an exploration of the proper role for women as they seek to assert their will and their sexuality.

At first glance, however, there is much in the film's plot which adheres to the formulas of the stereotypical Western. Critic Brian Garfield has called the film "fabulously melodramatic"[18] and certainly the use of melodrama is nothing new in the Western. Author Stanley J. Solomon also finds much in *Johnny Guitar* that fits the stereotypes of the Western, especially the ending, which "remains within the genre's tradition of the re-establishment of tranquillity and justice through the purging of vengeance and passion."[19] Nevertheless, Solomon argues that the Vienna/ Emma conflict is the central one in the story, and he believes the film is more psychological exploration than action-adventure, forcing us to pay attention "to the neurotic tensions that motivate the characters and their hostilities."[20]

In addition, whether intentional or not, there are frequent humorous moments in *Johnny Guitar* which have led many reviewers to label the movie as "campy." For instance, early in the film a showdown between Johnny Guitar and The Dancing Kid is avoided when the former plays his instrument so the latter may show off his eurythmic skill. And in a scene ripe with amusing symbolism, Vienna sits wearing a white dress and playing a piano when a lynch mob all decked out in black breaks into her saloon.

Such humor notwithstanding, *Johnny Guitar* does offer a psychological exploration of female sexuality and the limits society places on its expression. As lead character in all but the film's title, Vienna represents a strong-willed woman who refuses to be ashamed of her sexual history. Indeed, Johnny has come to reclaim her as a lover, but she refuses to apologize for the fact that in the intervening five years she has had other men. When Johnny asks her to lie to him about her affairs, she does so, but in a tone of voice which makes clear the lie even as she offers it. It is implied, moreover, that Vienna has used sex to gain her position and wealth. When Johnny confronts her on this point, she says simply, "I'm not ashamed of how I got what I have."[21] Later, in an exchange which makes explicit the double standard within society's established sexual roles, Johnny asks Vienna, "How many men have you forgotten?" And she answers, "As many women as you remember." Additionally, after Vienna insists that a man can perform any kind of deceit and still keep his manly pride, she says, "But let a woman slip once, and she's a tramp."

Not only is Vienna secure in her sexuality, but her refusal to conform to established gender roles is perceived as a challenge to traditional masculinity. At one point, one of her employees underscores Vienna's strength as well as her threat to the stereotyped masculine role: "Never seen a woman who was more a man. She thinks like one, acts like one, and sometimes makes me feel like I'm not." This threat to masculine identity appears later when a teenage outlaw tries to prove his manliness by shooting various objects in the bar. When Johnny over-reacts to this gunplay by shooting the pistol out of the boy's hand, Vienna chastises him as "gun crazy." If the ability to use a handgun is the mark of masculinity as well as the means of power in this society, then Vienna's appropriation of the Colt revolver as phallic symbol (she holds off a mob at gunpoint), as well as her later insistence that there be no killing, denies male exclusivity in running society. A more explicit exhibition of Vienna's power through repudiation of gun fighting occurs when she orders Johnny to leave his guns in his saddlebag—at least until she tells him to retrieve them.

The central conflict in the story occurs between Vienna and Emma, two women who represent very different sexual psychologies.[22] On the surface, their conflict is economic in nature. Vienna wants the railroad to build a depot in town so that she may profit from increased settlement. Emma, as representative of the ranching interests, does not want "sodbusters" infringing on range rights. In terms of its economic philosophy, then, the film is not subversive: Vienna is the individualistic entrepreneur fighting for economic progress in the form of increased development. But the sexual themes that the Vienna/Emma conflict reveals are subversive, for in the end, Vienna is able to assert her will and remain a woman unashamed of her sexuality; whereas Emma, as a symbol of repressed sexuality, is destroyed.

Vienna has slept with The Dancing Kid, an act which Emma resents because she harbors a passion for the Kid. Because of this repressed passion, Emma hates both Vienna and the Kid. Vienna recognizes the source of Emma's hatred when she says to her, "You want the Kid and you're so ashamed of it you want him dead." Later, Vienna tells Johnny that Emma wants to kill The Dancing Kid because "[h]e makes her feel like a woman. And that frightens her." In a reversal of stereotypical roles, the two women complete the film with a final shoot-out. In this battle, Emma kills the Kid, and Vienna shoots Emma. Symbolically, this scene represents the dangers of repressed female sexuality as well as the triumph of Vienna's brand of honest sexual expression. Significantly, the ranchers who have been supporting Emma resign the fight in the end, and Vienna and Johnny conclude the film by walking through a cleansing waterfall and exchanging a kiss.

Clearly, *Johnny Guitar* explores issues which most Westerns tend to overlook. Still, some critics dismiss this film as being unable to present an important social message, either because of its campiness or because they read the plot as merely a male construction. Historian Richard White, for example, contends that "the leading female characters become, in effect, male characters. The result is like watching a conventional western in drag."[23] Such a statement substitutes cheap shot for analysis, however, and White offers no support for his assertion. Yet he does raise an important consideration when one attempts to analyze the Western from a feminist perspective. That is, how can women truly be given voice in works which are not only produced by men but which frequently revolve around plot formulas which are largely male constructions? In other words, the very fact that Vienna and Emma shoot it out in the end could be read as a peculiarly male response to conflict resolution. Granted. Nonetheless, *Johnny Guitar* does offer trenchant commentary on the circumscribed nature of female sexuality in a society whose rules are created by men.

If one objects, however, that Westerns produced by men can never be accepted as feminist in their depiction of female characters, one need not necessarily condemn the entire genre as inherently sexist. Over the years women have written Western stories and novels, and, more recently, women are writing and directing Western films. Critic Norris Yates has recently "rediscovered" women writers of Westerns who worked during the first half of the twentieth century. While these women still wrote within established formulas, Yates discovers that their stories featured more female protagonists, depicted violence less often, and used more indoor settings. In addition, he argues that they managed "to some degree [to] resolve the conflict between the demands of the macho Western and their feminist leanings."[24] Furthermore, for Yates these writers "broadcast a message, however low the volume, that in adversity a woman could do almost anything a man could do—and maybe could do it just as well without the adversity."[25]

In addition, editor Vicki Piekarski has provided a long list of works by lesser-known women authors of Westerns in her anthology of short stories, *Westward the Women*.[26] Tellingly, Piekarski singles out many of these works for their attention to social concerns. She summarizes:

> *Women have helped to refine, reshape, and redefine the*
> *form of the historical novel to embrace wider frontiers.*

> *In their concern with history they have begun to unravel*
> *the tightly woven mythos of the American West. They have*
> *tackled social issues that others would have preferred to*
> *ignore. They have served as the conscience of our history*
> *by questioning actions and policies of the past. Treated*
> *as a minority themselves, women have often been sympa-*
> *thetic to the peoples native to this land. They have asked*
> *what the frontier offered and what it denied. And they*
> *have examined and explored the effects that the frontier*
> *had on women's constant search for a clearer identity.*
> *Women have not been afraid to break away from stereo-*
> *types, for they have understood from the very beginning*
> *that the frontier was both a masculine and a feminine*
> *experience—a human experience, for better or worse.*[27]

A novel which illustrates Piekarski's contention that Westerns by women tend to defy the stereotypes of the genre while portraying complex female characters is Mari Sandoz's *Miss Morissa: Doctor of the Gold Trail*. Published in 1955, the novel follows the adventures of Morissa Kirk in the wild North Platte region in the later 1870s. Morissa comes West because her wealthy fiancé has discovered that she is a bastard, and of course his family will not allow them to marry. But unlike other women in the genre who flee West to escape a failed love affair, Morissa is an educated physician. In fact, the novel is dedicated to three real women who are named and "a hundred others" who served as doctors "on our Western frontiers."

Morissa is determined to use her medical skills to make a difference in a strange and dangerous land. Her first act upon reaching a camp along the North Platte is to save a man from drowning in the spring-flooded river. Though she is shocked by the violence she witnesses—violence among the white men who are mining gold in the Black Hills and herding cattle on the north Nebraska plains, and violence against the Native peoples who threaten such fortune seeking—Morissa nonetheless decides to build a homestead north of the river. She administers to all who need medical attention, including outlaws shot in the night and Indians made ill during forced removals from their land. Her greatest medical triumph occurs when she rescues an injured settler from a well and mends his broken head with a plate she has pounded from a silver dollar. This feat earns her the respect of other doctors in the region, and she is eventually elected vice president of a new medical association.

In many ways, Morissa represents a civilizing influence in a raw country. However, she is not a threat to a kind of frontier purity depicted in so many male-authored Westerns which portray women as somehow taming a naturally exuberant West. On the contrary, Morissa's is the voice of reason and compassion in a harsh land. She is, for example, appalled by violence, not because she is skittish about bloodletting, but because it disturbs her sense of reason. When she sees a man who has been lynched as a warning to prospective outlaws, Morissa thinks "[The lynching] seemed a willful, a deliberate and dreadful violence; a sacrilege put upon the most beautifully balanced and artistic instrument, the human body; a defilement upon the finest, the noblest creation, the mind of man."[28] Furthermore, Morissa is sickened by the slaughter of Cheyenne and Sioux because she is capable, as few others in the region are, of recognizing the dignity and humanity of these Native peoples.

In the face of the lawlessness and greed she observes, Morissa begins to build something of value. She plants a ten-acre grove on her homestead. She builds a hospital and opens the first school. Along the way, she teaches herself to shoot a pistol and a Winchester, but only to protect her homestead from cattle ranchers who resent her presence on the range.[29]

Morissa grows as a character, too—from a girl who obsesses about her illegitimacy into a woman confident of her place and mission in her adopted territory. Impulsively she marries a dissolute man, only to discover that "[a] good man can have a bad wife, but no wife is better than her spouse."[30] Facing down such sexist stereotypes, including the notion that a woman cannot be a physician, Morissa sustains her idealism as she serves the sick and injured. In the end, her hospital burned to cinders, Morissa determines to stay in a country growing more violent even as it is becoming more settled.

In the end, too, it is suggested that she will gain the help of a man she loves, a man who sees her as an equal. Scorned by the rich Allston Hoyt, finally free of the cruel and childish Eddie Ellis, Morissa, it is implied, will wed Tris Polk, a rancher turned engineer who shares her vision of improving the North Platte valley. Of the man she will likely marry,

Morissa thinks "Husband. Not a father oversolicitous of his good name, or a warped and pitiful son seeking a mother, but a husband to stand beside her, a wife."[31]

In prose which realistically delineates the hardships of the Old West, and in a portrayal of a female hero more than up to the rigors of a dangerous frontier life, Sandoz provides a novel which challenges the notion that Westerns must center on boyish fantasies. Sandoz's vision of the Old West is neither sensational nor romantic. For her, moreover, the best aspect of America's frontier is the human character it helped to shape— the kind of character shown in a female protagonist capable of both action and love, endurance and compassion.

Two recent Western films, both written and directed by women and both based on true stories, additionally depict fully developed female characters struggling for independence and self-respect in a male-dominated West. Exceptional films by artistic measures, both *Thousand Pieces of Gold* (1991) and *The Ballad of Little Jo* (1993) also challenge the notion that the West was "won" by men, while women trailed docilely behind.

Based on a book by Ruthanne Lum McCunn and directed by Nancy Kelly, *Thousand Pieces of Gold* narrates the story of a Chinese woman whose father sells her into prostitution. Lalu is transported from northern China to San Francisco where she is purchased by a Chinese immigrant. At first Lalu, played by Rosalind Chao, believes that this man intends to make her his wife, and she is prepared to accept that fate. In a touching and meaningful scene, Lalu covers her face with a scarf in the traditional way of a Chinese bride. She is ready to be meek, to participate in a self-effacing gender role. However, Li Po, who in America calls himself Jim, has bought her for another man, and he takes Lalu, along with the other "supplies" in his pack train, to Gold Mountain, Idaho.

During the journey, Jim and Lalu form a bond. He teaches her a little English, and she recounts a Chinese legend based on the constellations. Jim tells her his Chinese name, and he boasts that he is saving to afford a return passage to China. He is proud that he has succeeded in America, that by working on the railroad for 12 years he was able to pay off his indenture. In English, he notes the keys to his success: "Learn English, carry a gun and start your own business. And don't let anyone push you around."[32]

When they arrive at the mining camp of Gold Mountain, Jim tells Lalu that the men will call her China Polly. Such an offensive renaming is a clear indication of the consideration Lalu will be granted. It is clear, too, that Jim is uncomfortable selling her to Hong King, a Chinese saloon owner who intends to use her as a prostitute. Again, Lalu believes she will be a wife to Hong King, so the first time a miner pays for sex with her, Lalu fights him off at knifepoint. She insists that she will be a wife only to Hong King.

To her defense comes Charlie Bemis, Hong King's business partner. Bemis tells Hong King that he cannot keep Lalu as a slave, threatening him with, "Break the law and you won't get your citizenship papers." Later Bemis teaches Lalu to say "no whore," and as more practical protection, he gives her a knife.

The rest of the story concentrates on Lalu's growing sense of herself as a free woman. When a black man comes to the saloon and tells her that she's free, the knowledge comes as a revelation. Immediately she insists that she wants to return to China. Bemis tries to make her see the reality of her situation as a Chinese woman in a place where people value neither her race nor her sex. "You just got to make your peace with the devil, Polly," Bemis says. "It's the only way to get along in this world."

Eventually, however, Bemis gambles with Hong King and wins Lalu's freedom. When Lalu returns to Bemis's cabin, he expects her to sleep with him, saying, "I ruined a good man for you. I thought you'd be happy." Lalu replies, "You want a Chinese slave girl; that what you want?" Bemis realizes that he is just as bad as Hong King, and, by way of apology he states, "I don't own you, Polly."

Significantly, love will not be possible between Bemis and Lalu until she is able to assert her independence, to become his equal and not his "slave girl." After Lalu moves out of Bemis's cabin and begins to work for herself, she and Bemis begin a courtship against the backdrop of a racist league of men working for the forced removal of all Chinese immigrants. In the scenes featuring this league's violent activities, the film adds an antiracist message to its feminist one.

All along, even as she and Bemis fall in love, Lalu has been determined to return to China. By the end of the film she is an independent woman with the means to pay her passage home. As all of the Chinese immigrants, including Hong King, are being driven out, Lalu begins to go with them. However, at the last minute she changes her mind and stays with Charlie Bemis. She chooses him. She is no longer the demure woman who veiled her head and prepared to marry a strange man in a strange country.

In this well-acted and quiet film, issues of self-identity and the limits of personal freedom for women are explored through Lalu's struggle to become more than a man's wife or whore, roles defined by men. Through sheer willpower, Lalu manages to create choices for herself. In the end she can stay or leave; she can be married or unmarried—options already open to men. By refusing to acquiesce to the "devil" of prescribed gender and racial roles, by learning how not "to let anyone push her around," Lalu gains control of her destiny.

In addition, Lalu's growing sense of independence challenges the idea implicit in many Westerns that self identity is gained at the expense of others. Think of those Westerns which feature a young gunslinger trying to gain a reputation by killing a man with a greater fast-draw reputation. In these Westerns, the identities of characters are predicated on how many men they have killed. And, understandably, a man who might kill at any moment tends not to have too many intimate friends. So personal identity for these characters is connected with violence, and their independence is really a kind of stark isolation. Not so with Lalu, who develops her inner strength and who forms a bond with Charlie Bemis. Ultimately, then, *Thousand Pieces of Gold* reveals that the image of Old West independence—and strength of character—can be discovered, not in the roaming cowboy or the loner lawman, but in a Chinese woman who chooses her own course in a new land.

In *The Ballad of Little Jo*, written and directed by Maggie Greenwald, the price a woman pays by having to serve in circumscribed gender roles is more keenly dramatized. The narrative follows Josephine Monaghan, the daughter of a wealthy Eastern family who flees to Montana after being shunned by her father for bearing a child out of wedlock. At first, Josephine is unaware of the dangers of being a woman traveling alone in a scarcely populated land. She trusts an itinerant peddler, only to have him "sell" her to two men. After escaping abduction and rape, Josephine gradually comes to see that her best chance for security and independence is to disguise herself as a man. Despite a woman storekeeper's comment that "it's against the law to dress improper to your sex,"[33] Josephine chops off her long hair and puts on men's clothing. To complete her disguise, she scars her face with a razor. Josephine becomes Jo.

Becoming a man, she discovers, will require that she alter her behavior. So she observes how the men in a mining camp saloon hold their forks, and she learns to smoke. However, the men, though they never question her true gender, still mark her as different, mistaking her refusal to make use of prostitutes as a youthful and virtuous abstinence. Shocked by the misogyny and casual whoring she witness among the men, Jo is pushed to leave Ruby City when Percy Corcoran, a man who has befriended her, viciously attacks a prostitute.

Sickened by all she has seen, Jo seeks isolation in a job as a sheep herder in a remote line camp. Alone with the sheep for four winter months, Jo learns to survive on her own. Significantly, she teaches herself to shoot so she can protect her flock from wolves. Later, after Jo returns to Ruby City, she discovers that Percy has learned her secret by reading a letter from her sister. Calling her a "whore," he tries to rape her, an attempt she prevents by threatening him with her pistol. Percy then decides to blackmail her for the money he needs to leave town.

Her one friend having betrayed her, Jo seeks further isolation working as a sheep herder. After five years, she saves enough money to quit working for Frank Badger and homestead her own ranch. It is clear at this point that Jo's desire for solitude is both a practical and psychological defense, and the film's principal theme revolves around her refusal to connect with the people around her.

This protective isolation is threatened, however, after she saves a Chinese man from a lynching. Frank Badger goads her into hiring Tinman Wong as a cook. Jo resists the idea, and even after she relents, she refuses to allow Tinman to sleep in the cabin with her. Eventually, Tinman discovers her secret, and the two become lovers. They live as a couple, each fulfilling opposite gender roles: He cooks and mends; she rides and tends the sheep. In one compelling scene, Jo's attraction for Tinman is underscored when she watches him standing in the river, bare to the waist, bathing and washing his long hair. This scene reverses so many familiar episodes in other Westerns which feature a male character spying on a nude female bather. Also, by casting the male as the object of sexual desire, the film offers a view of female sexuality which is on par with male sexuality.

By stepping out of a female gender role, Jo gains more than she loses. The other roles a female in the Old West could fulfill are shown to us. Staying largely in the background are women who are prostitutes and wives. Jo is freer than these women; she is able to choose her own course in life, to try to set her own rules. Still, there are certain aspects of the traditional male role with which she is uncomfortable. Being expected to kill disturbs her deeply. She must learn to shoot wolves when they attack her flock, but she does not want to fight the gunmen hired by intrusive cattle barons to drive sheep ranchers off of their land. Even though she sees these thugs murder an immigrant family she has befriended, she does not seek revenge—a course of action which would be typical in many other Westerns. Instead she decides to sell her ranch, turning down the sale at the last minute because Tinman is ill and would have no place to go.

Fear, on a number of levels, grips her. She is afraid of becoming too close to Tinman; she is afraid of having to war with the ranchers' hired killers; and she is afraid of being killed for concealing her gender and taking a Chinese lover. When she is drawn into a battle with the ranchers' gunmen, she participates reluctantly. The fight is instigated by Frank Badger, and she must defend herself, killing two men. But she feels no triumph, only remorse.

The Ballad of Little Jo certainly depicts a woman able to handle herself in a male-dominated milieu. As a woman living as a man, Jo is unlike any female character in the typical Western. She is free to live as she chooses, but with those choices come emotional and physical hardships. She is free to struggle in ways other women in the film are not. She must make an independent living and define her own relationships. And like all people, she must struggle with loneliness and fear and the uncertainty of belonging—belonging in a society which precasts one's gender roles, and, moreover, belonging in a world of one's own choosing even though, in many ways, that world operates on rules not of one's making. In the end, this richly photographed film suggests that while the struggle against society's mores often occurs along gender lines, the struggle for human dignity and self-fulfillment belongs equally to both sexes.

In a few exceptional instances, then, certain Westerns have given their female characters active roles and full voice. Those Westerns which can be labeled "feminist" belie the notion that the genre must merely pander to male fantasies. At their best, Westerns which portray fully realized female characters may challenge contemporary gender roles and inspire discussion of what it means to become a mature human being beyond the confines of societal type-casting. [34]

In addition, in a culture in which the popular arts receive so much attention, women may gain a certain measure of respect simply by being portrayed with depth in popular novels and films—obviously the arts most consumed by the majority of Americans. Moreover, by laying claim to a piece of the Old West, both fictional and real, women can gain claim to a vital piece of the national consciousness. Speaking through all Westerns which depict women as strong and significant is the message, "We were there. Whatever America was and is becoming, it belongs to women as well as to men."

FIVE

Beyond a One-Color Western:
Native Americans and
African Americans in Westerns

UNFORTUNATELY, WE KNOW THEM best from the movies. We sat in darkened theaters and watched as, sporting war bonnets and sitting astride painted horses, they charged circled wagons on expansive plains or lay ambushes in thick forests. In quieter moments they "parlayed" with whites in broken, buffoonish English. Once in a while they provided a near-mute sidekick who could put ear to ground and warn the white hero of far-off desperadoes. If these are the images of Native Americans with which we are most familiar, then at best they are caricatures; at worst they're the most flagrant of stereotypes.

That Western movies send a demeaning and incomplete picture of Native Americans is a common critical complaint. For one thing, until 1972 cinematic Westerns featured only the most war-like tribes. Less hostile tribes, the ones which "offered no substantial military resistance," were rarely, if ever, depicted on film.[1] It is no wonder, then, that non-Native Americans, particularly those who gained their historical insights from the movies and television, are charged with knowing so little about the people who were here first.

Cast most often in the stereotypical roles of "noble savage or . . . blood thirsty red devil,"[2] Native Americans in Western fiction, particularly cinematic fiction, often play foil to the dominant culture's aspirations. Many critics believe that stereotyping of Native Americans in popular fictions is inevitable, since these fictions are produced most often by non-natives who are more concerned with the dominant society than with Native ones. Historian Robert F. Berkhofer, for example, believes that no matter the extent to which portrayals of Native Americans changed over the years, these changing images still spoke more to white interests than to Native American issues:

> *About the only conclusion a historian can safely derive*
> *from the history of the Indian in the White imagination*
> *is that, even if new meaning is given the idea of the*
> *Indian, historians of the future will probably chronicle*
> *it as part of the recurrent effort of Whites to under-*
> *stand themselves, for the very attraction of the Indian*
> *to the White imagination rests upon the contrast that*
> *lies at the core of the idea. Thus the debate over 'real-*
> *ism' will always be framed in terms of White values*
> *and needs, White ideologies and creative uses.*[3]

Other critics concur, charging that Native Americans can never be presented unstereotypically in popular fictions. Authors Ralph E. Friar and Natasha A. Friar condemn even those Western films which purport to offer revisionist views of Native Americans.[4] And critic Raymond William Stedman argues that even supposedly positive portrayals of Indians are often still pernicious stereotypes.[5]

Even the so-called countercultural Western films of the late 1960s and early 1970s, films which have been viewed by some as attempts to alter negative portrayals of Native Americans, are dismissed by critics who see in them a kind of left-wing paean to white hippies rather than a serious depiction of Native cultures. Historian David Rich Lewis is one critic who scoffs at the pretensions to accuracy held by many of these films:

> *In the 1960s, the children of American excess made In-*
> *dians the romantic symbol of their revolt. Indians were*
> *tribal, spiritual, drug-using, and wronged, holdouts*
> *against conformity and an American political system*
> *gone mad with war. Hollywood reflected those images in*
> *movies like* Soldier Blue *(1970) and* Little Big Man
> *(1971)—films that told us more about ourselves, our*
> *countercultural desires, and the nightmare of Vietnam*
> *than about Native Americans.*[6]

Still other critics level even harsher charges, contending that portrayals of Native Americans in popular fictions are merely weapons in a conqueror's arsenal. This kind of criticism is expressed by Ward Churchill, et al.:

> *Stereotypical misrepresentations in media of Native*
> *American peoples and cultures has been comprehensive*

and systematic since the 1880s. The methods of such ste-
reotyping are known and the intent of their employment
has been the effective dehumanization of the peoples
depicted. This has been a fundamental aspect of the white
dominant culture's genocidal expropriation of Native land
and resources bases well into the twentieth century.[7]

Native Americans themselves have long taken exception to their portrayal in Western films. As early as 1911, for example, protesters went to
Washington to object to "the movies' use of whites dressed in war paint
and feather bonnets." In 1970, members of the American Indian Movement picketed the film *A Man Called Horse*, insisting that "'every dollar
going into the box office is a vote for bigotry.'" And, when asked his
opinion of the movie *Little Big Man*, Indian actor and movie consultant
Iron Eyes Cody snapped, "'It's a damned farce.'"[8]

Not all Native Americans object to every film by non-Natives, however. Native American novelist James Welch, for example, praises the
film version of *Little Big Man* for "humanizing Indians by depicting individuals living in a society, with its own special structure, mores and values."[9] By the same token, Welch cannot extend this praise to *Dances With
Wolves*. Of Kevin Costner's film Welch writes:

> *[its] main problem . . . is the homogeneity of, the inter-*
> *changeability, of the Indian characters. Graham Green is*
> *fine as Kicking Bird and Rodney Grant does a good job*
> *as the rebellious Wind in His Hair, but the other Indi-*
> *ans were so much background in their buckskins and robes,*
> *in their clean camp, even in dramatic scenes such as the*
> *feast after the buffalo hunt. . . . It is also worth pointing*
> *out that Costner's character . . . falls in love with the*
> *only other white—a captive woman with wildly teased*
> *hair and a thick tongue—in Indian country. It almost*
> *seems that Costner kept a shrewd eye out for what America*
> *would want (and wouldn't want) in an Indian movie.*[10]

Given this frequent and sometimes vehement criticism of the portrayals of Native Americans in Westerns, perhaps only Native Americans
themselves can make Western films which do not stereotype their people
and serve ideologies not of their making. Yet authors George N. Fenin

and William K. Everson report that the first film produced by Indians, *A Gunfight* (1971), contains no Indians. Funded by the Jicarilla Apache tribe, this film tells the story of a lawman/killer conflict.[11] However, it is certainly understandable if Indian artists eschew the Western genre altogether. After all, the story of the Old West is, in large measure, a story of the genocide of Native Americans.

Nevertheless, certain Native American novelists have chosen to write about the nineteenth-century West from an Indian perspective. Critic Charles R. Larson notes that in the late 1960s and early 1970s, three Native Americans wrote "revisionist" novels out of "the desire to record an event or historical perspective from the Indian point of view before it is forgotten, to demythify misleading concepts about the past."[12] *Tsali*, by Denton R. Bedford, dramatizes from a Cherokee perspective the outrage of the tribe's 1838 forced removal to Oklahoma. Dallas Chief Eagle, author of *Winter Count*, and Hyemeyohsts Storm, author of *Seven Arrows*, depict the steady extermination of the Plains Indians during the latter half of the nineteenth century. *Winter Count* depicts both the Battle of the Little Bighorn and the Wounded Knee massacre, its description of the former speculating that Custer committed suicide. In *Seven Arrows*, Larson finds an ultimate cautionary message for the dominant white society. Because Storm's novel shows that "[t]he Native American has survived in the white man's world precisely because of his ability to assimilate opposites," the message to "[t]he white man [is that he] will also have to learn to assimilate differing attitudes and beliefs if he is going to survive cultural diversity and heterogeneity."[13]

A more recent novel by a Native American conveys fully the richness of a nineteenth-century Native American world view. *Fools Crow*, by James Welch, immerses readers in the world of the Blackfeet in 1870s Montana. The story of the Lone Eaters, a band in the Pikuni or Blackfeet tribe, *Fools Crow* follows the development of the title character as he grows from a luckless young man into a leader of his people. While not shying away from describing the violence of war with other tribes—which, after all, was a part of life for the Pikuni—Welch is mostly concerned with depicting the familial and communal life of the Lone Eaters and the humanity and magic of their relationship to one another and with nature.

Welch effectively explodes the stereotype of the "savage" Indian, for here are a people with a spiritual life rooted firmly in cause and effect. Individual actions are governed by the real consequences these actions may have for the whole band. Ethics and morality are determined by the concrete rather than by the abstract. Honor is a real presence: "Honor is all we have, thought Rides-at-the-door, that and the blackhorns [buffalo]. Take away one or the other and we have nothing. One feeds us and the other nourishes us."[14]

This way of life is threatened by smallpox and soldiers, which also menace the Pikuni's spiritual life by threatening the surety of the cause and effect connection between the spiritual and physical worlds. In the end of the novel, having seen a vision of Pikuni children shunned by white society, Fools Crow wonders why the Above Ones have punished them. There is, of course, no answer.

In *Fools Crow*, Welch ultimately denies the dominant culture's mythic West. Immersed as the reader is with the sensibilities of the Pikuni, shown white culture rarely and then as an ominous encroachment, the white mythic West of conquests gained and destinies fulfilled vanishes. What's left is an intimate portrait of a people struggling to maintain physical and spiritual cohesion.

Novels like those by Bedford, Chief Eagle, Storm, and Welch are relatively rare in the canon of Native American literature. More often Native American authors prefer twentieth-century settings. This means, then, that views of pre-twentieth-century Indians are most often determined by white writers and filmmakers. Nevertheless, it is still possible to locate various attempts in literature and film by non-Natives to portray Native Americans sympathetically. However incomplete these sympathetic portrayals may ultimately be, they nonetheless do offer evidence that certain writers and directors of Westerns tried not to stereotype Indians and tried, moreover, to prod readers and viewers into rethinking their images of Native peoples.

In literature can be found the most earnest attempts to depict Native Americans with compassion and understanding. An example of this compassionate treatment can be seen in two novels that depict Native Americans with great respect and considerable insight. Douglas C. Jones's pair of novels, *Season of Yellow Leaf* and *Gone the Dreams and Dancing*, are set in

Texas and cover the conflict between white settlers and the Comanche. Without stooping to preaching, Jones is able to draw a balanced picture of the Comanche.

Season of Yellow Leaf opens in 1838 with the capture of ten-year-old Morfydd Annon Parry by a Comanche war party. Adopted by the tribe, she is given the name Chosen. Eventually, her white prejudices begin to disappear, and she comes to accept her captors as human beings for whom she cares deeply:

> She began to see the features of their faces for the first time, the broad copper and yellow and walnut-brown faces. And the blunt, powerful fingers on heavy hands, and the bodies and legs and feet and hair. Before, all she had really been aware of were black eyes, bloodshot usually, from wind-swept sand. But now she saw it all, the solid flesh and bone that made these beings people like herself.
>
> Not animals. Not demons sprung from the depths of earth, but people who talked and walked, who laughed and ate and drank and raised their children to the only life they knew. Who loved and died and were mourned, and who had fears just as she herself had.[15]

In the end of *Season of Yellow Leaf*, after Chosen has lived with the band for 16 years and borne two children, Texas Rangers attack the village, killing most of the men and horses and scattering the women and children. When the Rangers take Chosen to live again among whites, her son, Kwahadi, escapes and vows to bring her back to what he considers to be her people.

Gone the Dreams and Dancing is the sequel to *Season of Yellow Leaf*. It follows Kwahadi's life as he tries to help the defeated Comanche adapt to the "white man's road." This novel, too, is respectful of the Comanche way of life, and it conveys that respect through the narrative voice of Liverpool Morgan, a confederate veteran living at Fort Sill who witnesses the "pacification" of one of the last Comanche tribes, one led by Kwahadi.

Morgan's sympathy for the Comanche comes through his understanding of European history. He is aware that peoples have been conquered before, and he is not willing to accept the popular version of the newly conquered Comanches as savages. The first historical comparison comes early in the novel: "[They were] defiant still, I thought that day as I waited for them to come, in some ways akin to my own ancestors in Wales with the English industrialists sucking out the lifeblood."[16]

Because the Comanche and Morgan have both fought "the soldiers in blue coats," Morgan feels "a sense of closeness to these wild tribesmen."[17] More important, he sees in them a dignity he has not seen in peoples found in his study of European history. After troops burn the scalps from Kwahadi's war lance, for example, Morgan thinks:

> *In that moment I recalled some of my reading and imag-*
> *ined the spectacle of severed heads, dripping, being car-*
> *ried through the streets of Paris during the days of the*
> *revolution. It seemed to me that these scalps, heathen*
> *trophies of hard-won victories, perhaps, were more taste-*
> *ful, more easily stomached, being oiled and brushed and*
> *groomed and gleaning in the sun, showing respect at*
> *least for those who had once worn them.*[18]

Able to imagine the Comanche's place in world history, and capable of seeing beyond the self-serving cant of the times, Morgan is impressed with the "dignity and courage" of the Comanche as, even confined to a reservation, they maintain their collective identity. This identity and nobility is suggested in Morgan's musings on the Comanche language:

> *Maybe most of all I remembered their speaking, the*
> *Comanches. The words coming in bits and pieces from*
> *the past but always reminding me that here was a people*
> *who were called ignorant savages and yet whose lan-*
> *guage had all the nuance of diplomatic French, all the*
> *power of Mr. Henry Morton Stanley's English, all the*
> *tones and timbre of exquisite expression. . . . So much*
> *for those who called them ignorant savages!*[19]

In these two novels, Jones tries to correct racist images of Native Americans, and his attempted correction comes in two stories full of the kind of action most readers of Westerns could appreciate.

Perhaps one of the more well-known, positive portrayals of Native Americans comes in Thomas Berger's novel *Little Big Man*. Narrated by

111-year-old Jack Crabb, who lived the Old West experience as both a white man and as a member of the Cheyenne, *Little Big Man*, however, is more of a satire on white notions of civilization than a serious depiction of Native American life. As Jack tells his story, white ideals of progress and civilization are undercut. Indeed, the two most famous white characters in the novel, the icons Wild Bill Hickok and George Armstrong Custer, come off as little more than mad, though their portrayal in the book is more subtle than their depiction in the film version.[20]

Still, the Cheyenne characters in *Little Big Man* are more fully realized than their white counterparts. Since Berger seeks to satirize white culture, it stands to reason that his white characters would be more two-dimensional. The Indian characters, on the other hand, are allowed a balance between strength and foible. Beginning with the chief Old Lodge Skins and continuing through Jack's Cheyenne wife Sunshine, these characters are shown approaching life with wisdom and dignity, as well as their share of human folly. Old Lodge Skins, for example, leads his people—called Human Beings in Jack's translation of their name for Cheyenne—with an almost mystical grace. For one thing, he has a near supernatural ability to locate game, yet he is also prone to lust after other men's wives and daughters, which is the main reason his little band lives separately from the main tribe.

Above all, the Native American characters in the novel are perfectly centered; they know where lies "the center of the world, where all is self-explanatory merely because it *is*."[21] In contrast is Jack Crabb, who is mostly doomed to the white perception of progress defined by technological innovation and Victorian notions of "civilization," notions which lead to the worst kinds of hypocrisy. In the white world live hypocrites who praise feminine sexual virtue while making prostitution one of the more profitable Old Western enterprises, who justify the destruction of Native peoples to open the land to the greedy and the homicidal.

But *Little Big Man* is not a simple diatribe. It is, rather, the work of an author concerned with discovering the best in human nature while refusing to pander to the sentimental. Like most satirists, Berger is an idealist. Disappointed perhaps, but hopeful. And the prayer that Old Lodge Skins offers in the end of the novel speaks to the value to be found in the full scope of any life, lived by man or woman of any race.

Novels aside, Western movies seem to trouble critics most when they examine the portrayals of Native Americans through the years—probably because film is a more pervasive medium in our visual age. Attempts have been made, however, to prevent stereotypes in Western films. As early as 1950, in fact, a committee formed by the Association on American Indian Affairs began to advise filmmakers on ways to avoid Native American stereotypes.[22] Coincidentally, perhaps, one of the films most praised for its attempt to portray Native Americans with depth and sympathy, Delmer Daves's *Broken Arrow,* was released that same year.

For a thorough discussion of the films of the 1950s, 60s, and 70s which offer noteworthy portrayals of Native Americans, one can turn profitably to historian John H. Lenihan's *Showdown: Confronting Modern America in the Western Film.* Based on a viewing of hundreds of films, Lenihan's study offers to researchers an extensive list of Westerns which attempted to explore racial prejudice in America. Lenihan argues that 1950s Westerns which depict Indians sympathetically are implicitly responding to the burgeoning Civil Rights Movement of the era. He contends that Westerns could safely supply anti-racist messages in a form "with which a contemporary audience could identify."[23]

In this formulation, then, Westerns about Indians are really about America's treatment of blacks. While many of these films may not depict Native Americans all that realistically, at least in the aggregate they represent an attempt to offer a general critique of racism. Further, Lenihan's work demonstrates that early on, certain 1950s Westerns attempted an integrationist message by demonstrating "that no real basis exists for treating one race as inherently different from, and hence inferior to, another."[24] Into this category of integrationist film Lenihan places *Broken Arrow* (1950), *White Feather* (1955), *Taza, Son of Cochise* (1954), *Sitting Bull* (1954), *Chief Crazy Horse* (1955), and *Walk the Proud Land* (1956).

For Lenihan, the integrationist ideal is questioned in later films such as *The Broken Lance* (1954) and *Apache* (1954). Still later films are outright skeptical of America's ability to deal successfully with racism: *Reprisal* (1956), *The Last Hunt* (1956), and *Run of the Arrow* (1957). Of *Run of the Arrow*, Lenihan writes that director Samuel Fuller portrays "cruelty and hatred [as] . . . universal traits that render questionable the chances for racial harmony and peace." Furthermore, "Fuller wished no one to miss the point that the happiness of these sympathetic characters is dependent upon the nation's solving its racial prejudices. In lieu of the standard 'The End' title, he substituted 'The end of this story will be written by you.'"[25]

By the 1960s the integrationist ideal was openly rejected in Western films. To Lenihan, these films "emphasized the cruelty and intolerance of white society that discouraged racial harmony and provoked the Indian to violent resistance."[26] *Geronimo* (1962), for example, showed the righteousness of the famous Apache warrior's attempts to resist "American public forces [until] its political representatives . . . investigate[d] injustices on the reservation."[27] According to Lenihan, the "degeneracy of white society" is more fully underscored in the later countercultural films: *A Man Called Horse* (1970), *Soldier Blue* (1970), *Little Big Man* (1970), and *Jeremiah Johnson* (1972). By the time of *Ulzana's Raid* (1972), Westerns had completely revolted from the notion that races could live peacefully with one another. Of *Ulzana's Raid*, Lenihan contends, "[director] Aldrich . . . emphasized the inevitability of bloodshed between two totally disparate cultures."[28]

A more in-depth analysis of four films, each covering the United States Army's battles with the Apache, will reveal more fully the changing attitudes toward race to be found in Western movies. The amount of social critique in each of these films is clear; moreover, in their respective eras, each film stood out as an attempt to re-define racial attitudes. These four films are *Broken Arrow*, *Apache*, *Ulzana's Raid*, and the recently released *Geronimo* (1993).

Broken Arrow is cited in studies of 1950s Westerns as an early example of Hollywood's attempt to treat Native Americans compassionately. It is not the first film to endeavor such a serious treatment, however. In fact, even a few silent-era movies attempted serious Indian portrayals.[29] *Broken Arrow* is, however, widely credited as a "revisionist" film. For one thing, writer-director Delmer Daves lived with Indians as research for his motion picture.[30] This seems to have lent an authenticity to the film that critics have noted.

And *Broken Arrow* has been praised often. Author William K. Everson, for one, calls it "the best" film "on Indian-white problems."[31] Even Peter Biskind, who objects to the integrationist message sent by the film, credits *Broken Arrow* for its recognition of worth in a Native American people.[32]

Broken Arrow is set in Arizona in 1870. Narrator Tom Jeffords, played by James Stewart, recounts his role in the peace process between the Cochise-led Apaches and the U.S. government. From the beginning, *Broken Arrow* announces its intention to treat the Apache considerately. Jeffords tells us that in his tale, presumably for convenience, the Apache characters will speak English instead of their own language. This consideration continues in the story as when Jeffords nurses a wounded Apache boy back to health and begins to have a deeper, more human appreciation for a people he has previously seen only as an enemy. After the boy tells Jeffords that his mother will be longing for her son's return, the white man thinks, "'My mother is crying,' he said. Funny, it never struck me that an Apache woman would cry over a son like any other woman. Apaches were wild animals, we all said."[33]

The boy tells Jeffords that he will pray to his gods for him, and later he is able to talk a band of Apache out of killing Jeffords. Jeffords then thinks, "I learned something that day. Apache women cry about their sons. Apache men had a sense of fair play."

Soon, however, Jeffords witnesses an Apache attack on a group of white miners. One of the miners is carrying Apache scalps, and he is staked to an ant hill for his offense. In this scene, the cruelty of war is underscored, as Jeffords notes that such brutality has occurred "on both sides." Because he has seen too much killing, Jeffords returns to Tombstone with the desire to effect peace between the whites and the Apaches. In this effort, he is scorned by some of the town's citizens who believe peace without total victory is impossible.

Still, Jeffords learns Apache, and he sets out to find Cochise to negotiate the safe passage of white mail carriers through Apache land. When Jeffords first meets with Cochise, the peacemaker asks the chief, "Is it not possible that your people and mine cannot live together as brothers?" Cochise is skeptical, but—impressed with Jeffords's willingness to learn about Apache culture and seeing an opportunity to enhance his sense of personal power—agrees to let the mail riders through.

But the war is not over, and Cochise leads a well-coordinated attack against a wagon train, his men killing 50 soldiers. Back in Tombstone, Jeffords is blamed for his association with the man who led this attack, and a mob begins to hang him as "an Indian lover." He is saved, however, by a Bible-reading general, and Jeffords convinces the general to seek peace with the Apache. However, this cessation of hostilities must not demean Cochise and his people. As Jeffords explains it, any peace treaty must be based on "equality. The Apaches are a free people. They have a right to stay free on their own land."

Along with the theme of peace between races, *Broken Arrow* tries to address interracial love. Jeffords has fallen in love with Morning Star, a young Apache woman. Cochise attempts to talk them out of marriage, asking, "Is it not better to live with your own?" But the two are committed to marrying. And Jeffords, who now sees himself more intimately connected with the Apache, pushes harder for peace: "I wanted [peace] for my country. I wanted it for Cochise and his people. And I wanted it because I loved a girl."

Central to the integrationist message the film sends, then, is the love story between a white man and an Apache woman. Symbolically, they represent the union of two cultures, of two enemies. Unfortunately, the film has a real 1950s uneasiness about interracial marriage: Morning Star is killed in an ambush by white peace-breakers. In this, the fear of miscegenation is revealed. While esteeming the film overall, author Everson objects to the ending: "If one has cause for complaint at all, it is only at the censorship-dictated ending. Racial barriers being what they were at the time, an 'important' white star still was not permitted to marry an Indian woman and have it turn out happily."[34] In fact, Biskind notes that in many 1950s Western movies which featured a white man married to a Native woman, the woman died or was killed in the end.[35]

Broken Arrow is unwilling to push its depiction of harmony between white and Native Americans beyond the sexual taboos of the time. In the end, a troubled peace is kept by a determined Cochise. The hate-filled whites and the Apaches who follow Geronimo are portrayed as extremists. For these reasons, Biskind calls *Broken Arrow* a "centrist" film, and he argues that the cooperation between Jeffords and Cochise—two moderates from two different races—ultimately denies uniqueness to the Apaches.[36]

Biskind is right: *Broken Arrow* carries its integrationist message only so far, and from the perspective of 40 years of continued racial violence in this country, the message "why can't we all just get along" may seem quaintly idealistic. Still, for its time, *Broken Arrow* was daring to portray a

Native American people with understanding, as human beings rather than as savages. Objecting after all of these years that it doesn't go far enough is to lose sight of the positive gains it did make in the depiction of race relations.

Where *Broken Arrow* calls for peace and understanding, director Robert Aldrich's *Apache* takes a more critical view of white racism and its effects on Native Americans. *Apache* opens in 1886 and tells the story of Massai, an Apache warrior who refuses to surrender. Massai, played by Burt Lancaster in the era's tradition of casting white actors in Native roles, is so against peace that he shoots the surrender flag out of Geronimo's hand. When captured, Massai insists that he would rather die fighting: "If an Apache cannot live in his home mountains like his fathers before him, he is already dead."[37]

To Massai's wish to die in battle and have future generations of Apache sing his praises, army scout Al Sieber replies: "You're not a warrior anymore. You're a whipped Injun. And nobody sings about handcuffs."

Geronimo's band is rounded up and placed on a train to be transported to Fort Marion, Florida. The whites pride in having captured Geronimo is revealed in a scene which has an excited photographer eagerly taking pictures of the subdued Apache chief.

Massai, however, escapes the transport train. Wandering the noisy streets of St. Louis, he comes in contact with a white society in which he does not belong. When some young trouble-makers jeer him, a crowd forms and Massai is chased through the streets. The intolerance of white society is made clear here, and in a few subtle shots a class system based on race is also shown: Massai passes a black man in ragged clothes with his back pressed against a wall and sees Chinese immigrants working in a laundry, next door to a fine restaurant in which a well-dressed white man is dining.

Eluding the crowd, Massai escapes the city. Eventually he comes to the house of a Cherokee man who has become a farmer. This man takes Massai in and tries to teach him the value of living in harmony with white ways. This character represents the integrationist view, as he says: "Here Cherokee and white man live side by side. There is no difference." Giving Massai seed corn, a symbol of making peace by adopting white ways, the Cherokee man encourages the Apache warrior to stop fighting. However, with a kind of sad resignation the Cherokee tells Massai, "We found we could live with the white man only if we lived like him."

Massai takes the corn and returns to his reservation. Upon arrival he sees enslaved Apaches building a road, cruelly overseen in their labor by a white reservation agent. Wishing to restore "pride" to his people, Massai tells chief Santos that he plans to plant the corn: he plans to make "a warrior's peace. A peace between equals." Santos, however, turns Massai over to the army, and this betrayal inflames Massai's warrior spirit. He will continue his fight, alone.

Massai escapes from the reservation agent who had planned to murder him. Kidnapping Santos' daughter, he flees to the mountains. There, in a mimic of the outlaw/schoolmarm dynamic which appears in certain Westerns, Massai is tamed by his love for a woman. Together they plant corn, and Massai becomes a provider for the woman, who is now his wife, and for his unborn child.

Still, as his wife says, "There is a gun in Massai's mind." He has not renounced his war with the army. In the end, Sieber discovers Massai's hidden cabin and he brings troops to capture the warrior. Sieber and Massai fight in the grown patch of corn. Massai is about to kill Sieber when he hears the cry of his newborn child. In this moment, Massai's rage drains away, and the soldiers let him return to his wife's side, the general believing that the corn Massai has planted represents a changed, more docile Apache.

It is a wholly unbelievable ending, and not the finish that Aldrich wanted. According to Biskind, Aldrich wanted to take the film to its logical conclusion: showing Massai being killed. But he was forced by the studio to append a happy ending,[38] which is too bad, because the hokey finale undercuts much of the film's commentary on white racism. Nevertheless, in its portrayal of a dignified warrior who cannot be tamed, and in the love story between two Apaches, Native Americans are shown to be human beings worthy of respectful treatment. Moreover, the notion that Indians should simply be able to adopt white ways is questioned. Massai belongs to a particular culture and way of life. To get peace, he must seek it on his own terms, something which the white conquerors will not allow. Peace, for Massai, can only be found in a place far from white civilization.

That whites and Natives can co-exist at all is questioned in *Ulzana's Raid*. Again, some critics do not believe that this film offers a realistic portrayal of Native Americans. Critic Geoffrey O'Brien, for instance, argues that "[a]lthough [*Ulzana's Raid*] makes some motions in the direction of ethnographic understanding, the film is clearly not about Apaches but about the dread of Apaches."[39] Such a criticism, however, should not automatically devalue *Ulzana's Raid* as a motion picture worthy of study, for this film does offer suggestive commentary on race relations.

In fact, the ability of members of one race to understand another is thoroughly doubted in *Ulzana's Raid*. Coming at the end of an era which saw the rise of racial pride movements, this film supports the idea that minority races in America cannot possibly co-exist with the dominant white society because that dominant society is simply incapable of accepting the differences to be found in other cultures.

Representing the most sympathetic members of white society is Lt. Garnett DeBuin, an idealistic army officer who has been charged with capturing a war party led by the reservation-jumping Apache Ulzana. The commanding officer of Fort Lowell admits that he does not understand the Apache, so he assigns a veteran scout to DeBuin's command to help the inexperienced lieutenant. DeBuin and the scout, McIntosh, are opposites: DeBuin, who has no knowledge of Apache culture, wishes to treat the Indians with "Christian sympathy"; McIntosh, who speaks Apache and lives with an Apache woman, has no illusions about his ability to understand this warrior tribe. While respectful of the Apache, McIntosh nonetheless recognizes that their ways cannot be changed. Indeed, even he does not fully comprehend the Apache mind. When Ulzana's men kill a trooper and a rancher's wife, but spare the woman's son, DeBuin cannot understand why the boy would be allowed to live. McIntosh cannot explain it either, offering only the belief that the boy was saved by "a whim. The Apaches got lots of whim."[40]

This inability to comprehend the Apache is expressed later when the army troop finds a rancher who has been tortured to death and left with a dog's tail in his mouth. DeBuin wants to know the significance of the dog's tail. To his question, McIntosh responds, "Apaches got a sense of humor. Nothing you'd recognize. They just find some things funny."

Horrified by the killing and torture he has seen, DeBuin seeks answers. He questions the troop's Apache scout, urgently wanting to know why the Apache are "so cruel." The Apache scout, Ke-Ni-Tay, is clearly reluctant to address the lieutenant's questions. But eventually, in a compelling soliloquy, Ke-Ni-Tay tries to explain:

> *Ulzana is a long time in the agency [reservation]. His power is very thin. The smell in his nose is old smell of agency. . . . The smell of woman, the smell of dog, the smell of children. Man with old smell in nose is old man. Ulzana can be loose now. Pony running. The smell of burning, the smell of bullet. For power!*

Ulzana has been emasculated by the reservation. What he seeks on his raid is a revitalization to be found in expressing his warrior psychology. This is, of course, a psychology completely alien to white men, especially the would-be do-gooder Lieutenant DeBuin. DeBuin, the son of a minister, cannot understand why the Apache "do these terrible things. After all, they are men made in God's image like ourselves." His sergeant rejects the lieutenant's attempts to treat the Apache with Christian charity. Because he is a veteran of the wars with the Apache, the sergeant declares, "Ain't nobody gonna tell me to turn the other cheek to no Apache."

Ultimately, DeBuin is thwarted in his attempts to apply his own religious and cultural ideologies to an understanding of the Apache. Abandoning his desire to understand, DeBuin comes to hate the Apache instead. But McIntosh cautions him against hate, because hate interferes with reason and because such an emotion will not change the differences between the respective races. McIntosh says that hating the Apache would "be like hating the desert 'cause there ain't no water on it."

In the end, DeBuin is helpless. He cannot stop the slaughter without McIntosh and Ke-Ni-Tay's help, and he cannot understand the enemy he is fighting. All he can do is insist that the Apache warriors his men kill be buried. Ke-Ni-Tay plays the biggest role in killing members of Ulzana's war party to end their raid. When Ulzana sees the cavalry bugle that his son carried, his eyes tear up, and he sinks to his knees to sing a mourning song. Then he is shot by Ke-Ni-Tay, the only witness to Ulzana's grief.

No white man sees Ulzana's death, just as no white man understands his need to make war. The only common ground these two races can find is one based on respect for the other's ability to kill. Such is the respect that occurs between Ke-Ni-Tay and McIntosh. That the two races will never comprehend the other is underscored in the filmmaking decision to have the Indian characters speak Apache without subtitles.

In many ways, *Ulzana's Raid* marks an acceptance of the beliefs raised by such movements as the Black Panthers, for the film not only negates the integrationist view point, but it also doubts that peaceful co-existence is possible. Races are doomed to remain separate, incapable of mutual understanding or appreciation. In *Ulzana's Raid*, respect and power can be gained only through violent opposition to oppressors. Such a view of race relations is still with us, alive in much of the real race-based violence which occurs in this country.

If *Ulzana's Raid* openly scoffs at the possibility for a peaceful, multicultural America, the recently released *Geronimo* is more hopeful that the various races in the United States can discover a common bond. Tellingly, director Walter Hill insisted he would not make his version of the Geronimo story before he could find a Native American to play the title role, which went to Wes Studi.[41]

Even more significant, *Geronimo* is subtitled *An American Legend*. This subtitle is thematically suggestive, for in places this film attempts to speak to what makes America special: tolerance, idealism, and an Old West which contained heroes both red and white. The two principal characters are presented heroically, and not surprisingly, they become allies against a repressive racism. Geronimo is presented here as a warrior learning to lead his people. The other main character is Lt. Charles B. Gatewood, a soft-spoken Virginian who has "sympathy and knowledge of all things pertaining to the Apache."[42]

Early in the film, Gatewood is sent to bring Geronimo onto the reservation. With him is the film's narrator, 2d Lt. Britton Davis, an impressionable officer fresh from West Point. Geronimo and Gatewood become almost instant allies. When a posse from Tombstone threatens to take Geronimo and lynch him, Gatewood supports the Chiricahua Apache warrior in a near-violation of the law. Together, the two men manage to scare off the posse.

Later, an army policy to suppress Apache medicine men who preach against the government leads to a skirmish which sends Geronimo off the reservation and into a series of bloody raids. In the film, neither white nor Apache violence is condoned. The ugly side of violence is carefully balanced: an Apache attack on a stagecoach parallels a massacre of innocent Yaquis by white bounty hunters. That neither side is morally superior is underscored in an exchange between Geronimo and General Crook, an officer who has sympathy for the Apache. When Crook exclaims that Geronimo has "killed women and children," the warrior retorts, "so did you." To this, Crook has no answer.

While not excusing Apache violence, the film is still clearly sympathetic to them as a people. Geronimo's longest speech illustrates this sympathy:

> *When I was young, the white eye came and wanted the land of my people. When their soldiers burnt our villages, we moved to the mountains. When they took our food, we ate thorns. When they killed our children, we had more. We killed all white eye that we could. We starved and we killed. But in our hearts we never surrendered.*

In the end, General Nelson Miles is assigned to bring Geronimo back onto the reservation. Crook is forced to resign, and as he does so, he recognizes that he is being forced out by politicians who use the army to kill Apache and protect white economic interests. When Geronimo surrenders to Gatewood, he gives up because he has tired of killing. Once Geronimo is back on the reservation, Nelson has the Apache scouts the army has employed arrested and removed from military service. Such a dishonor disturbs young Lt. Davis, and he resigns his commission. To Miles, Davis is merely unrealistic, as he says, "I hate an idealist. There's always something messy about them."

As Geronimo and the other Chiricahua Apache are being shipped to exile in Florida, Davis's voice-over sounds a sorrowful note: "A way of life that had endured for a thousand years was gone. This desert, this land that we look out on, would never be the same." This sense of finality is stressed in an exchange between Geronimo and an Apache who had scouted for the army. On the train east, the former scout insists that he was wrong to serve the army, because everything whites had told him turned out to be a lie. Geronimo concludes the discussion and the film by stating, "Now, maybe the time of our people is over."

The ending is significant, because it underscores the film's attempt to offer social commentary. In a way, this is a somewhat confused film. Does it want to be an action picture or a critical examination of racism? There certainly is a great deal of violent action in the movie, something not unusual in a script by John Milius. At times, then, the social commentary is lost amid gunplay and detours into the kind of macho showdown so familiar to the Western genre. For some viewers, then, it may be difficult to consider *Geronimo* as anything more than an action yarn.

Nevertheless, there are enough reflective moments in the film to sustain its attempts at social commentary. Its main theme, emphasized by the ending, is this: America lost something when it subdued such a proud and noble people. America lost, too, when it compromised its ideals, by forcing soldiers like Gatewood and Crook to kill for the greed of politicians, miners, and land speculators. At one point in the film, Gatewood speaks of his father and brothers who served the Confederacy in the Civil War. When the war was over, Gatewood's father sent him to West Point to serve the one America. That one America, *Geronimo: An American Legend* suggests, must pay homage to all of its courageous and principled men regardless of their race. In this way, a truly multicultural nation is possible.

That awareness of a multicultural or multiracial West is often missing from most Westerns. On film, the West seemed to belong mostly to white cowboys or settlers who often warred with Indians. Missing from the bulk of these cinematic Westerns were others who shared in the Westward expansion: Asians who built railroads, Mexicans who founded missions and cattle ranches, blacks who went west to become independent farmers and cowhands.

Asian-Americans have been least represented in Western films and television programs, at least as central characters. And, given the popular nineteenth-century perception of Asians on the frontier, perhaps such under representation could be considered a kind of blessing. The popular misreading of a poem by Bret Harte illustrates the nineteenth-century stereotype of Asians. In "Plain Language from Truthful James," published in 1870, Harte introduces the character Ah Sin.

Unfortunately, the poem became popular for reasons unintended by the author. Widely published in its day, the poem's irony was lost on most readers. Instead of seeing in the verse a cowardly excuse for violence done to a Chinese man who has out-cheated a cardsharp, readers accepted the poem as confirmation of their prejudices.[43] In the poem, Ah Sin is thus maligned by the speaker, friend to the man who has beaten him: "That for ways that are dark / And for tricks that are vain, / The heathen Chinee is peculiar." That readers accepted this sentiment at face value distressed Harte. According to biographer Richard O'Connor, Harte "had always been vigorously opposed to any form of racial prejudice and was especially, and out-spokenly, disgusted by the harsh treatment of the Chinese in northern California."[44]

Modern exceptions to the under-representation of Asians in Westerns include the movie *Walk Like a Dragon* (1960) which features "a Chinese immigrant [who] Americanizes himself by learning the arts of the gunfighter."[45] Even though he was half white, Kwai Chang Caine, the lead character in the television program *Kung Fu* (1972-1975), did offer a portrayal of a strong Asian man in the Old West. Played by David Carradine, Caine roamed the West, searching for a long-lost brother and righting wrongs. The recent film *Thousand Pieces of Gold* also places Asian-American actors in complex leading roles.

Hispanics also get short shrift in Westerns; they are rarely portrayed as anything more than killers or victims. In many movies they are both; for example in *The Magnificent Seven* (1960) the Mexican characters come in two types: helpless farmers who must hire protection and vicious outlaws who prey on innocent villagers. Exceptions to these stereotypes include the Spanish-made *Valdez Is Coming* (1971), which features a strong Mexican-American protagonist. A later film, *The Ballad of Gregorio Cortez* (1982), also gives a central place to Hispanic characters in its depiction of white racism directed at Mexican-Americans.

The Ballad of Gregorio Cortez, based on a true story, narrates the pursuit and capture of a Mexican man in South Texas in 1901. Accused of killing a sheriff who had come to arrest him, Gregorio eludes over 600 pursuers for 11 days. When he is finally caught, his court-appointed attorney learns that Gregorio shot in self defense. Because the interpreter for the sheriff did not properly distinguish between the Spanish words for male and female horses, the sheriff believed Gregorio to be guilty of horse thievery. During the attempted arrest, the sheriff shoots Gregorio's brother, and that is when Gregorio shoots the lawman.

To the Mexicans of South Texas, Gregorio becomes a folk hero, featured in a popular ballad. To the majority white society, however, Gregorio is a dangerous killer. White fear and racism are so strong that Gregorio has to be saved from a mob out to lynch "that damn greaser."[46] Although sentenced at his first trial to 50 years in prison, Gregorio is tried six times, serving 12 years before being pardoned in 1913. So along with portraying a Mexican-American hero, the film reveals how racism and hatred can lead to injustice and repression.

More prominent than Asians or Hispanics in Westerns have been blacks, but even here the depictions have been subject to stereotyping and misinformation. Authors David Daly and Joel Persky sum up the portrayals of African-Americans in Western films this way:

> It is reasonable to assume that black-white interaction did indeed have some importance in shaping a frontier culture in the late nineteenth century. But this fact has not played any truly significant role in the evolution of the Western. For example, the cinema has almost totally avoided dealing with the historical reality and national significance of slavery or abolition issues. Nor has there been any meaningful exploration of the relationship between white settlers (many of whom were from the slave-owning South) and blacks seeking their freedom in the West.[47]

Still, African-Americans have appeared in Westerns more frequently than Asians and Hispanics, thanks largely to the so-called "race" movies of the early twentieth century. These films, featuring black actors, were made by blacks to be shown to African-American audiences. One noted director of these "race" films used a Western setting and theme as the basis for his first movie. Director Oscar Micheaux made *The Homesteader* in 1918, shooting it in South Dakota.[48] Another early "race" Western, *The Trooper of Troop K* (1916), told the story of a black cavalry troop. By providing a black hero, the film "reverse[d] the then-common racist imagery blacks suffered in mainstream movies."[49]

However, because they were meant for an African-American audience, and because they often merely patterned themselves on "white" films, "race" movies certainly did not change the dominant view of blacks to be found in white America. In fact, these "race" films may have contributed to racial stereotypes within the African-American community, as Daly and Persky contend of the films which starred black singing cowboy Herb Jeffries:

> But "race" movies often continued to perpetuate some of the objectionable racial stereotypes so often found in mainstream films, like the slow-witted, eye-rolling Negro, a Hollywood staple for many years. Significantly, Jeffries played a light-skinned black hero while the villains were generally darker-skinned. At the end he would always get the girl, who was usually light-skinned herself. What this did was help to perpetuate the class system of color that generally exists in black society right up to the present.[50]

The stereotyping of blacks in Hollywood Westerns shows up in two of the few films which featured central African-American characters during the Golden Age of postwar Westerns. In *Stars in My Crown* (1950), star Juano Hernandez plays a black man saved from vigilantes by a white man. But Lenihan argues that the film "was more a justification of the Southern dream of harmonious segregation than a forceful indictment of social discrimination."[51] Ten years later, John Ford's *Sergeant Rutledge* also sent the message that only through white intervention could African-Americans succeed. In this film, a black cavalryman, played by Woody Strode,[52] is saved from false murder and rape charges by a white officer.

Nevertheless, in the 1960s and early 1970s African-American actors did turn up in lead roles in Hollywood Westerns. Sidney Poitier co-starred with James Garner in *Duel at Diablo* (1966).[53] Jim Brown starred with Raquel Welch in *100 Rifles*. Sammy Davis Jr. is the most memorable part of the eminently forgettable *Little Moon and Jud McGraw*, playing with relish a leather-clad gunslinger.[54] And Bill Cosby played a father in the Western *Man and Boy* (1971).

A more significant film than these, however, is the Sidney Poitier-directed *Buck and the Preacher* (1971). In this movie, Poitier also starred as a leader of a wagon train of freed slaves pursued by white racists. While he does not praise Poitier's acting, Donald Bogle, an authority on African-Americans in film and television, believes that Poitier's role offered to African-Americans a strong character who does not sell out to white society: "After having starred for years as the liberal fantasy model integrationist hero (always conciliatory and 'reasonable'), Poitier re-established his roots with the black community with this [film], the first of his movies pitched directly at the black market."[55]

Bogle also notes the social significance of *Buck and the Preacher*: "The blacks [in the film] unite with American Indians at one point to battle the white man, their mutual oppressor. Could politically conscious audiences have hoped for more from commercial cinema?"[56]

In addition to these mainstream Hollywood films, so-called "blaxploitation" Westerns of the early 1970s "attempted to remake the West in black terms and appeal directly to black audiences."[57] However, Daly and Persky believe that most of these films offer mere escapism, singling out just two—*The Legend of Nigger Charley* (1972) and *Boss Nigger* (1974)—as offering "serious social and political issues."[58]

Bogle's opinion of these "blaxploitation" films offers insight into their appeal for African-American audiences, particularly males. For Bogle, these films follow a set "formula": "a strong aggressive black man bests Whitey and waltzes off into the sunset—with a cache of money and his old lady, too."[59] In his review of *The Legend of Nigger Charley*, for example, Bogle argues that even though the filmmakers were motivated more by money than by a desire to paint an accurate historical portrait of African-Americans in the West, the movie and its sequel, *The Soul of Nigger Charley* (1973), at least offer a portrayal of a powerful, independent black man.[60]

However, despite these Westerns' attempts to place African-American men in central roles, Bogle is skeptical of their merit as tools for social change. While he acknowledges that these films may try to set right the mistaken notion that there were no blacks in the West, and while he allows that they may give to African-American children the kind of "mythic structure and heroic struggles" that white kids can find in Westerns starring white actors, he is concerned about the gender roles found in all formulaic Westerns:

> But in the 1970s and afterwards if a black western
> couldn't go beyond the dynamics (and the built-in fail-
> ures) of the familiar formula white western of past film
> history, then there doesn't seem to be much point in mak-
> ing one. Who wants a black child to grow up with the
> same distorted macho and territorial values many white
> children have had foisted on them (values that contrib-
> uted to bigotry and racism).[61]

Bogle's argument helps to make the point that those Westerns which are
most capable of offering social critique are often the ones which subvert
established formulas in the genre.

Unfortunately for Bogle's concern over the image of masculinity found
in the genre, the most recent attempt to portray African-Americans
in the Old West does nothing to change the macho-driven plots of so
many Westerns. The Mario Van Peebles-directed *Posse* (1993) is a male-
dominated action flick straight from a Hollywood adman's dream. Nevertheless, while Van Peebles freely admits that he wanted to make an
exciting film which would have mass appeal, he also believed that by
making a Western he could more easily offer social commentary "without being preachy."[62]

The social commentary here is about the nature of racial violence in
America. In fact, certain scenes in *Posse* are intentional parallels to
the Rodney King beating and the violence which erupted after the King
trial.[63]

Marketed as "The Untold Story of the Wild West," *Posse* begins with an
old black man, played by Woody Strode, talking about the various African-
American Western heroes who have been overlooked by history. Laced
throughout this opening segment is the indication that the historical record
has been controlled by whites to enhance their power. As the old man
says:

> History's a funny thing. They got us believing that Co-
> lumbus discovered America and the Indians were already
> here. That's like me telling you, and you're sitting in
> your car, that I discovered your car. Then they want to
> call 'em the evil red savages because they didn't give up
> the car soon enough.[64]

Immediately, then, in its use of modern imagery, *Posse* connects past racial injustices with current ones. This connection of past with present is made, too, in the film's use of contemporary musical styles and modern slang and profanity.

Posse opens in Cuba in 1898. On the front lines in the Spanish-American War is the all-black tenth cavalry; behind the lines is an egotistical white colonel. This Col. Graham orders Jesse Lee, played by Mario Van Peebles, to raid a Spanish supply train. During the raid, Jesse discovers the train was carrying gold coins, gold for which Col. Graham will kill Jesse and his men. But Jesse's "posse" escapes from Graham and his henchmen, taking the gold with them to the United States.

In the States, Jesse goes West, looking to kill the white racists who murdered his minister father. Posse in tow, Jesse eventually arrives in Freemanville, an all-black town. Here, he becomes embroiled in a fight between the residents of Freemanville and the all-white, Klu Klux Klan-dominated Cutterstown. Because the whites want to drive off the citizens of Freemanville to sell the town site to the railroad, Jesse leads the black townspeople in a fight to defend their homes.

The citizens of Freemanville decide to fight after witnessing the beating of the posse's only white member, Little J. In this scene, which has white racists beat a white man, a parallel is established with the Rodney King beating. Van Peebles has admitted that he wanted the audience to identify with the white character.[65] So in this scene, the injustices of racial violence are shown to have victims of all colors. Subtly, Van Peebles has suggested that justice must be fought for by all races. In fact, Van Peebles is uncomfortable with the suggestion that his is merely a "black" Western. As he quipped to an interviewer, "We have more white people in *Posse* than *Unforgiven* had black people, but they didn't call that a *white* western."[66]

That may be so, but in its white-town versus black-town plot, *Posse* does establish a largely two-sided racial conflict. In this conflict, three positions for blacks are offered. First, they can give up on America and return to Africa, as one resident of Freemanville decides to do. Second, they can act like Freemanville's sheriff and sell out to white interests, putting personal gain before racial justice. Or third, they can act like Jesse: They can fight to eliminate racial injustice and secure their rightful place in the West. In the end, Jesse wins, killing both the racist sheriff from Cutterstown[67] and the persistent Col. Graham. Jesse vows, then, to rebuild Freemanville.

In many ways, the plot of *Posse* is sophomoric, full of cardboard characters and mindless action. Nevertheless, particularly in its opening and closing scenes which feature the old black man, the film underscores the rightful place African-Americans should have in the history of the Old West. The titles which appear on the screen in the end emphasize the connection between Old West and contemporary African-Americans, making explicit the connection between past and present racial and economic injustice:

> The majority of Black towns [in the Old West] were destroyed, partly due to laws like the 'Grandfather Clause,' which kept African-Americans from voting on the basis that their Grandfathers as slaves had not voted. Often intimidated or lynched if they tried to own property, and discouraged from educating themselves, most of the early Black settlers were successfully kept from power.
>
> Today, approximately twelve percent of Americans are African-Americans. However, that twelve percent owns less than one-half of one percent of America's wealth.
>
> Although ignored by Hollywood and most history books, the memory of the more than 8,000 Black cowboys that roamed the early West lives on.

Clearly, *Posse* attempts to correct a long-distorted view of blacks in the Old West. That it makes this attempt amid the kind of hyperkinetic violence currently favored by Hollywood movies should not detract from its social message. To date, *Posse* marks the most explicit endeavor to reach a mass audience with the message that racial intolerance and race-motivated violence occurred in the Old West, and that it is incumbent upon those who inherited a land founded and developed by all races to assert themselves to ensure racial justice.

Fundamentally, those Westerns which portray racial minorities as strong central characters worthy of respect can help to empower members of those minority groups in the contemporary United States.[68] At stake in any Western is the dominant society's view of an American past which is most credited with shaping our national character. Even if one does not wholly accept Frederick Jackson Turner's thesis that out of the "crucible" of Westward expansion came the great American character, one should be able to see that the Old West has lent to our national consciousness much of the mythology through which we understand certain national ideals. The image of the independent cowboy or farmer, for example, gives form to the idea that Americans are a nation of individualists. And the cliché "pull yourself up by your own bootstraps" has more than a little Old West in it. Suggestively, Dee Brown, author of *Bury My Heart at Wounded Knee*, is convinced that "Americans know neither their country nor themselves unless they know the story of the old Wild West."[69]

That fictional accounts of the Old West can function as cultural myths with contemporary significance is a point made by James K. Folsom in *The American Western Novel*. Folsom argues that since Westerns are "fable[s]" not subject to criticism as realistic fiction, they are able to address ongoing questions of American character, are able to attempt answers to the question: What is an American?

> It has not been sufficiently recognized that [the Western's] nature is finally unrealistic; that the Western is usually a 'myth' or 'fable.' The material of this fable is based . . . upon American history, but the purpose of the fable is not the realistic explication of a colorful chapter of the American past. It is rather a metaphorical parable of the inconsistencies and contradictions which inhere in the American's paradoxical views about himself, his country, and his destiny. At bottom the Western depicts— often shallowly, sometimes profoundly, but always clearly—the argument . . . about what the American experiences should be.[70]

If it is accepted that the Western addresses the American character, then by laying claim to a piece of the past, both actual and imagined, present day American minorities can claim their contributions to a national character. Simply by claiming "we were there," Native Americans as well as those of African, Hispanic, and Asian heritage, can achieve greater access to the consciousness of white Americans. The notion of the American character as depicted in so many Westerns is generally one based on white, Protestant, patriarchal values. Over the years, however, certain Westerns have attempted to include other points of view. Given today's increasing attention to the multicultural make up of America, it is easier for producers of Westerns to include sympathetic portrayals of Americans of Native, African, Hispanic, and Asian birthright, as well as of women. But the effort to include these various points of view has been, in smaller measure, occurring in Westerns at least since 1950.

S I X

Commercialization and the Loss of Personal Integrity

A COMMON, IF SIMPLISTIC, criticism of Westerns is that they are frequently tinged with nostalgia.[1] Notions that Westerns frequently fashion a past without ambiguity—free of moral dilemma and ethical confusion—give rise to the critical generalization that "the Western rarely makes a truly profound or transcendent statement about the conflicts it expresses. Also, the highly conventionalized tradition of the Western does not encourage new interpretations of the American past."[2] However, critic Christine Bold, discovering one instance when Western artists used their material "subversively," locates in the work of Owen Wister, Frederic Remington, and Emerson Hough an impulse "to oppose the course of history."[3] Ultimately, Bold argues, these artists fail to keep out of their work hints that the real West was not at all like the one they tried to create. For Bold it is "the next generation of formulists—Zane Grey and the like, who were one stage further removed from the nineteenth-century frontier" who finalize the stereotypical Western with its unambiguous characterizations, standard plot, and happy ending.[4]

Nevertheless, it can be argued that the twentieth century's seminal Western, Wister's *The Virginian*, did romanticize the past, and, as Bernard de Voto argues, a partial cause for this romanticization was the attempt to disguise the real role the large ranchers played in the Johnson County War. Even in Bold's reading, whether or not they were wholly successful, Wister, Remington, and Hough did try to create a romanticized view of the Old West, styling it as a place where adventure and glory were possible. Such a view, perhaps disseminated more thoroughly by later writers and artists, not only prevents a more factual exploration of the past but also may lead to thematic stagnation.

However, one kind of idealized vision of the Old West offers implicit critique on the ways in which American society developed. In many Westerns, an idealized past is based in part upon the repudiation of moneymaking. The belief that civilization is founded on economic expansion is a threat to certain ideals frequently advanced in Westerns. Contradictorily, while often that quintessential individualism found in so many Western heroes is transformed into the cultural myth that undergirds American capitalism, Westerns have a long suspicion of capitalistic enterprise. In many Westerns, capitalists, be they merchants or railroaders or large ranchers looking to protect their economic dominance, are seen as threats to a Western character which advocates fair play and the democratic belief that every hard-working individual deserves an equal chance.

According to critic James K. Folsom, many Westerns oppose modern-day capitalism by seeking to establish a new set of "values":

> *The Western mirrors the persistent nagging doubt in American life about whether the choice which America made to become a great, capitalist, industrial power was indeed a wise one. Not surprisingly, objections to modern American life have often taken the form of myths about alternative American destinies, destinies which at least for artistic purposes Americans like to think they positively chose against. The Western, therefore, is not so much true to the facts of American Western history as a mirror image of modern American life, in which the virtuous Westerner, representative of an older and different order, is contrasted with a morally inferior modern— and often Eastern—world. To say, as many critics have, that Westerns are "nostalgic" is to miss the point. They do not so much yearn for an older and simpler life as attempt to set up an alternative standard of values to the often shabby ones of modern finance capitalism.*[5]

To oppose capitalism and to establish this "alternative standard of values," certain Westerns take the view that rich men, and not Indians or outlaws, are the enemy. Richard Slotkin locates an early instance of this kind of socio-economic critique in the film *Jesse James* (1939). Credited with beginning the "cult of the outlaw," this film can also be read as anti-capitalist. Slotkin writes, "[Henry] King's folk epic took the gangster film's dark and critical view of American capitalism, gave it populist appeal by shifting the action from the modern city to the agrarian past and managed to blend a critique of economic exploitation into a story that still ends by celebrating American progress."[6] Done by sympathetic characters, then, the robbing of trains and banks in Westerns can be read as a symbolic attack on repressive moneyed interests.

In addition to bankers and railroad magnates, ranchers who hire gunmen to drive settlers off of the range often become villains in many Westerns. What makes these ranchers so despicable is not just their inability to fight for themselves, but their greed: They believe that the range belongs to them, and that they have the right to keep the natural resources of the West to themselves. Moreover, as large outfits, they use their size and strength of numbers to prevent individual entrepreneurs, farmers, from getting their start in a new land. There is something odiously un-American about large cattle concerns preventing a noble yeoman farmer from building a sod cabin and raising a family on land he has homesteaded.

A variation of this kind of anti-capitalist theme can be seen in the movie *Invitation to a Gunfighter* (1964). In this one Yul Brynner plays a crisply composed gunman who stops off in little Pecos, New Mexico. The year is 1865, and the Civil War has recently ended. Home from the war comes Matt Weaver, one of two local men who fought for the Confederates. The other man was Matt's father who was killed in action. Matt's sorrow is increased when he discovers that his mother has died, his girlfriend has married another man, and his family's farm has been stolen by the local rich and powerful banker.

This banker soon hires Brynner's character to kill Matt. Guilty of standing up to Bruster, the banker, and accused of killing a man, Matt poses a threat to the town. One townsman puts the conflict in purely economic terms when he exclaims, "We can't wait a year [to apprehend Matt]; business will go to pot!"[7] At first, Jules, the Creole hired gun, agrees to the job. As the story progresses, however, Jules begins to despise Bruster for waving the bloody shirt—exploiting animosity toward the Confederates—to further his own power and economic position.

Soon Jules begins to take advantage of the Pecos residents and shop-keepers. He knows that none of them has the courage to try to kill him, so he cheats openly at cards and he steals from a shopkeeper who is unctuously acting as middleman for war widows desperate to sell their jewelry to survive. Jules, it turns out, possesses an egalitarian spirit. Because his mother was a quadroon slave, Jules, despite his education and talent, has often been considered "not human." He therefore hates social injustice, and in Pecos to be a Mexican or a "Reb" is to be a social outcast.

To redress the town's social and economic sins, and to express his contempt for the shopkeepers' hypocritical greed, Jules rampages down Main Street, smashing shop windows and throwing merchandise in a Mexican's burro cart. The businessmen are too frightened to stop him, so to protect their economic interests they conveniently alter their principles: They hire Matt to kill Jules.

In the requisite final shoot-out, Jules is killed, but his death brings the town together, for Bruster's hypocrisy is revealed before he, too, is killed. Free from the banker's tyrannical rule, both Mexican residents and members of the white establishment can unite. In a symbolic conclusion, Mexicans and whites bear away Jules's body. Certainly this unity is too pat. Nevertheless, *Invitation to a Gunfighter* is an entertaining dramatization of a frequent Western theme: The greed and selfishness of the few is a danger to the happiness and harmony of the many.

Other Westerns are not so blatantly anti-capitalist; rather they are merely uneasy with money, either because it blinds people to injustice or because the pursuit of it is depicted as somehow tainted. In *Broken Arrow* a character equates civilization with the goods he can sell, in particular whiskey. But the Apache are preventing him from importing these goods, so he wants them killed or at the very least imprisoned on a reservation. In *High Noon* it is implied that one reason the residents of Hadleyville don't want trouble is that new business may be coming to town, and gunplay in the streets is bad for business. Uphold law and order, fine, but don't turn enforcement of the law into a public relations fiasco.

The making of money in many Westerns often demeans individuals and prevents them from living freely. For example, in *Big Jake* (1971)

John Wayne plays a millionaire cattleman who has forsaken his financial empire to roam the countryside, free from the difficulties of having to operate his vast holdings. It's a good thing that such a man exists, too, because when outlaws abduct Big Jake's grandson, only he, and not men who have grown soft in a mercantile economy, can track down the kidnappers. Even a movie as lighthearted as *The Cheyenne Social Club* (1970) implies that money is a personal devil. In this film a cowboy, played by James Stewart, inherits his brother's brothel. But although the cowboy tries to play the part of the successful businessman, he discovers that he is not cut out for such a role, and by the end of the film, he and his sidekick have returned to a more fulfilling labor: punching cattle.

A more extensive critique of commercial culture can be found in two excellent novels and one intriguing film. In their novels *True Grit* and *Roman* Charles Portis and Douglas C. Jones both question the purity of motives held by postbellum Westerners as they settled and operated in the West, for it is clear in both novels that economic gain is the primary motivation behind such settlement. Furthermore, by revealing the loss of personal integrity which occurred when the Old West became tainted by commerce and financial concern, Portis and Jones offer a critique of a contemporary commercial culture in which financial success takes precedence over spiritual gain.

In *True Grit*, the insistence on pay for every service rendered and on cutting the best deal in a trade operates as a motif which highlights the increasing rarity of the charitable gesture in modern society. In *Roman*, a parallel is drawn between the economic expansion in the post-Civil War West and the freebooting financial practices of the 1980s to underscore the difficulty of maintaining an ethical and moral compass in a society in which making money has supplanted the cultivation of personal integrity.

On film, Sam Shepard's *Silent Tongue* (1992) dramatizes the madness of possession and the spiritual aridity of a materialistic society. A darker tale than the ones offered by Portis and Jones, *Silent Tongue* explores the existential results of a society in which monetary transaction and selfish possession replace compassion and self sacrifice.

As a novel, *True Grit* is remarkable for a number of reasons, but the primary one lies in its voice—that of Mattie Ross, an older woman recounting her adventures as a 14-year-old. The novel is set in 1878

Arkansas, the site of Fort Smith and the home of Hanging Judge Isaac Parker. Mattie journeys to Fort Smith to find her father's killer and hires one of Parker's marshals to guide her into the Territories and help her hunt down the murdering Tom Chaney. Though paid by her, Marshal Rooster Cogburn, joined by a Texas Ranger named LaBoeuf, reluctantly takes Mattie along on his search. In the novel's stirring end, Tom Chaney and the thieving gang he rides with are discovered. Rooster, with his reins in his teeth and pistols in each hand, confronts four of the outlaws on horseback, shooting three of them and escaping death from the fourth when LaBoeuf shoots Lucky Ned Pepper from afar. Immediately after this gun battle, Rooster rescues Mattie from a pit full of rattlesnakes and carries her back to Fort Smith, where her snake-bitten arm is amputated to save her life. Certainly, the novel provides a rousing tale of adventure, and viewers of the film version, which stars John Wayne as Rooster Cogburn, will recall vividly the celluloid depiction of the story's action.

But what the film adaptation leaves out is the voice of Mattie Ross as narrator, the personality which enlivens the printed story. At the end of the novel we discover that she has become a successful businesswoman, that she has never married and never wanted to—in short, that she possesses the kind of "grit" which allows her to succeed in a commercial world. Such grit becomes clear early in the novel as Mattie describes her quest for her father's killer. Her memory is phenomenal; these are not the confused ramblings of an old woman romanticizing her personal history. And some of her more detailed memories involve her financial transactions as she hires Rooster and prepares to journey to the Territories.

Money becomes a theme from the first paragraph when Mattie informs us that "Tom Chaney shot my father down in Fort Smith, Arkansas, and robbed him of his life and his horse and $150 in cash money plus two California gold pieces that he carried in his trouser band."[8] Throughout her narrative, Mattie mentions how much she pays for things, from an (to her mind) overly expensive boarding room to the cost of her father's coffin and the charge to ship his body home by railroad. Indeed, it seems that commercial opportunities abound in Fort Smith: When Mattie attends a hanging she spies "[a] noisy boy . . . going through the crowd selling parched peanuts and fudge. Another one was selling 'hot tamales' out of a bucket."[9] But there is something suspect in all of this bustling commerce, and it is not just a matter of two enterprising young boys profiting by the hunger of gawkers at a hanging. Mattie's father is shot while in the company of "drummers" or salesmen, and it is clear that these men are cowards because they do not pursue Chaney:

> Now the drummers did not rush out to grab Chaney or shoot him but instead scattered like poultry while Chaney took my father's purse from his warm body and ripped open the trouser band and took the gold pieces too. I cannot say how he knew about them. When he finished his thieving he raced to the end of the street and struck the night watchman at the stock barn a fierce blow to the mouth with his rifle stock, knocking him silly. He put a bridle on Papa's horse Judy and rode out bareback. . . . He might have taken the time to saddle the horse or hitched up three spans of mules to a Concord stagecoach and smoked a pipe as it seems no one in that city was after him. He had mistaken the drummers for men. "The wicked flee when none pursueth."[10]

From this account, while these drummers represent the new breed of commercial man, they seem incapable of dealing with the violence of the older West.

If the new commercial man is ill-equipped to function in a less pacified society, even as that society is passing away, older men like Rooster have become anachronisms in a rapidly developing commercial economy. At one point Mattie finds Rooster laboring over his "fee sheets," or itemized expense accounts. He has trouble filling out the ruled pages because his "handwriting was so large and misguided that it covered the lines and wandered up and down into places where it should not have gone."[11] Rooster underscores his lack of preparation for the emerging commercial economy:

> What you see is an honest man who has worked half the night on his fee sheets. It is the devil's own work and Potter is not here to help me. If you don't have no schooling you are up against it in this country, sis. That is the way of it. No sir, that man has no chance any more. No

> *matter if he has got sand in his craw, others will push*
> *him aside, little thin fellows that have won spelling bees*
> *back home.*[12]

Later, Rooster tells Mattie of his failed attempt to run a restaurant in Cairo, Illinois: "I tried to run it myself for a while but I couldn't keep good help and I never did learn how to buy meat. I didn't know what I was doing. I was like a man fighting bees. Finally I give up and sold it for nine hundred dollars and went out to see the country."[13]

Rooster clearly belongs to an era that is fast disappearing. This theme of the increasingly anachronistic position of certain people as the new consumer culture becomes dominant appears among the outlaws as well. After she is captured by Lucky Ned Pepper's gang, Mattie is forced to sign banknotes that the train robbers have stolen. Because he doesn't understand what banknotes are, Lucky Ned must have Mattie explain them to him. He then forces her to sign the bank president's name to the notes, using a stick and gunpowder mixed with saliva. As she signs, Mattie looks at her handicapped effort and wonders, "*Who will believe that Mr. Whelper signs his banknotes with a stick?*"[14]

The person most capable of negotiating her way in a commercial society is Mattie herself. In fact, she frequently bargains to her advantage. Early on, for example, she convinces Col. Stonehill to buy back the ponies her father bought from him and even to pay for her father's horse and saddle that Chaney stole from Stonehill's stable. Later she buys from Stonehill one of the ponies at a price cheaper than what he had originally paid her per head.

At the end of the novel, Mattie has Rooster's body shipped back to her hometown where she can provide his grave with an expensive headstone. Even in this she swings a deal:

> *I had Rooster's body removed to Dardanelle on the train.*
> *The railroads do not like to carry disinterred bodies in*
> *the summertime but I got around paying the premium*
> *rate by having my correspondent bank in Memphis work*
> *the deed from that end through a grocery wholesaler*
> *that did a volume freight business.*[15]

In a society built on buying and selling, everything becomes commodity, including people. Rooster will not track down Tom Chaney unless he is paid extra for his effort, and he bargains with Mattie to receive $100 to perform a job that as Federal Marshal he should already be paid to do. The Texas Ranger LaBoeuf is after Chaney because the outlaw has shot a Texas state senator whose family has offered a $1,500 reward for Chaney, dead or alive. When LaBoeuf makes this reward known to Rooster, it is uncertain whether the marshal will work solely for Mattie who wants Chaney tried in Fort Smith.

Near the end of the novel, in the year 1903, Mattie reads that Rooster has become part of a Wild West circus. Rooster's part in the show is advertised in a Memphis newspaper:

> *HE RODE WITH QUANTRILL! HE RODE FOR*
> *PARKER! Scourge of Territorial outlaws and Texas cattle*
> *thieves for 25 years! "Rooster" Cogburn will amaze you*
> *with his skill and dash with the six-shooter and repeat-*
> *ing rifle! Don't leave the ladies and little ones behind!*
>
> > *Spectators can watch this unique exhibition in per-*
> *fect safety!*[16]

The Wild West has not only become spectacle for sale, and Rooster Cogburn's reputation has not only become the only thing left for him to trade on, but both have become packaged and tamed. For the "Wild" West can now be experienced in "perfect safety" and Rooster has become an absolute good guy—never mind that he was forced to resign his Federal badge over some questionable killings and that later he participated in the Johnson County War as a hired thug.

When Mattie reaches Memphis to find Rooster, she discovers that he is already dead. The show itself turns out to be a disappointment: Though she doesn't attend, she later learns that "people grumbled" about the performance of the two headliners—Frank James and Cole Younger—"who did nothing more than wave [their] hat[s] to the crowd."[17]

In a society which commodifies everything, including personal reputations, Rooster's selfless act in saving Mattie's life stands out in noble relief. Perhaps that is why Mattie admires him enough to want to have his grave near her in Dardanelle. Through the experiences of Mattie Ross, Charles Portis has offered a criticism of a society dependent on a consumer economy, for when everything becomes commodified, the truly altruistic act becomes increasingly rare, and precious. In the end, *True*

Grit attributes the passing of the West to the rise of commercialism, and emphasizes that what is lost in this passing is a certain grace, courage and nobility in human life. A rose-colored view, certainly, but all the more poignant in that it underscores the fragility of ideals in a world where everything is for sale.

A second novel which offers a critique of commercial culture is Douglas C. Jones' *Roman*. Opening in 1865, the novel traces the rise of Roman Hasford, who at 18 leaves his mother and father in Arkansas to go West. Roman moves to Leavenworth, Kansas, because he wants to see buffalo and Cheyenne Indians. While the story of a young man moving West for the sake of adventure is certainly not unique in Western fiction, *Roman* alters the Western formula by providing a bildungsroman, the story of a young man's education. What Roman learns is that greed can rob one's soul. What he gains is a sense of personal ethics in a world where rapacious profiteering has eroded old moral codes. Ultimately, Jones' novel can be read as a repudiation of the cut-throat business practices and ethical erosion of the 1980s.

While Roman experiences the kind of adventure recognizable in so many Westerns, that is, participating in a battle against Indians, his frontier trials are not unambiguous. For example, in the Battle of Beecher's Island, Roman kills the Cheyenne warrior Roman Nose, and he learns that the reality of frontier violence is a matter of survival and waste. Through his guilt over having killed a man, Roman loses his fanciful vision of frontier adventure; he is matured by a painful confrontation with the very Indians that he has idolized. In his struggle to discover the reasons for violence, Roman is led to explore his own moral code. His education, then, becomes a matter of self-examination.

The second main plot line of the novel revolves around the financial success Roman gains in Leavenworth by raising hogs and selling them to the army. However, while Roman is portrayed as energetic and industrious, Jones makes it clear that his financial success comes just as much from his meeting well-to-do people as it does from his willingness to work hard. In addition, Roman makes money even though he is not primarily concerned with financial gain; he is not a crass materialist. Rather, a native intelligence born from his experiences in nature blends with his childhood exposure to the Bible and classical history to create in Roman a rather sophisticated point of view which allows him to transcend mere material concerns. He is ultimately an idealist, if only in the sense that he expects more from life than physical comfort and thrilling adventure.

Because he is not wholly interested in financial profit and because he is repulsed by the violence which often accompanies such success (Roman meets both a stage-robbing murderer and a professional killer hired to protect a rich railroad tycoon), Roman achieves the ability to understand, in moral terms, the causes of evil and destruction in life. After witnessing a slaughter of buffalo by tycoon August Bainbridge's wealthy partners, and after killing a man and escaping death himself, Roman questions the existence of a benevolent God. Feeling guilty about his skepticism, he searches for some kind of resolution to his doubt. Looking for answers, he attends a church service, but there he grows uncomfortable with the minister's "calling out of sinners," and he is disturbed by "the fact that he himself had never made peace with any God."[18]

Then, offhandedly, he purchases a pamphlet from a disheveled peddler. Entitled "Defense for the Rational Adorers of God," this tract advocates Deism, "the religion of John Adams and Thomas Jefferson." Roman becomes convinced that faith is revealed "through the force of reason,"[19] and his embracing of a God who cannot be held accountable for man's wickedness gives him a needed explanation for man's destructive impulses. In this way, Roman transcends the violence in which he is both witness and participant. However, exhibiting a touch of literary Naturalism, Jones has the peddler who sells Roman the pamphlet freeze to death in an alley. In fact, Jones' whole world is one in which nature is indifferent to the plight of humankind. Yet the author supplies a palliator to a harsh world: He has Roman become a committed philanthropist. It is clear, however, that philanthropy is not a panacea.

Jones creates a character, then, who becomes moderately wealthy while maintaining an ethical and moral compass. Likewise, Roman successfully balances his individualism with his belief in community. To hold himself apart from corruption, Roman refuses to take part in a kickback scheme with crooked Army procurement officers. Additionally, while August Bainbridge helps him to make money, Roman declines the tycoon's offer to make him a state legislator or even a U.S. Senator.

Refusing to be a puppet, Roman tells Bainbridge that he plans to move back to Arkansas—which he does, taking two friends with him.

Effectively, Roman moves back to the settled South, back to his home. He does not keep wandering West, away from civilization, as a Huck Finn or a Shane would. In Arkansas Roman plans to reunite with his mother and father, begin a horse ranch, and marry the young woman he has saved from an orphanage. The theme of family is strong here, as is the importance placed on community. It is significant that Roman's greatest successes occur in town and not on the frontier. Jones has given us a character who can be autonomous while also allowing himself to be nurtured by family and friends. This connection with community serves as a buffer to the greed and violence found in an expanding commercial society.

Significantly, Jones has written a historical romance that responds implicitly to the concerns of Ronald Reagan's 1980s. The parallels between Reagan's America and the postbellum West that Jones creates are striking. In both greed runs rampant; government fosters financial empire building; and unscrupulous business practices seem to be the norm. Indeed, in Bainbridge and in the procurement officers one recognizes the inside trader. Ultimately, then, in *Roman* we have Jones' answer to a very modern dilemma: How does one become financially successful while maintaining an individual code of ethics?

The threat of a consumer culture is the uncritical embrace of materialism, the surrender of the ideal. Jones shows us the dangers of such a surrender: the loss of ethical guideposts. In a world where economic gain is all that matters, violence and exploitation may reign unchecked by moral codes. Jones's critique of consumer culture along these lines may seem quaint to those who scoff at absolutes in human behavior; however, such a critique does suggest that reform of capitalism, or at least the development of safeguards against such a system's excesses, becomes more than a matter of more equitable distribution of wealth— this reform must account for the loss of personal integrity and self-control that a profit-at-any-cost economy induces.

Thematically, these two novels offer a conservative critique of American society as one without clear ethical codes—individual rules of conduct which have been sacrificed in a society where what you buy is more important than who you are. But at a fundamental level, Portis and Jones critique the commodification of ideas and self-image. As writers of Westerns, they are surely aware of the genre's roots in the dime novel, one of the first mass-marketed forms of escapist entertainment. As professional writers, they are both caught in an ironic situation: They must sell their stories in a marketplace which is less than encouraging of original work while preserving the intellectual integrity of their fiction. Ultimately, each author addresses this ironic position by offering a glimpse of a world, however mythified, before the dominance of consumerism—a world which did not insist on selling us images of ourselves, but which allowed, presumably, individual autonomy in self-definition.

Clearly in certain Westerns the critique of capitalism can be more sophisticated than the simple championing of financial underdogs. Westerns can demonstrate the effects a strictly material response to the world can have on one's spiritual life. One recent Western film, written and directed by Sam Shepard, dramatizes the spiritual loss that occurs when selfish materialism supplants self-sacrifice and self-understanding. Effectively, *Silent Tongue* underscores the existential pain which accompanies the madness of possession.

Set on the Great Plains in 1873, the film opens with a young man guarding a corpse. Talbot Roe, played by River Phoenix, refuses to relinquish his wife's body. It is implied that Talbot, unstable to begin with but demented now, is afraid to part with his wife's remains because he is afraid of living without her. In Talbot the film's theme of existential stasis is immediately established. He is afraid to live or die, so he focuses on a single, ultimately impossible task: keeping his wife's corpse from decomposing.

That Talbot is acting selfishly is underscored by his wife's ghost. In life Awbonnie, a half white, half Kiowa woman, was sold to Prescott Roe to become his son's wife. Her ghost's anger, then, stems from having been treated as a possession in both life and death. By haunting Talbot, Awbonnie hopes to gain her freedom. In one scene she moans to Talbot, "You're a low dog to tie me here. . . . You keep me bound here out of your selfish fear of aloneness. I'm not your life. . . . It's you that must release me. Throw my body to the wind. Let them feed me to their young."[20] But Talbot will not free her spirit by relinquishing her body. To do so would mean sacrificing his only reason to live.

To help his son, Prescott Roe attempts to buy a second wife for him. Prescott seeks out Eamon McCree, Awbonnie's father and the alcoholic leader of a traveling medicine show. Eamon previously traded Awbonnie to Prescott for horses the circus needed. Since Prescott tried to save his son's sanity by buying Awbonnie for him, he thinks nothing of attempting to save his life by bargaining for Eamon's other daughter, Velada. Prescott pleads with Eamon: "My son is dying of grief. His mind is gone. I will pay you anything you ask. What more can a father do?"

Eamon, however, is not sure he wants to sell Velada. He is reluctant, not because he loves her, or because his son Reeves loves her. Of Reeves, Eamon, says, "He's always carried an unnatural fondness for his half sisters." Eamon's reluctance to sell his remaining daughter is purely a business calculation: As an accomplished trick rider, Velada is Eamon's "main attraction."

Unable to purchase Velada, Prescott kidnaps her, and Reeves and Eamon set out in chase. Reeves instigates the pursuit because Velada is his sister; Eamon joins his son because the horse Velada was riding is valuable, as he snarls to Reeves: "That paint [horse] was worth more than both daughters and you thrown into the bargain."

The urge to satisfy selfish desires rules *Silent Tongue's* characters. Even Reeves, who along with Prescott comes closest to expressing unselfish emotions, pursues his sister's kidnappers in part because "she belongs to us." Eamon's need to serve his own desires knows few bounds. In a flashback sequence, Eamon is shown raping Silent Tongue, a Kiowa woman who had her tongue cut out for "lying to her headman." Eamon excuses this rape by boasting that he at least made Silent Tongue his wife.

Yet not even the little guilt that these characters show for their actions will allow them to transcend their self-serving ways. Prescott cannot bear to hurt his son, for the son's pain becomes his. Velada, once she has bargained with Prescott to try to help Talbot, cannot act to free her sister's spirit. Not only is she afraid of Awbonnie's ghost, but she has also taken four horses and an amount of gold to serve Prescott's attempt to "save" his son. Eventually Awbonnie's spirit is freed, but not out of consideration for her eternal torment.

Among the issues it raises, two themes seem clearest in *Silent Tongue*. The first is that personal profit without regard to others leads to spiritual death. This connection is symbolized in a scene which has Prescott playing dead to trap Velada. To bait his trap he covers himself with gold coins, placing two over his eyes and posing as if laid out in an Old West funeral parlor. Eamon is also spiritually dead, for the only spiritual life he knows of is a lie. To help sell his patent medicine, he spins a wild story about visions of a Kickapoo medicine man who spoke to him in the "language of the spirit world."

The second theme comes through in the film's emphasis on alienation and existential stasis. Because they emphasize personal gratification, none of these characters is capable of intimacy or self-understanding. This theme of existential alienation is symbolized most directly through the character of an old man who wanders the plains pushing a wheelbarrow full of possessions. In the end, as Prescott and Talbot plod horseless across an empty landscape, this old man stops to yell after them, "Where to?" Of course, he receives no answer.

Because there are few easy answers in *Silent Tongue*, and because there is no catharsis in the conclusion, the film may be unsatisfying to many viewers. Certainly as a Western it defies most of the plot conventions of the genre. The film's significance, therefore, lies in the themes it raises. Above all, *Silent Tongue* critiques not so much capitalism per se, but a worldview which sees worth only in the senses and which measures progress only in material terms. Though often a difficult film to watch, it can be seen as a disturbing indictment of a culture bereft of value.

S E V E N
Metafiction and Parody:
An Undermining of Cultural Assumptions

IF ONE ACCEPTS THE commonplace that something is truly established only after it has been spoofed, then Mel Brooks's movie *Blazing Saddles* (1974) can be seen as unequivocal evidence of the pervasiveness of Western formulas in American popular entertainment. Although a hilarious film in its own right, at least one commentator has noted that *Blazing Saddles* has made it impossible for "many viewers . . . to take the genre seriously since [seeing the film]"[1]— if indeed they ever did at all. Herein lies the critical aspect of parody: its ability to lead readers or viewers to question the validity not only of an entire genre but of the assumptions upon which a genre's dominant formulas are based.

Built on irony, parody is a mode of expression which can have it both ways: It can spoof or look askance at something while at the same time it brings to the foreground, if only momentarily, that which is being satirized. In other words, one of the best ways to subvert a formula is to parody it, but the very life of such a discourse is dependent upon audience recognition and recall of familiar plots and characters. Seen in this light, then, parodic uses of the Western become both wry critique of and sly tribute to the very formulas which have been appropriated—even when such critique is mild and such tribute is given only by way of acknowledging the pervasive status of the Western in American popular culture.

Blazing Saddles is both a recognition of the popularity of the Hollywood Western and a satiric critique of racism and sexism. Much of the movie's humor comes from the conflict between bufoonish white characters and the urbane black sheriff played by Cleavon Little. Bart, Little's character, is a man so sophisticated that he plays chess, drinks wine, and boasts a pair of Gucci saddlebags. In contrast are white dimwits: the risible Headly Lamarr who serves as the chief villain; the oversexed and gullible governor, played by Mel Brooks, who seems a prescient parody of so many politicians to come; and the Slim Pickens-led gang of clods who are both mentally deficient and gastro-intestinally distressed.

The movie's savaging of racial stereotypes[2] begins when white over-seers demand a "darky" song from black railroad workers, only to have the workers croon "I Get No Kick from Champagne" instead of the expected "De Camptown Ladies." Later, before Bart will save an all-white, racist town, he insists that the community accept the black and Chinese railroad workers. When one townsman exclaims, "All right, we'll take the niggers and the chinks, but we don't want the Irish," Bart forces the bigot to back down.[3] For some, *Blazing Saddles'* satire on race may be offensive, with its Yiddish-speaking Sioux Indians and its frequent use of the word "nigger." But the intelligence and panache of Cleavon Little's Bart combined with the clownishly moronic white characters should ensure that if the movie offends, it will do so on grounds other than its attempt to satirize white racism.

The satire on sexism in *Blazing Saddles* is much less apparent than its lampooning of racism. While the governor's secretary is an obvious sexual prop, the saloon singer played by Madeline Kahn offers musical comment on the sex-object status of so many women in so many Westerns. Kahn plays Lili Von Shtupp, the Teutonic Titwillow. A clear takeoff of Marlene Dietrich's character in *Destry Rides Again* (1939), Kahn's Lili burlesques through a song titled "I'm Tired." With lines like "[I'm] Tired of being admired / Tired of love uninspired," the song spoofs the stock role of the dance hall entertainer who appears in a number of Hollywood Westerns. Even in less explicit times, the saloon girl in Western movies was an object of sexual desire. In these movies men often treated her as a prize, fighting for her attention; or they resisted her tainted allure, trying to save her from an unseemly life. But think of it from her perspective: Being the object of all of that sexual attention had to be downright exhausting.

As a parody, then, *Blazing Saddles* not only confronts racism and sexism, but it also undercuts certain plot clichés found in a host of Western movies. And since these clichés so often give form to questionable values, a comic treatment of them makes it easier to re-examine what we believe and why.

Since parody is self-conscious, a discussion of parody and the Western can lead to an examination of metafictional approaches to the genre. On film or in prose, parody and metafiction are linked through the common denominator of self-consciousness. In simple terms, a metafictional work is one which reminds the reader or viewer that what is unfolding is merely a story, merely an artificial narration of the actions of fictional characters. Because in metafictional works the artificiality of storytelling is foregrounded in some way, the audience is never completely able to suspend disbelief and is therefore prevented from taking the plot of a metafictional story too seriously.

In literature, writers are operating metafictionally when they remind us that what we are reading is just a story. They do this in a number of ways, employing a narrative within a narrative, for example, with one narrative more suspect than the other. Or writers might interject into their stories an authorial voice to make apparent certain plot devices or writer's tricks. On film, metafiction most often occurs when characters directly address the audience, often for comic effect but always to remind them that what they are watching is, after all, only a movie. *Blazing Saddles* is blatantly metafictional, especially in the end when the movie's action spills off of its studio set and out into the streets of modern Los Angeles.

However it is manifested, in both novels and films metafiction often results in social critique. Literary critic Patricia Waugh notes that authors who write in this mode frequently begin with familiar and "well-worn conventions" of storytelling in order to establish a connection with an audience.[4] However, metafictionalists then undermine these conventions through parody, thus exposing the artificiality not only of modes of storytelling, but of any "form" of belief one may choose. Waugh argues that metafiction is a "lever of positive literary change" which "by undermining an earlier set of fictional conventions which have become automatized . . . clears a path for a new, more perceptible set."[5] In other words, authors who employ metafictional techniques—that is, authors who build into their narratives an awareness of the artificiality of their narrative form—reveal their belief that literary conventions must change to usher in not only new modes of storytelling, but "new, more percep-tible" ideas as well.

In addition, by parodying narrative conventions, metafictionalists ex-pose the cultural assumptions which underlie these conventions. Waugh writes:

> [I]n metafiction, a convention is undermined, or laid
> bare, in order to show its its historical provisionality: to
> show, for example, that the use of an implicitly male
> omniscient author in popular continuations of realism
> is tied to a specific ideological world-view which contin-
> ues insidiously to pass itself off as "neutral" or "eternal"
> or "objective", and which has its historical roots in the
> late eighteenth and early nineteenth centuries.[6]

Such a function gains extra importance when metafictionalists choose to parody the most widely read popular fictions—the spy novel or the Western, for example—because their satirizing of such forms provides critique of the most widely held cultural assumptions. Relying on Cawelti,[7] Waugh makes the connection between formula fiction and es-cape or "release" from ambiguity. However, she finds in the metafictional uses of popular fiction a different dynamic, that is, one which deliber-ately makes apparent the fictional nature of storytelling and of the com-mon assumptions which make such stories appealing:

> Formulaic fictions . . . provide collective pleasure and
> release of tension through the comforting total affirma-
> tion of accepted stereotypes. What is interesting about
> their use in metafiction is that, when they are parodied, the
> release effect of such forms is to do with disturbance
> rather than affirmation. The reader is offered the tem-
> porary consolation of a release from contingency: the
> comfort of a total 'sense of an ending.' However, meta-
> fiction always simultaneously undermines such satisfac-
> tions and thereby reminds the reader of the necessarily,
> but not always apparent, selective restriction of any 'formu-
> lation'. Thus the reader may escape vicariously into the
> comforts of aesthetic certainty but he or she is certainly
> not allowed to rest complacently in this condition.[8]

By exposing the "selective" nature of the ideologies we wish to embrace, metafiction can be seen to be offering social critique. Our assumptions, authors of such fiction reveal, can and should be examined precisely because they are chosen rather than given, are created categories of thought rather than absolute natural modes of thinking. In the end, it could be argued, such critique can be liberating in its effects, for once we discover that society is based upon beliefs that are preselected, and not necessarily on ideologies inherent in being "American" or "Mongolian" or whatever, then we may be more able to make decisions to alter belief and, hence, society.

To examine how metafiction and parody have worked in Western novels to offer social critique, one can turn to E. L. Doctorow's *Welcome to Hard Times*. Christine Bold notes that Doctorow wrote this novel "as a direct counterpoint to all the very conventional, repetitive Westerns he encountered as a script reader for the movie companies in the 1950s."[9] However, she errs in reading the metafictional nature of *Welcome to Hard Times* as merely a comment on the sterility of conventional Western formulas and their inability to offer anything more than repetitive plots.[10] By seeing metafiction as simply a means of exploring the limitations of a particular mode of storytelling, Bold's reading ignores metafiction's fundamental desire to expose the artificiality of societal assumptions. *Welcome to Hard Times* mercilessly satirizes the acceptance of freedom, individualism, and progress, beliefs which can be seen to inform both the formulaic Western and American society itself.

Set in the Dakota Territories in the 1880s, *Welcome to Hard Times* provides a bleak picture of Western life and conditions. Nothing is romanticized in this tale told by Blue, the unofficial mayor of Hard Times. In chapter one, the Bad Man from Bodie terrorizes the town, raping two of its women; killing numerous people, including the father of the only child in town; and setting fire to most of the buildings. Hard Times' citizens are powerless to stop the Bad Man, though Fee, the carpenter, attacks the outlaw and is killed and Blue tries to shoot him but is run off by a spray of bullets. Eventually the Bad Man either kills or scares away most of the town's inhabitants. Only four stay: Blue; Molly, a prostitute whom the Bad Man has raped and who has been burned; Jimmy Fee, the twelve-year-old son of carpenter Fee; and John Bear, an Indian who doctors Molly's burns.

Blue, Molly, and Jimmy form a family; indeed, Molly eventually comes to wear an old wedding dress which symbolizes her union with Blue. But it is clear that Molly hates Blue for his inability to kill the Bad Man, and she teaches Jimmy to despise Blue, too. When people start to stumble across the town, Blue encourages them to stay and help rebuild Hard Times. The first to arrive are a Russian whoremaster named Zar and his group of prostitutes; a greasy character named Jenks whose only skill is with firearms; and Isaac Maple, the brother of the departed storekeeper. Blue persuades all of them to stay by promising that profit is to be had by rebuilding the town. Indeed, after this small cast survives a harsh winter, the town does revive as people flock to Hard Times with the hope of profiting from the construction of a road that a gold mining company is supposedly planning.

This story will not end happily, however. Obsessed with destroying the Bad Man, Molly pays Jenks to teach Jimmy how to use a Colt revolver, and she makes Jimmy her personal bodyguard, turning his affection for her into a suspicion of Blue. Ultimately it is discovered that the gold in the nearby hills has played out and that the road will not be built after all. In the riot which follows this news, Blue tries to kill the Bad Man from Bodie, who has suddenly reappeared like an apparition drawn to violence. Blue fails, however, and he gets the affable Swede killed in the process. When the Bad Man comes for Molly, Jimmy shoots at him wildly, killing him and Molly and wounding Blue. As Blue sits dying in the street, penning the last words to his story, surrounded by corpses and buzzards, accompanied only by Helga, the insane wife of Swede, he recognizes the futility of all his efforts: "[N]o matter what I've done it has failed."[11]

The metafictional aspects of *Welcome to Hard Times* are manifested in two ways. First, Doctorow frequently reminds the reader that this is a story. In fact, Blue is writing his tale down in ledgers, and the novel is divided into three of these. Moreover, as a first-person narrative the novel underscores the subjective nature of storytelling. Indeed, Blue himself wonders if he has recorded everything accurately:

> And now I've put down what happened, everything that
> happened from one end to the other. And it scares me more
> than death scares me that it may show the truth. But how

> *can it if I've written as if I knew as I lived them which*
> *minutes were important and which were not; and spoken*
> *as if I knew the exact words everyone spoke? Does the*
> *truth come out in such scrawls, so bound by my limits?*[12]

Expressed here is the author's concern over truth even as he recognizes that truth is relative and that his story is an artificial construction.

The second metafictional quality of the novel, however, must move us beyond mere considerations of authorial legitimacy into the realm of social critique. By offering such a relentlessly bleak tale complete with an ending almost naturalistic in its hopelessness,[13] Doctorow has undermined an entire set of Western formulas. The inevitable happy ending of the stereotypical Western, the kind of 1950s B Western that Doctorow sought to satirize, has been inverted; now the story is not only repetitive (the town is burned and abandoned, then re-inhabited, only to be burned and abandoned again), but it is relentlessly pessimistic as well. When Blue recognizes "that we were finished before we ever got started, our end was in our beginning,"[14] he underscores the futility of individual effort, and not just the predictability of formula fiction.

In this sense of futility lies Doctorow's critique of all the happy assumptions which support so much of American society. Notions of freedom, individualism and progress are negated. Instead of offering a view of an individualistic hero who saves a budding civilization from destruction, Doctorow shows us a "civilization" in which everyone is inevitably isolated, in which freedom is impossible, alienation masquerades as individualism, and progress is just the dream of hopeless optimists like Blue.

The town of Hard Times itself, Blue says, has "no excuse . . . except that people naturally come together."[15] Later, after the town has been burned, the optimistic Blue responds to the realism of Ezra Maple: "'We got a cemetery. That's the beginnings of a town anyway.'"[16] Hard Times is not the kind of "civilized" community for whose preservation the "classic" Western hero will sacrifice himself. Before it is burned the first time, its economic center consists of one saloon and one store, and it contains only one child.

The main freedom in the novel is the ability to drift in and out of town. Additionally, there is no triumph of free will. Though Blue tries to rebuild the town, his efforts inevitably fail. His free will extends only so

far, and though he persists in his efforts despite glimpses of his "unend-
ing futility," Blue finally must come to terms with his total lack of freedom to control his destiny:

> *Of course now I put it all down I can see that we were*
> *finished before we ever got started, our end was in our*
> *beginning. I am writing this and maybe it will be re-*
> *covered and read; and I'll say now how I picture some*
> *reader, a gentleman in a stuffed chair with a rug under*
> *him and a solid house around him and a whole city of*
> *stone streets around the house—a place like New York*
> *which Molly talked about one night, with gas lamps on*
> *each corner to light the dark, and polished carriages*
> *running behind horses, and lots of fine manners . . . Do*
> *you think, mister, with all that settlement around you*
> *that you're freer than me to make your fate? Do you*
> *click your tongue at my story? Well I wish I knew yours.*
> *Your father's doing is in you, like his father's was in him,*
> *and we can never start new, we take on all the burden:*
> *the only thing that grows is trouble, the disasters get*
> *bigger, that's all.*[17]

By exploding the belief in mastery of one's fate, Doctorow also undercuts the notion of rugged individualism. Individualism in *Welcome to
Hard Times* appears mainly as a form of isolation. Blue cannot connect
with Molly and Jimmy, for example. A Christmas party ends in individual isolation as each person present contemplates death at the hands
of the Dakota winter. Near the end of the novel, Blue underscores the
meaningless nature of the town: "It had no earthly reason for being there,
it made no sense to exist. People naturally come together but is that
enough? Just as naturally we think of ourselves as alone."[18]

Significantly, each character is haunted by past experiences which prevent him or her from connecting with anyone else. Blue cannot forget
his cowardice. Molly is doomed to constantly remember being raped,
and her fear of the Bad Man from Bodie guides all of her actions. These
characters are bounded; they cannot transcend themselves. Blue expresses
the plight of all of the characters when he notes that he could not think
beyond himself.[19]

If true community is not possible among such circumscribed characters, then neither is the kind of successful autonomous action that the notion of rugged individualism often connotes. Jimmy Fee's father cannot stop the Bad Man, and Blue cannot prevent Swede from being killed when a trap for the Bad Man is sprung. But Blue's greatest failure, perhaps, is his inability to help Jimmy become anything more than an outlaw. In the end, Jimmy becomes another Bad Man; ironically, then, the only successfully autonomous characters are the Bad Man from Bodie and Jimmy, who becomes a wanderer himself.

A lack of individual control over one's fate has one major consequence in the novel: Nothing good can be accomplished. Blue longs to do good, to leave a positive mark on the world. But even early on he senses the futility in this desire. Gazing at a skeleton he laments, "I had to think what an indecency it is that leaves only the bones to tell what a man has been."[20] All belief in progress is negated in *Welcome To Hard Times*. There is no moving forward to a better life; no one is capable of either creating a true community or of preserving what little society there is in Hard Times. In the final analysis, Doctorow offers a bleak vision of human existence: We are all, ultimately, powerless and alienated.

As social critique, *Welcome To Hard Times* seeks to explode certain categories of thought, certain assumptions which Americans hold to so blithely. Doctorow refutes the doctrine that "progress" is possible through individual effort. For him, individualism, that brand of it which is encoded in the Western hero's ability to save civilization and ensure its progress, is a cruel joke. It is oxymoronic to insist that community can be created within a system which insists that each person work for his or her own benefit. The belief in the freedom to act independently, to be a rugged individualist, to ensure progress through personal gain is the foundation of capitalism. To Doctorow, if such an ideology is acted upon, then the only result can be cycles of destruction and rebuilding, but no real progress toward individual fulfillment. If we act only upon our greed, then when the gold in the hills gives out, no one will be safe from the riot which will inevitably ensue.

A second novel which employs metafictional touches to expose the artificiality of storytelling and hence to offer social critique is Robert Ward's *Cattle Annie and Little Britches*. Contemporary reviewers of this novel about two teenage girls who join the Doolin-Dalton gang in 1895 Oklahoma recognize in it a social message immediate to mid-1970s American life. Indeed, their commentary was used in book-jacket blurbs designed to promote the novel. James Baldwin called the book "[a] fable for our children, from Jesse James to Patty Hearst. A love story connecting the failure of love to the failure of the social contract." Reviewer Helen Van Slyke noted that "Mr. Ward has been clever enough to put two young girls in a runaway, 'drop-out' situation that's like today's teenagers, but set a hundred years ago. [Ward's] West could be today's 8th Avenue, with its crime, sex, pot, loyalty and love." And critic James Whitehead saw in Ward's novel a "recogni[tion] that violent death is still a terrible solution deep in the imagination of this country."[21]

However, *Cattle Annie and Little Britches* provides social critique which transcends its era of publication—paralleling a similar dynamic seen in *The Ox-Bow Incident* which certainly speaks to the concerns of the 1930s and 40s, but whose political message resonates today. Part of what allows Ward's novel to speak to today's readers is his caution that when people substitute stories for actual experience, they lose the ability to effect real social change.

To warn of the dangers of allowing popular fantasies to inform one's existence, Ward supplies 15-year-old Annie McDougal (Cattle Annie) and 14-year-old Jennie Stevens (Little Britches) as teenagers fed on the romanticized tales of dime novels. Annie wants to join the local band of outlaws because she has read of their adventures in Ned Buntline's *The Amazing Exploits of the Doolin-Dalton Gang*. Moreover, she expects her fantasy to conform with reality, so when she does finally become part of the gang, she encourages them to act in the ways Buntline has characterized them—in other words, as latter-day Robin Hoods or populist heroes[22] who rob banks and trains largely for the excitement and the attendant celebrity. Annie is caught up in the "romance" of being an outlaw, and she is entranced by the gang's fame. She tells Jennie that while she knows Bill Dalton is just "'flesh and blood,'" she is certain that he is "greater than that . . . [that he has been] turned into something greater . . . like in the fairy stories we used to read."[23]

However, because Annie's fantasy is so strong, she is unable to confront directly the brutality which accompanies the gang's outlawry. For example, when Bill Doolin is captured and shot, Annie believes that his fame will continue, helping to make him greater than he was in real life: "Lemme say this, . . . [Doolin] won't be forgotten. He was a real man, a great man, and they will write books and songs about him . . . as long as there are people on this earth. And in that way, he'll go on living."[24]

Jennie, who narrates the novel, eventually sees through Annie's fantasy world, and she objects to a psychology which can justify any violent action as long as it will make one famous:

> [T]here ain't nothing glorious or romantic about what I
> saw on that slab in that sheriff's office. It's cold and it's
> bloodless and it ain't Bill Doolin at all. . . . All you
> see, Annie, is a goddamned dime novel. . . . A dime novel
> with you on the cover. But behind the cover . . . behind
> it, every one of us will be dead. What difference does it
> make if we live on in somebody's song?[25]

Ward identifies two major sacrifices that occur when one forsakes actual experience in order to live a fantasy life fed by popular fiction and the desire for fame. One is that the truth can be twisted and put up for sale. So when an old man lies that Jesse James used to hide out in a near-by cave, Annie doesn't argue with him but just tosses him a penny and says: "You see. . . . He really believes it. Now you tell me it ain't true. It'll be true as long as people got money to spend and stories to tell."[26]

Second, along with jeopardizing the ability to trust in "facts," mixing fantasy with actual life confuses one's personal identity. Jennie expresses this loss of reliable identity when she says that "up till [Bill Doolin's death] we was actors in somebody else's book. Whose? Ned Buntline's maybe. But I had a feeling that Ned Buntline wasn't to blame exactly. Because he was only borrowing something that was floating around."[27] The danger in creating a sense of identity out of the bits and pieces of a popular culture is the potential for becoming detached from a secure inner life. So Jennie comes to feel "like . . . a dozen people at once. That is, when I wasn't feeling like a ghost."[28]

In a scene which symbolizes Ward's anti-fantasy theme, Jennie confronts a flock of swans:

> They would come right up and peck at you, and looking
> at them made me feel strange as hell. For some reason

they frightened me, for at a distance they seemed so beau-
tiful, all white and wonderful. . . . But when you got
closer to them, you could see meanness in their eyes, a
meanness and a wildness which made my hands shake.
Plus, they had a strange odor, these swans. . . . They
smelled of sweat and blood, as if they had just eaten some-
thing terrible, and its death was still on their breath.[29]

Here, using an animal familiar to a child's fairy tale, Ward makes concrete the danger of believing too much in popular fantasies: In a world in
which the only reality one knows comes from stories, disseminated in
everything from dime novels to television sitcoms, the ability to penetrate surfaces and apprehend deeper truths is lost.

Even after the gang is massacred by Pinkerton agents at the Chicago
World's Fair,[30] Annie believes that the continuation of their fame in the
popular imagination will lend immortality to them all, and this belief
sustains her. But Jennie, precisely because she has confronted real suffering, eventually comes to work at a New York settlement house. In the
final analysis, Ward demonstrates that social inaction is supported by a
culture fed on popular fictions. For as long as these fictions supply escape from real hardship, and as long as one can retreat into fantasy—
indeed, as long as fantasy becomes a major preoccupation for people—
then society will continue to deteriorate while the nation sits narcotized
in front of "Gunsmoke" or "The A Team."

A third and final novel which bears examination as a work which paro-
dies Western formulas in order to supply social critique is Richard
Brautigan's *The Hawkline Monster: A Gothic Western*. Written bluntly in sen-
tences almost entirely simple or compound in form and full of a dark,
sardonic humor, Brautigan's novel resembles a stylistic kinship with some
of Kurt Vonnegut's satires. Thematically, Brautigan's parody of formulas
found in the Western and Gothic genres undercuts a dominant concern
found in both types of fiction: the characterizing of good and evil. For
Brautigan, both good and evil in these respective genres is too fantastic
to be taken seriously. In the *Hawkline Monster*, Brautigan's parody explodes
the assumption that evil can be traced to concrete forms—individual
people or monsters—and not to actions which society as a whole participates in or condones.

The plot here follows two professional killers, Greer and Cameron, who are summoned in July of 1902 to a remote part of Eastern Oregon to do a job. Upon arrival, Greer and Cameron discover the fantastic Hawkline mansion which, since it supposedly rests on ice caves, is much colder than the surrounding environment. The identical-twin Hawkline sisters want Greer and Cameron to kill a monster which has disposed of their scientist father—a chemist who has been working on secret formulas which he believes will benefit mankind. Naturally, in keeping with any good Gothic, strange things have been occurring within the house, all caused by the monster's ability to alter people's thinking. As stoical Western heroes (or anti-heroes) Greer and Cameron agree to the job, but after breaking out their arsenal and descending to the basement, they come to discover—after some more weird interruptions—that the "monster" is really a light accidentally created by Mr. Hawkline which feeds on the chemicals he has concocted. This light is followed by a clumsy and harmless shadow which feels guilty about the light's evil actions. In the climactic scene, the shadow blocks the light's vision while Cameron pours whiskey into the light's chemical food supply, thus fragmenting the monster into thousands of diamonds.

In outline, it's a goofy story, but one made compelling by Brautigan's reportorial style and dark sense of humor. More important, as a parody of formulas frequently found in two popular genres, *The Hawkline Monster* suggests that our notions of evil are too benign. In the stereotypical Western, for example, evil just exists in the form of a character or two—with maybe some requisite henchmen working at the behest of the main bad guy. Rarely is there any attempt to examine why these characters are evil. In the Gothic, evil is frequently located in a scientific experiment which somehow goes wrong. This kind of evil is so fantastic that it can become laughable, as ridiculous as making a strange light one's monster. In both genres, the stereotypical plot has the evil eventually destroyed, presumably so good can reign unchecked—at least until the next bad hombre or mad scientist blows into town.

In Brautigan's novel, the characters pursue this fantastic evil while ignoring the very real evil which surrounds them. Greer and Cameron kill people for a living. Sure, in the first chapter they refuse to shoot a Hawaiian because he has a wife and child, but murder is still their business. They are matter of fact about it, too, though at times they have had bad experiences, for example:

> *the time they shot a deputy sheriff in Idaho ten times*
> *and he wouldn't die and Greer finally had to say to the*
> *deputy sheriff, "Please die because we don't want to shoot*
> *you again." And the deputy sheriff had said, "Ok, I'll*
> *die, but don't shoot me again."*
> *"We won't shoot you again," Cameron had said.*
> *"Ok, I'm dead," and he was.* [31]

The consequences of evil in society surround Greer and Cameron. Passing through Oregon they witness the results of a war between cattle ranchers and sheep herders. Traveling on the stagecoach to the town of Billy, Greer and Cameron see a man hanging from a bridge, a sight which everyone accepts as common:

> *Just outside of Gompville a man was hanging from the*
> *bridge across the river. There was a look of disbelief on*
> *his face as if he still couldn't believe that he was dead.*
> *He wouldn't believe he was dead until they buried him.*
> *His body swayed gently in the early winds of morning.*
> *"There's a lot of that going on around here now," [a fel-*
> *low stage coach passenger] said, pointing at the body.*
> *"It's those gunmen from Portland. It's their work."* [32]

In this most matter-of-fact style, violence is regarded as a matter of fact; moreover, it seems to be no one's responsibility to prevent it. Significantly, the characters accept violence; indeed they profit from it in any way they can. Later, Cameron and Greer meet the town marshal of Billy, Jack Williams. Williams is a Western stereotype, someone "known far and wide as a tough but fair man," and Greer and Cameron admire him. But Williams, too, accepts violence, as long as it doesn't happen in his town: "I don't care what those cattle and sheep people do to each other. They can kill everyone of themselves off if they're going to be that stupid, just as long as they don't do it in the streets of Billy." [33]

When Greer and Cameron and Magic Child (their "Indian" guide who later turns into one of the Hawkline sisters) ride through the Dead Hills to the Hawkline mansion, they experience another concrete fact which they choose to gloss over:

> *Finally they came across something human. It was a grave.*
> *The grave was right beside the road. It was simply a pile*
> *of bleak rocks covered with vulture shit. There was a*
> *wooden cross at one end of the rocks. The grave was so*
> *close to the road that you almost had to ride around it.*
>   *"Well, at least we've got company," Greer said.*
>   *There were a bunch of bullet holes in the cross. The*
> *grave had been used for target practice.*
>   *"9," Cameron said.*
>   *"What was that?" Magic Child said.*
>   *"He said there are nine bullet holes in the cross," Greer*
> *said.*

In his unreflective style and in his characters' shallow responses to the world, Brautigan fashions a critique of a worldview which refuses to penetrate surfaces. Cameron's main approach to life is to count things, to enumerate experiences but not to think about them. This is precisely the kind of automatic approach which is encouraged by certain Western and Gothic formulas. Because in both genres evil is often just accepted as a given, as a necessary part of the plot, no serious attempt is made to explain its source. In actuality, though supposedly made concrete in the form of the villain or the scientist, evil might as well be as silly as a beam of light. What difference does its source make, if in the end evil is inevitably vanquished?

Moreover, if evil is so immediately located in a gunslinger or a monster, then one can ignore the deeper causes of corruption in favor of enjoying a simple morality tale full of exciting action. Such a simple formula encourages a simplistic approach to actual experience. Evil can become the other; it can become a matter of easily defeated externals. And more difficult questions can be ignored—for example, what accounts for a society in which violence is tolerated? Ultimately, Brautigan suggests that a failure to probe the causes of evil has made Jack Williamses of us all: We have become people interested only in peace within our own little spheres; we have abdicated the responsibility to take action against the horrible results of a very human and universal tendency toward evil acts.

As can be seen from the above examples, parodic and metafictional approaches to the formulaic Western, one of the more prevalent story formulas in our culture, can explode assumptions which help shape our personal realities. If recent theorists are correct in their belief that a society's stories embody not only a sense of its past but a concrete formulation of the actions its people should take in creating their future,[34] then an imperative action for those who want to effect social change is to make apparent the ideologies embedded in a society's popular fictions. In other words, if people are attached to beliefs or worldviews which are continually reinforced by popular fictional formulas, then change must in part begin with attempts to make conscious these unconsciously accepted ideologies. One value granted to the novelists discussed above is that they attempt to reshape the thinking of readers through their self-conscious revelation of ideas which are so blithely accepted without critical examination.

E I G H T
Stories of the Modern West:
Values, Character, and Freedom

IN *THE MISFITS* (1961) Clark Gable tells Marilyn Monroe: "I guarantee you'll have something out here you won't find on every corner." The "here" he refers to is the West, and his comment, though in some ways belied by the film, suggests the continued belief in the exceptional qualities of the American West. As an idea, even the modern West still has a hold on us. The peripatetic Sal Paradise in Jack Kerouac's *On the Road* seems to be continually driving or hitchhiking West to find good friends, cool jazz, and existential satisfaction; indeed both his first and last trips find him out West. On film, recent road movies—e.g., *Thelma & Louise* (1991), *Boys on the Side* (1995)—feature characters hitting the modern highway and heading West to find a fuller life. Few American movies reverse the direction, say, having characters start out in Illinois and driving to New Jersey to find personal fulfillment. Shot through modern American literature and film is the idea that we can still go West to gain something we cannot find anywhere else.

Generally, fictional representations of the modern West respond to cultural notions of Western exceptionalism in two ways. On the one hand are stories which implicitly reject the heroic and mythic status the West has been granted over the years, instead finding the region intriguing for the same reason most regions are important: for the human lives which unfold there. In contrast are stories which employ the West as an ideal or a symbol, which see the region as America's best hope or as its lost best hope, cast in terms of promises fulfilled or of dreams denied.

Illustrative of the first category of modern Western story are two films. *The Misfits*, written by Arthur Miller, is at once a character study and a debunking of Old West notions that life is somehow purified through a struggle with nature. The story follows a small cast of characters in and around Reno, Nevada, in the early 1960s. While the male characters are latter-day cowboys who plan to hunt wild mustangs with an airplane, the principal female character, played by Marilyn Monroe, finalizes a divorce and seeks a new, more meaningful life. Thus the film explores the struggle between masculine and feminine sensibilities. As the men recklessly hurtle toward death, riding bulls and wrestling stallions, Monroe's Rosalind becomes symbolic lover and substitute mother to them all. Her life-affirming nature eventually allows Clark Gable's character to renounce his emotionally truncated ways and to recognize the cruelty in his cowboy life. (He hunts wild horses to sell them for dog food.) Certainly, a woman's taming of a man is a long-familiar Western theme. But in *The Misfits*, Gable's character is saved rather than emasculated by his embracing of Rosalind and her female sensitivity.[1]

Like *The Misfits*, *The Last Picture Show* (1971) also updates our view of the West. Based on a Larry McMurtry novel, *The Last Picture Show* is about love and the death of innocence in a small town in Texas in the early 1950s. In many ways the film's themes of adolescent yearning and thwarted desire help to shape a more modern vision of the West. The story focuses on the characters' search for love and permanence and on their acceptance of loneliness and death. Depicted is not a mythic West but a real place where the universals of human experience play themselves out. Indeed, in its gritty, black-and-white realism, *The Last Picture Show* rejects the sentiments found in stories which idealize the West. It is no accident that the last picture show presented in the Anarene, Texas, movie-house is the classic Western *Red River*. In this subtle touch, the contrast between the mythic and the actual West, however mediated by Hollywood images, is underscored.[2]

Certain novels set in the modern West critique the notion that the region is somehow America's promised land, where all dreams are possible. In this vein is John Steinbeck's *The Grapes of Wrath*. After heading West to California to find a better life, the Joad family finds continued poverty and economic exploitation, and not America's Garden of Eden. As critique, *The Grapes of Wrath* operates on several levels: economic, political, and social. The novel depicts the West, with the exception of the government-run camp for economic refugees, as no better than the rest of the country. Likewise, the lure of the golden West is critiqued in

Nathaniel West's surrealistic novel *The Day of the Locust*. Here West satirizes America's ultimate dream-factory, Hollywood, styling it as a place inhabited by grotesque misfits in the grip of a stultifying boredom, hardly the land of stardom and riches.

Another realistic portrayal of the twentieth-century West occurs in Wallace Stegner's *The Big Rock Candy Mountain*. Though it is mainly a powerful story of a Western family, Stegner's novel can be read as a critique of the American dream. At the center of this minor masterpiece is Harry "Bo" Mason, a domineering husband and father who drags his family throughout the West in search of easy wealth. His wife, Elsa, longs for a permanent home, but restlessness and rootlessness seem to be bred into Bo, so when one financial scheme after another collapses, the family is forced to move in constant search of "some Big Rock Candy Mountain where life was effortless and rich and unrestricted and full of adventure and action, where something could be had for nothing."[3]

Bo's monomaniacal pursuit of this dream destroys the Mason family, but there is a social cost, as well. Late in the novel as Bruce, the younger son, drives across the West, he connects his family's woes with the price then being paid by Americans caught in the Great Depression. Wondering "when [Americans would] get enough sense to quit looking for something for nothing," Bruce sees his family's restlessness in national terms. He believes that having a true home is something

> not only his family, but thousands of Americans had missed. The whole nation had been footloose too long, Heaven had been just over the next range for too many generations. Why remain in one dull plot of earth when Heaven was reachable, was touchable, was just over there? The whole race was like the fir tree in the fairy-tale which wanted to be cut down and dressed up with lights and bangles and colored paper, and see the world and be a Christmas tree.
>
> Well, he said, thinking of the closed banks, the crashed market that had ruined thousands and cut his father's savings in half, the breadlines in the cities, the political jawing and the passing of the buck. Well, we've been a Christmas tree, and now we're in the back yard and how do we like it?[4]

While this passage is as close to outright social philosophy as the novel gets, it does place Stegner's characters within the context of a national character. In the figure of Bo Mason, then, can be seen Americans past and present whose insatiable drive for personal wealth has not only cost them emotional security and family happiness, but also has helped to create a society founded on hollow values.

In contrast to these novels and films are stories of the modern West which have a thematic kinship with tales of the Old West. Often these works perceive the West as a special place, a place in which American values and a national character are forged. Often, too, these stories posit the West as an area where personal liberation is possible, where experience is unique and more self-fulfilling. And, to the extent that their authors see the West as living up to its promises, these novels and films frequently contain social critique.

Simply costuming the clichés of the stereotypical Western in modern garb is nothing new. Stories, particularly movies, set in the twentieth-century West frequently employ the hackneyed scenes and conflicts of so many Old West tales. Sometimes these modern "Westerns" play it straight. The movies which feature San Francisco police detective Dirty Harry, for example, make blatant use of the Old West plot which sees a lone gunman standing between civilization and chaos, preserving the former through superior violent force even as the use of that force makes him unfit for the society he saves. Other movies make ironic use of Western plot devices. One such film is *Delusion* (1990), a movie in which clichés are inverted to reveal the moral ambiguity in modern life. The story of a computer executive whose embezzlement scheme is complicated by a hit man and his girlfriend, *Delusion* not only revels in shots of desolate desertscapes in which, as one character claims, "they made John Wayne movies,"[5] it also updates the stock scenes of formulaic Westerns. So a stage coach heist becomes a car-jacking, the tenderfoot Easterner comes in the person of a yuppified computer whiz, and the final showdown in the street stalls when one man cannot fire because he is afraid and the other can't shoot because he's out of bullets.

Yet other novels and films do more than just borrow the plot clichés: they also appropriate the myth of the Old West. One recent example of this can be seen in the popular film *City Slickers* (1991) starring

Billy Crystal. Central to this film is the idea that in the West survive values more honest than the ones found in urban centers. In *City Slickers*, Crystal plays a New Yorker named Mitch who is dissatisfied with his life. He despises his job because as an ad time seller for a radio station he doesn't do anything real, as he says to his wife, "I sell air." Too, Mitch is depressed about aging and worried about dying. "I just feel lost," he claims.[6]

The solution to all of this urban angst, then, is to go West. Mitch and his buddies Ed and Phil take a novelty vacation to New Mexico, where they will spend two weeks driving cattle. At the ranch the men meet Curly, the trail boss. Played by Jack Palance, Curly is the last of the boot-leather-tough cowboys. The film plays on the contrast between the pampered "city slickers" and the self-reliant Curly. In one scene, Mitch sets off a stampede when he starts up a battery-operated coffee grinder. Curly single-handedly stops the stampede by firing a single shot and glaring at the rampaging cows. While the city slickers are initially afraid of Curly, the old cowboy does embody the kind of certainty in life that Mitch and his friends seek. After Curly dies, Mitch eulogizes him by saying, "You lived life on your terms: simple, honest and brave."

Alone without an experienced guide, the three friends decide to finish the cattle drive. When, despite their inexperience, the city slickers push the herd across a river and into the valley, they triumphantly hum the theme from the television Western *Rawhide*. This scene, as well as the bulk of the film, is a tribute to Westerns by people who grew up on a diet of TV oaters. The West in *City Slickers* is like that of the simplest 1950s television Westerns: it is a place where all answers are clear, where action is more self-defining than thought, where endless renewal is possible. This attitude is both escapist and subtly critical of a confining modern society. In the end, as a natural result of their adventure together, each of the three friends gains the courage to face his fears, becoming more determined and less anxious about the future. Their western experience has made them new men.

That the West builds character is a common idea in many modern Westerns. Because Western experience is unique, these modern stories suggest, it fosters extraordinary men and women. Movies like *City Slickers* reveal that in the popular mind the West can still be a place where character is best developed and tested. Sometimes character issues even become a source of conflict in modern Western stories. Such is the case with the film *Hud* (1962).

While it is also a film about family relationships, *Hud*, based on Larry McMurtry's *Horseman, Pass By*, is mainly a study of its shiftless title character. Paul Newman plays Hud Bannon, the last son in a Texas ranching family, a heavy drinker and unashamed womanizer. While Homer, Hud's aging father, stays mostly on the ranch, working and worrying, Hud spends much of the story roaring off to town in his pink Cadillac to sop up liquor and cavort with married women.

The contrast in character between Hud and his father is revealed early in the film. When it is discovered that a heifer might have died from the contagious hoof and mouth disease, Hud wants to sell the rest of the herd quickly. Homer opposes this move as unethical, but Hud argues that cheating has become an American way of life. "How many honest men do you know?" Hud asks. "You take the sinners away from the saints you're lucky to end up with Abraham Lincoln. I say let us put our bread in some of that gravy while it's still hot." To this Homer responds sadly, "You're an unprincipled man, Hud."[7]

Hud's selfishness not only destroys his relationships with his father and nephew and their female housekeeper, but his lack of character is seen as perilous to society. To many in town, Hud is a popular figure; he is greeted enthusiastically whenever he walks into bars, for example. To Homer, however, Hud's popular image threatens societal values. In a dramatic scene Homer confesses to Hud that he dislikes him—not because he was driving when a car crash killed his older brother—but rather because Homer is disgusted by Hud himself. He tells his son,

> *You don't care about people, Hud. You don't give a damn about them. Oh, you got all that charm going for you, and it makes the youngsters want to be like you. That's the shame of it. You don't value nothing. You don't re-spect nothing. You keep no check on your appetites at all. You live just for yourself and that makes you not fit to live with.*

When Lon, Homer's grandson, offers the defense that many people in the area are like Hud, Homer emphasizes the societal cost of such a widespread lack of character: "Little by little the look of the country changes because of the men we admire."

Conveyed in this exchange is a very modern question: What is the effect on society when its role models are revered for their cynicism and self-interest? It is not difficult to believe that the role models in question are the movie and rock stars adored by a youth culture and admired for their stylishly dissolute ways.

This social critique was apparently not lost on certain contemporary viewers of *Hud*. Writing in the *New York Times*, movie critic Bosley Crowther called Hud a character "fully diseased with all of the germs of materialism that are infecting and sickening modern man." And for Crowther, *Hud's* social message was meant for the entire nation: "[T]he place where [Hud] lives is not just Texas. It is the whole of our country today. It is the soil in which grows a gimcrack culture that nurtures indulgence and greed."[8]

Other modern Westerns approach the character issue differently. In these works the kind of West which previously built extraordinary men and women is being pushed aside by modern technology and societal values. This theme often occurs in novels and films which offer a kind of conservative lament about what is lost when the new West dominates the old.

One recent novel that explores the encroachment of society upon what is believed to be purest in our lives is Cormac McCarthy's *All the Pretty Horses*. Set in Texas and northern Mexico in 1949, the story follows 16-year-old John Grady Cole and his 17-year-old friend Lacey Rawlins as they leave home in search of a life worth believing in. John Grady's future has changed with the death of his grandfather and his mother's sale of the family ranch. Instead of operating the ranch which has been in the Grady family for generations, his mother wishes to pursue a career as an actress. Trying to understand the life his mother has chosen, John Grady secretly attends one of her performances. But in the play he can find no answers: "He'd the notion that there would be something in the story itself to tell him about the way the world was or was becoming but there was not. There was nothing in it at all."[9]

John Grady is drawn to a more immediate and less artificial way of life. Upon the land he feels the traces of a consecrated past—of Comanche on the move, of forebears killed young. Carried to his thoughts "like a grail,"[10] these past lives bless a way of life best pursued by "the ardenthearted."[11]

To find that which is elemental and constant, John Grady and Rawlins ride into Mexico. There they meet a 13-year-old horse thief who calls himself Jimmy Blevins. Rootless and temperamental, Blevins is at first a nuisance to John Grady and Rawlins; later his actions will endanger their freedom and their lives. But other threats exist as well. When the boys get work at the large ranch owned by a man named Rocha, they at first feel at peace, meaningfully connected to their work. Later, however, after John Grady falls in love with Alejandra, Rocha's daughter, the boys' peaceful lives are upset by the dictates of Mexican upper-class society. Betrayed and sent to prison, John Grady and Rawlins learn of the cruelty to be found in societies, both respectable and criminal, where truth is relative and created by those in power, like the police captain who arrests the boys or the convict-king Pèrez who rules the prison yard.

When the boys are bought out of prison, Rawlins leaves for home. But John Grady goes back to Alejandra, only to discover that culture and social caste make their love impossible. Later he seeks retribution against the police captain who arrested them, but circumstances and conscience prevent John Grady from exacting his revenge, although he does manage to retrieve the horses that were taken from them.

While there is much in the novel about what is lost in human experience, ultimately, *All the Pretty Horses* is about what lasts. The land and the stars, the pleasure and heartache of direct experience, the desire for purity symbolized in the horses John Grady so often dreams of—these endure, as do human courage and cruelty. The legacies of society can be cruel, too, as the Duena Alfonsa, Alejandra's grandaunt and protector, says: "What is constant in history is greed and foolishness and a love of blood and this is a thing that even God—who knows all that can be known—seems powerless to change."[12] Though individual friendships and loves are challenged by time and experience, immutable value can be discovered by refusing to surrender one's ideals, one's honest sense of the proper relationship between people and the land.

Not surprisingly, certain critics have called Cormac McCarthy a religious novelist in that his characters seek something transcendent in a harsh and cruel life. Gail Moore Morrison believes McCarthy's work is archetypal, concerned often with journeys and quests for meaning the world cannot automatically provide.[13] For Edwin T. Arnold, "McCarthy's protagonists are most often those who, in their travels, are bereft of the voice of God and yet yearn to hear him speak."[14] Other critics note that in his attempt to convey the elementals in human experience McCarthy fashions a world separate from the ordinary. So Denis Donoghue writes that McCarthy "isn't good with village Romeos and Juliets or indeed with any lives that have entered upon communities, cultural interests, attended by customs, proprieties, and laws. . . . He is one of those writers who exhibit in their truest work, however they act as citizens, a refusing imagination: it refuses to give credence to the world as it has come to be in its personal, social, and political forms."[15]

McCarthy finds little in modern civilization which can sustain the human spirit. For him life is truest when it confronts directly the immensity of nature and the danger of violent destruction. In a rare interview, McCarthy alludes to a philosophy which is dramatized in his fiction: "There's no such thing as life without bloodshed. . . . I think the notion that the species can be improved in some way, that everyone could live in harmony, is really a dangerous idea. Those who are afflicted with this notion are the first ones to give up their souls, their freedom. Your desire that it be that way will enslave you and make your life vacuous."[16]

Finally, then, the power that John Grady seeks can come only from a brave determination. There is honor in his sense of endurance, even in the guilt he feels over having killed a man, no matter the justification of self-defense. In the end, when he rides away from a part of Texas that he can no longer call his, John Grady is more than an echo of the solitary outcast typical to Westerns—rather he is man who has chosen a destiny, apart from a corrupting society. Evoked in the novel's poetic final passage is the sense that John Grady's refusal to conform to shoddy values makes him the kind of man who has vanished from the modern world even as his spirit of defiant self-definition lives on like a shadow upon the land.

The increasingly anachronistic place of certain values in modern society is at the heart of the film *Lonely Are the Brave* (1962). Starring Kirk Douglas as the individualist cowboy Jack Burns, *Lonely Are the Brave* is quietly anti-establishment. Set in New Mexico in the early 1960s, the film opens with a shot of Jack Burns asleep in open country, his horse hobbled nearby. This scene could have come from just about any Western with a frontier setting. Soon, however, the modern world intrudes, as Jack's sleep is disturbed by the sounds of jets overhead, and he awakens to see three fighters streaking across the sky. From there the film builds on images of the "progress" of a technological society as it pushes aside a simpler Western past. For example, to ride cross-country, Jack must cut a barbed-wire fence to open a trail, and later when he begins to cross a busy highway, his horse is frightened by the traffic.

Jack has come to the town of Duke City to see his childhood friend. But Paul, a writer and social activist, has been sentenced to two years in prison for aiding illegal Mexican immigrants. Jack cannot understand why helping people should be illegal. He likens the borders between states and countries to fences which only prevent individual freedom, and he believes that he and Paul, as true Westerners, do not recognize artificial barriers between people. It seems natural to Jack that Paul would help people no matter where they came from. This attitude angers Paul's wife, Gerry, who blames both Jack and her husband for being hardheaded and foolish. "Either you go by the rules or you lose, you lose everything," Gerry says. To which Jack replies, "You can always keep something."[17]

For Jack, there is honor in defying rules you cannot believe in. Wishing to visit Paul, who is being held temporarily in the local jail, Jack doesn't wait for visiting day. Instead, he gets into a bar fight so he will be arrested. In this scene, Jack's sense of honor is made clear. As he fights with a one-armed man, Jack keeps his right arm behind him, even when he is close to being strangled.

In the jail scenes, the inequalities of the law are shown. An elderly man, for example, complains of being jailed for vagrancy. Indignant he asks, "Just because I got no money, that's a crime?" But while the old man is booked into an overcrowded jail, the desk sergeant is inclined to let Jack go. Of course, that's not in Jack's plans, so he slugs an officer, increasing his sentence from 10 days suspended to one year.

Once inside the jail, Jack plots an escape, and he wants to take Paul out with him. But Paul refuses, in part because he believes he must pay society's penalty even though he is not contrite about his actions. Mainly, however, Paul does not want to add five years to his sentence for breaking jail. He cannot further burden his wife and son. Jack, on the other hand, must break out, because he has been marked for brutal treatment by a sadistic jailer and because he believes he could not keep his sanity if he spent a year pinned behind bars.

After escaping, Jack is pursued by a laconic sheriff, played drolly by Walter Matthau, who secretly sympathizes with him. In the end, after escaping authorities who hunt him with jeeps, radios, and a helicopter, Jack's flight ends as his horse panics in the middle of a highway and a violent collision ensues. What saves this scene from being a transparent symbol of the modern world crushing a more wholesome past is the realistic depiction of a rain-driven night, a horse screaming in agony, and the unnatural stare of Jack's eyes as he goes into shock.

Questioned in *Lonely Are the Brave* is the complacency that modernity brings progress. This theme will not surprise readers of Edward Abbey, who wrote the novel *The Brave Cowboy* upon which *Lonely Are the Brave* is based. But this is not a reactionary film, for it does not simply call for a return to the past. Rather, the film raises doubts about the direction of modern society. By asking if technology automatically enhances our lives, if the rule of law always results in justice, and if true personal freedom is possible in the absence of human compassion, *Lonely Are the Brave* sought to jolt viewers out of the self-contented notion that America in the early 1960s was inevitably perfect.

One of the more pernicious threats to a wholesome West as a special place that can continue to forge America's principles is racism. In the 1950s at least two modern Westerns took on anti-racism themes: the enduring epic *Giant* (1956) and the taut classic *Bad Day at Black Rock* (1954).

Based on an Edna Ferber novel, *Giant*, set in Texas during the first half of the twentieth century, tells the story of the wealthy Benedict family. When Jordan Benedict goes East to buy a stallion for breeding stock, he falls in love with and marries Leslie Lynton, a daughter of Maryland. To a less-refined West, Leslie, played by Elizabeth Taylor, brings courage and a sense of old world noblesse oblige. As the wife of one of the richest men around, Leslie sees it as her duty to help poor Mexican-Americans. At first, Jordan derides his wife's efforts as undignified and unnecessary, but her convictions win out. She pressures a white doctor to save a Mexican child, and eventually she sponsors a Mexican-American physician in his desire to improve public health.

Giant's strongest comments on racism, however, occur in the film's homage to those twin 1950s American ideals: love of country and love of family. A strong patriotic message is added to the movie's anti-racist concerns when young Angel, son of the Mexican-American ranch foreman, is the first local boy to enlist in the army and fight in World War II. One of the strongest visual scenes in the film begins with a silhouette shot of Angel's flag-draped coffin left on a railroad siding. At Angel's funeral, his father is presented with a Texas flag from the Benedict household. Here the themes of national, state, and family unity are emphasized.

And thematically *Giant* upholds an old-fashioned belief in family, for it is the Benedict family which endures. It survives the inclusion of the spunky Leslie, the revolt of children who do not want simply to follow in the family's ranching tradition, and the economic challenge presented by the upstart Jett Rink. In Jett, played by James Dean, can also be seen the film's major threat to wholesome values. An alcoholic and a bigot, Jett is a playboy whose lifestyle is deglamorized in his ultimate humiliation.

However, what clinches the film's pro-family and anti-racism message is Jordan's acceptance of his son's Mexican-American wife and son. In a last big scene, Jordan has so changed his bigoted inclinations that he fights a racist diner owner who refuses to serve a Mexican family. The film concludes with a lingering shot of the elder Benedicts' two small grandsons, one blond and blue-eyed and the other dark and brown-eyed, standing side by side.[18] What more obvious appeal could there be to the sentiments which support love of united country and family?

Bad Day at Black Rock also critiques racism for its threat to community. Starring Spencer Tracy as a one-armed stranger who mysteriously comes to an Arizona town, the film makes use of the well-worn Western convention of the outsider who must secure justice in a corrupt community. When John J. Macreedy steps off of the streamliner in tiny Black Rock, he is received with open suspicion and hostility. At first Macreedy is puzzled by this reception, though he remains mild-mannered and purposeful. The town's inhabitants seem afraid, and though outwardly they question Macreedy's reasons for coming to town, they seem to know why he is there.

The viewer must wait to learn Macreedy's purpose, however, and that helps to build suspense. Clearly, Macreedy is looking for something or someone, and he resists all attempts to frighten him off. When the town's dominant force, wealthy rancher Reno Smith, tries to pry answers out of Macreedy, the one-armed stranger wonders why everyone is so suspicious of him. Smith answers, "We're suspicious of strangers. A hangover from the Old West." Macreedy's reply to this casts the conflict in social rather than personal terms: "I thought the tradition of the Old West is hospitality."[19]

Eventually, Macreedy reveals that he is looking for a man named Kokomo. The year is 1945; World War II has just ended. At first, then, Macreedy is told that Kokomo was sent to a relocation camp. But Macreedy has seen Kokomo's burned-out farmhouse, so this answer does not satisfy him. As he keeps pressing for the truth, Macreedy uncovers a seething racism. When Smith asks "Why would a man like you be looking for a lousy Jap farmer," Macreedy speaks of loyal Japanese-Americans. This sets Smith on a tirade: "Loyal Japanese-Americans, that's a laugh . . . . There's a law in this county against shooting mad dogs, but when I see a mad dog I don't wait for him to bite me." Smith's xenophobia is summed up when he snarls, "It's our West, I just wish they'd leave us alone."

Macreedy, however, finds this attitude anomalous. "There aren't many towns like this in America," he says. "But one town like this is enough." Eventually, with the help of a sympathetic local doctor and a hotel clerk shamed into telling the truth, Macreedy learns that soon after America entered the war with Japan, Smith and his henchmen burned Kokomo's house before Smith shot him. For four years the entire town has conspired to cover up the murder. In the movie's climax, Macreedy ensures justice when, after being lured into an ambush, he kills Smith.

In the end, *Bad Day at Black Rock* emphasizes the themes of tolerance and community. It turns out that Macreedy came to find Kokomo to present him with a medal earned by his son. During the war, Kokomo's son saved Macreedy's life. Driven by racism, the townspeople murdered the father of an American hero. While Macreedy is skeptical that such people can ever be redeemed, he does give the doctor the medal as a

symbol of community pride and as a token of the better instincts necessary to Black Rock's survival as part of a truly American society.

If a film like *Bad Day at Black Rock* seems confident about achieving a
racially integrated society, other modern Westerns aren't so sure. Fiction by Native Americans, for example, frequently dramatizes the sense
of displacement felt by twentieth-century Indians in modern society. The
lyrical, Pulitzer-prize winning novel *House Made of Dawn* evokes well the
difficulty Native Americans often have in belonging to two cultures.
Written by N. Scott Momaday, a Kiowa and professor of literature, *House
Made of Dawn* follows a young Native American named Abel who returns
to the reservation after serving in World War II. Abel comes home a
sullen and misunderstood man. Having left the continuity provided by
the land and his culture to fight as an infantryman, Abel, like so many
veterans, is unable to take up his old life. He is a man who has "lost his
place. He had been long ago at the center, had known where he was, had
lost his way, had wandered to the end of the earth, was even now reeling
on the edge of the void."[20]

Abel's personal crisis turns violent. First he stabs a man to death. Sent
to prison, Abel is later released and "relocated" to Los Angeles. In the
city, despite meeting other Indians who befriend him, Abel still cannot
find peace. Unable to connect to the workaday demands of white, urban
society, Abel drifts into an alcoholic nihilism. When he is brutalized by a
policeman, Abel seeks revenge, only to be badly beaten. His friends then
help him to return to the reservation. There, the novel's ending suggests,
he has a chance to save himself, to re-connect to a meaningful life and
come to "a house made of dawn."

Indeed, several critics have read the novel's ending as a case of "spiritual renewal and/or cultural rejuvenation,"[21] but critic Charles R. Larson
insists on the ending's ambiguity. Noting that in the end Abel can escape
his tortuous life only by running to his death, Larson argues that a main
theme of the novel is "cultural irreconcilability."[22] Because the novel's
Native characters can neither recapture their ancestral spiritualism nor
find wholeness in white society, their lives eventually reach a brutal existential finality. As Larson puts it, for Momaday's Indian characters "existence is not even a matter of simple endurance; rather they are slowly
being obliterated. Their world is dead-ended."[23]

A different reading of the novel is offered by Susan Scarberry-Garcia. She argues that in its use of Native American oral traditions and mythologies, *House Made of Dawn* is essentially "a novel of healing." In this reading, Abel's final run becomes an opportunity to transcend physical and psychic pain, an offering of the self to a larger spiritual tradition which allows Abel to rise above his suffering.[24] While different from Larson's reading, Scarberry-Garcia's interpretation suggests the social critique which is also part of the novel. Only a return to the traditions of his people and not the adoption of white values can save Abel.

A poetic portrayal of a man's life, *House Made of Dawn* is also a critique of white societal values. Not only can these values not be forced on Native Americans, but they tend toward disintegration and disharmony. A contrast of scenes illustrates this theme well. In one, a group of Indians, led by the Priest of the Sun, comes together under the influence of peyote to discover "that something holy was going on in the universe."[25] In the very next scene, however, Abel awakens alone after an alcoholic binge to find his memory blank and his hands horribly broken. Thus, subtly, Momaday contrasts Native and white cultures.

For Larson, *House Made of Dawn* ultimately reveals

> the subtle and insidious ways that one ethnic group slowly strangles another: by words (legal methods), by deed (historical patterns), by culture (spiritual beliefs). Taken together, along with the overriding images of death and destruction, these issues make Momaday's [novel] the most searing indictment of the white world by a Native American novelist.[26]

While it is a gross oversimplification to call Native American fiction mere "protest" literature, often such fiction dramatizes the difficulty Native Americans have in living freely in both white and Native cultures. However, modern Westerns born of the counterculture, a movement largely by and for whites, have little difficulty in invoking the Old West myth of the greater freedom possible in the West. Perhaps the most well-known countercultural/protest movie of the Vietnam era is the contemporary Western *Billy Jack* (1971). Yet what most people casually remember about the film, that it contained the hit song "One Tin Soldier" by Coven and that it featured a karate-kicking title character, cannot fully explain the movie's popularity. Made for less than one million dollars, the film "earned tens of millions, making it one of the most profitable films up to that time."[27] As a highly popular product of its times, *Billy Jack* probably resonated with audiences because it tried to be both an action movie and a social tract.

Set in the West and unafraid to evoke certain idealistic Western images (the film opens with horses running freely across a landscape), thematically, *Billy Jack* was clearly spawned by 1960s social idealism. Most of the values of the countercultural movement can be found in it. It tries hard to be pro-inclusion and anti-racist, pro-spiritual and anti-material, pro-peace and anti-violent. In addition, some lessons from the 1960s cultural turmoil are blended in, as the movie also makes statements against drug use and for inter-generational understanding.

Title character Billy Jack is an ex-Green Beret who now lives on an Indian reservation in Arizona. There he protects the students at a unique school from the racist residents of a nearby town. In a voice-over, the director of the Freedom School labels Billy Jack "a half breed, a war hero who hated the war and turned his back on society by returning to the reservation where he watched over the Indians, the wild horses and the kids at my school."[28] The townspeople hate the students at the Freedom School presumably because they're all troubled kids from diverse racial backgrounds. Jean Roberts, the school's director, runs the place on three rules: "no drugs, everyone had to carry his own load, and everyone had to get turned on to creating something . . . preferably something that made one proud of one's own heritage and past." To help show the creative side of the school's students, the film features a young girl singing an anti-war song about a brother who was killed in Vietnam.

Into this creative, multicultural atmosphere comes the teenage daughter of a deputy sheriff. Barbara has been beaten by her father for returning from Haight-Ashbury pregnant by an unknown man. At the school she is given refuge, and she falls in love with Martin, a young Indian boy.

Meanwhile, in town Billy Jack must save some of the students from a racist attack. Exhibiting his karate skills, Billy battles with several men, along the way incurring the wrath of Bernard Posner, son of the richest man around. This fight leads to a scene designed to show the intransigence of established authority. When the city council decides to seek an injunction forbidding the school's students from coming freely to town, the students protest. The girl who sang the anti-war song even reads a quote attributed to Adolph Hitler but which echoes the rigid law and order sentiments of the council members. However, something positive results from this confrontation: two council members agree to visit the school. There, by participating in a role-playing exercise, they begin to understand the students' point of view as their generation's social hypocrisy is dramatized.

Along with its desire for better communication between the generations, *Billy Jack* also presents an anti-drug, pro-spiritual message. Billy has turned to Native American mysticism. These days the picture of Native Americans as the keepers of a spiritual reservoir in counterbalance to a spiritually parched white society seems like a cultural cliché. In 1971, however, the idea was probably still more or less novel—at least to whites, who seem to be *Billy Jack*'s target audience. Hence we see Billy participating in a Native American rite which requires that he be bitten repeatedly by a rattlesnake. After surviving this ordeal, he speaks to the assembled host about the nature of Indian spirituality. Contending that white people take drugs because white religion has failed to provide them with true spiritual peace, Billy lauds the ancient Native American religion which seeks a spiritual life in the natural world and which binds people to that world and to each other. He then leads the people in a sacred dance which proceeds in a complete human circle, ostensibly a symbol of the unity created by Native American spirituality.

All of these other themes aside, *Billy Jack* tries mainly to be an anti-violence movie. This may surprise those people who remember the film mainly for the martial arts expertise of its lead character. The main dramatic tension in the film, as is the case in so many American movies, is the escalation of violence. In intensity, the violence in the story builds from Billy's unarmed fight with the townspeople and from his earlier armed confrontation with a group of wild mustang hunters. As Barbara's father and Bernard Posner seek revenge, the violence escalates through beatings, kidnappings, a rape, and a murder.

For a supposedly pacifistic film, *Billy Jack* does depict a great deal of violence. Nevertheless, a non-violent message is attempted. Amid the mayhem, Jean tries to prevent Billy from responding violently. Billy at first rejects her argument that "you just can't keep making your own laws." To Billy, the fact that laws are unequally administered justifies a violence which seeks justice. In one of the film's few direct acknowledgments of the decade to which it responds, Billy asks Jean to consider the assassinations of Martin Luther King, Jr. and John and Bobby Kennedy. For Billy, these men are "not [just] dead. Their brains [were] blown out because your people wouldn't even put the same controls on their guns as they do on their dogs, their cats, their bicycles . . . " At this point Jean seems to be merely the unrealistic idealist, whereas Billy comes off as the hardened realist who sets out to right wrongs in the only way they can be righted—through superior violent force.

Still, the film bravely tries to retain its pacifistic message. While Billy kills both Bernard and Barbara's father, he does so in self-defense. Later, refusing to be captured for these killings, Billy holes up in a church. After holding off an attack by state police, Billy is talked into giving himself up. He is prepared to die fighting, but he is eventually convinced that the publicity from his trial would do more than his death to help the Native American cause. Billy surrenders because he loves Jean and the kids at her school. In exchange for keeping the school open and publicizing its progress, Billy walks out of the church and into a pair of handcuffs. It is clear that this act has taken more courage than his previous desire to die fighting. Billy Jack's heroic status is underscored when the squad car he rides in is saluted, in raised-fist fashion, by the students who line the road.

Watching *Billy Jack* today, it's sometimes difficult to understand the popularity it enjoyed 25 years ago. Along with low production values and loose scripting, its social messages could seem garbled to today's viewers. It's at once obvious and confused. Billy Jack: Native American mystic or karate-chopping avenger? Spokesman for harmony or Chuck Norris's cinematic granddad?

Despite its flaws, there is an honesty about the film. If nothing else, *Billy Jack* is at least an earnest attempt to speak to the concerns of the counterculture and to portray the era's "wayward" youth as decent and caring. Its popularity could only have been enhanced by the kind of action movie-goers then and now expect to see. In addition, in its plot elements the film offers a familiar vision: freedom and self-determination are still possible, at least out West and given the protection of principled men like Billy—who in certain ways is just a hippie version of Shane. Both are violent defenders of vulnerable people trying to develop a communal way of life.

The countercultural themes of freedom and societal improvement find a Western setting in Tom Robbins's novel *Even Cowgirls Get the Blues*. While stylistically it revels in unabashed punning and witty juxtapositions, *Even Cowgirls Get the Blues* could be considered a novel of ideas. Ultimately, Robbins supplies his solution to an America troubled by divisive political, religious and racial strife: If every individual pursues inner happiness, a better society will follow.

The plot of *Even Cowgirls Get the Blues* follows Sissy Hankshaw, a beautiful young woman who possesses inordinately large thumbs and a concomitant gift for hitchhiking. On one of her cross-country trips, Sissy hitchhikes to the Rubber Rose Ranch in western North Dakota, where she encounters a feminist utopia in the form of an all-female combination ranch and commune. The prevailing pursuit at the Rubber Rose is personal freedom as its resident cowgirls seek to escape a sexist and chauvinistic world.

The social critique in the novel is simply put: "If you want to change the world, change yourself."[29] This advice comes from the Chink, a philosophical hermit who lives near the Rubber Rose. In many ways the Chink is a convenient device through which Robbins can espouse his ideas on such things as human sexuality and the nature of time. But as an author Robbins is not bound by literary convention: If he wants to include an idea, he'll stop the narrative and include a mini essay. One such essay comes in the form of a dialogue between a brain and a thumb.

Robbins's main idea is that any obstacle to personal freedom should be recognized and overcome. These obstacles would include everything from repressive social mores and government bureaucracies to one's own limited capacity for reason. All social change should tend toward greater personal freedom, and for that reason Robbins is opposed to group solutions. Rejecting collective ideologies, Robbins calls for each individual to pursue a truly fulfilling life. In this way, social change must occur. As Delores del Ruby, one of the Rubber Rose's principal figures, says toward the end of the novel:

> *The enemy of women is not men. No, and the enemy of*
> *the black is not the white. The enemy of the capitalist is*
> *not communist, the enemy of homosexual is not hetero-*
> *sexual . . . We all have the same enemy. The enemy is the*
> *tyranny of the dull mind. . . . The enemy is every ex-*
> *pert who practices technocratic manipulation, the enemy*
> *is every proponent of standardization and the enemy is*
> *every victim who is so dull and lazy and weak as to*
> *allow himself to be manipulated and standardized.* [30]

For Robbins there is a tyranny in the collective solution. Even governments, he argues, must be open to constant change. At one point,
Sissy paraphrases the Chink's ideas on the government's attempts to
"stabilize" every situation:

> *Stabilization to them means order, uniformity, control.*
> *And that's a half-witted and potentially genocidal mis-*
> *conception. No matter how thoroughly they control a*
> *system, disorder invariably leaks into it. Then the man-*
> *agers panic, rush to plug the leak and endeavor to tighten*
> *controls. Therefore, totalitarianism grows in viciousness*
> *and scope. . . . [A] stable culture, government or insti-*
> *tution has built into it its own demise. It is open to change,*
> *open even to being overthrown. It is open, period. . . .*
> *That's stability.* [31]

Ultimately, by challenging our notions of stability, Robbins questions
a central epistemology of American society. Indeed, for critic Robert
Nadeau, "Robbins's intent . . . is to hammer away at those assumptions
about self and world in Western cosmology which he feels are injurious
to our emotional well-being and a threat to our continued survival as a
species." [32]

In Nadeau's reading, Robbins borrows a central premise from recent
studies in physics—the idea that "[o]rder in nature is always accompanied by disorder" [33]—to challenge our "continue[d][belief] that rational
analysis, predicated upon a belief in abstractions and either-or categori-
cal thinking, can answer 'Ultimate Questions.'" [34] Thus, the Chink builds
into his clockworks an element of random disorder to symbolize
humankind's real relationship to the natural world.

In most Westerns, however—indeed, in most societal goals—establishing order is precisely the point. Think of the classic Western plot which sees a stranger ride into town to rid the community of a de-stabilizing force, say, greedy ranchers who kill farmers for encroaching on the range. These Western plots are built upon a careful duality between good and evil, civilization and savagery, order and disorder. However, *Even Cowgirls Get the Blues* refutes the idea that "progress" is a dialectical outcome; for Robbins evolution is random and unpredictable, so complete freedom—especially from a mindset and a political ideology which operates on an either/or principle—is necessary to personal and social health.

While Robbins is concerned about a perception of reality which oppresses individual freedom, his fellow author Edward Abbey lashes out at governments and businesses that seek to develop the West in defiance of individuals who wish to preserve the region's natural state. As a writer and thinker, Abbey became a spokesman for environmentalists who oppose the industrialization of the West. This debt was acknowledged after his death in a eulogy published in the magazine *Sierra* where he was lauded as a writer who "voice[d] . . . concerns that were stirring in our [environmentalists'] own breasts" and as a man who "was smack in the middle of traditional American nature writing, carrying forward its heat and light, and the smoke of its magical trickery, into our own decades."[35]

Further, Abbey's novel *The Monkey Wrench Gang* supported an environmental movement which would use destructive means to stop road building, strip mining, and clearcutting. Released in 1975, *The Monkey Wrench Gang* became "an underground classic, selling half a million copies."[36] Said to have inspired the formation of the radical environmental movement Earth First!,[37] the novel has been called "an ode to individual liberty and the preservationist ethic of saving the land and the life it sustains from the cancerous political and economic machine."[38]

Often hilarious, *The Monkey Wrench Gang* follows a group of four saboteurs as they make their way across the Southwest destroying any industrial threat to a pristine environment. In many ways the novel is an instructional manual for would-be "eco-raiders." Want to know how to start a bulldozer and drive it off a cliff, or how to set a charge to blow a coal train off its tracks? Turn to Abbey for details.

Yet amid the gang's destructive hijinks there is a serious message. Each of the gang members opposes industrialization for different reasons. For Seldom Seen Smith, the industrial blight on the land has just become too monstrous. For George Washington Hayduke the "developing" of the West is reminiscent of the complacent destruction his government unleashed in Southeast Asia. And for Doc Sarvis the perceived rape of the West's natural resources exemplifies an elaborate corporate world indifferent to the rights of individuals. Thus when Doc looks upon a coal mine the gang has targeted, he thinks

> *of the plain of fire and of the oligarchs and oligopoly beyond: Peabody Coal only one arm of Anaconda Copper; Anaconda only a limb of United States Steel; U.S. Steel intertwined in incestuous embrace with the Pentagon, TVA, Standard Oil, General Dynamics, Dutch Shell, I. G. Farben-industrie; the whole conglomerated cartel spread out upon half the planet Earth like a global kraken, pantentacled, wall-eyed and parrot-beaked, its brain a bank of computer data centers, its blood the flow of money, its heart a radioactive dynamo, its language the technetronic monologue of the number imprinted on magnetic tape.* [39]

As if this weren't scary enough for Doc, he has also witnessed the direct human cost of the increase in industrial pollution. Reflecting on a recent lung-cancer patient, Doc muses, "[t]he Southwest had once been a place where Eastern physicians sent their more serious respiratory cases. No more; the developers—bankers, industrialists, subdividers, freeway builders and public utility chiefs—had succeeded with less than thirty years' effort in bringing the air of Southwestern cities 'up to standard,' that is, as foul as any other."[40]

As social critique, Abbey's work identifies a central conflict in values which is at the center of our nation's debate on the proper approach to our natural resources. In Abbey's writing can be found an exemplum of what A. Carl Bredahl, Jr., calls the Western imagination. For Bredahl, the Western American view of the world is different from the Eastern in that "[t]he imagination of the American West . . . finds essential value in surface because surface is at the heart of the western experience. . . . [T]he western eye regards surfaces as neither hollow nor artificial. Distant from eastern structures and challenged by the big sky, the westerner finds himself accepting the landscape and indeed embracing it for physical and spiritual sustenance."[41] Thus for Abbey the natural world should not be exploited because the Western landscape has value all its own. Behind his immediate criticism of the industrialization of the West lies Abbey's critique of the view that nature is valuable only if it can be used to serve economic ends.

Finally, the idea that the West is still an exceptional place where one can somehow be a freer individual is reflected in one of the more controversial films of the 1990s. The critical storm surrounding *Thelma & Louise* (1991) seems surprising, especially since many of its themes had been occurring in Westerns for years. The film supports freedom and self-reliance; it values self-definition and commitment to friendship. It also contains clear-cut bad guys, a modicum of violent action, and the thrill of traveling the open country: All the traditional elements of an action/adventure Western. So why did it become so controversial? Because its main characters are two female anti-heroes, and that fact fed a national debate on the nature and direction of feminism.

As befitting a road picture, the plot of *Thelma & Louise* is episodic. Thelma, played by Geena Davis, is a housewife married to a controlling, philandering husband. Susan Sarandon's Louise is a waitress in love with a commitment-wary musician. Together they set out on a weekend camping tramp, each eager to experience a little freedom. Along the way they stop in roadside honky-tonk. Even though the more experienced Louise knows that nothing good can come of it, Thelma insists on drinking too much and dancing with a creepy barfly. When the creep takes Thelma into the parking lot and tries to rape her, Louise stops him at gunpoint. Then she shoots and kills him.

This is where the film requires its largest suspension of disbelief, for Louise shoots the would-be rapist after he has released Thelma. Later the audience learns of an unspecified but horrible sexual assault which Louise suffered. So has she shot the man in self-defense or out of a need for revenge? Either way, the film needs a reason to put the two women on the run. Afraid that the authorities will not believe the story of attempted rape, Thelma and Louise hit the open road, pushing their '66 T-bird convertible for the Mexican border.

Though they seem to be running from the law, in essence they are fleeing a repressive, male-dominated world. In many Westerns, the male heroes keep riding west because they cannot abide a world tamed by women. Here the roles are reversed: It's the men who stultify the women. Only one decent man stands out in the film, and that's Hal, the Arkansas state policeman who tries to talk the women into giving up. Most of the other men in the women's lives, from Thelma's loutish husband Daryl to an officious highway patrol officer to a crude and moronic truck driver, depict the worst to be found in the masculine gender. One sees these guys and thinks, no wonder Thelma and Louise light out for something better.

The other two principal men in the story represent something more problematic. The first is Jimmy, Louise's boyfriend. When Louise asks him to wire money to her, Jimmy flies out to meet her instead. Jimmy then proposes to Louise. Why she refuses to marry him is not so clear. Perhaps it's because Jimmy waited too long, deciding to make a commitment only after he grew afraid of losing her forever. Or maybe Louise has simply moved on to something more thrilling: a life on the lam. The reason probably doesn't matter, because naturally if she accepts the proposal the show's over.

The other male character who isn't completely without charm is the young hitchhiker Thelma picks up and has sex with. Fittingly, in a film which reverses so many standard plot elements, it's the man who becomes the sex object. But who has used whom? The drifter turns out to be a paroled stick-up man, and he absconds with all of the money Jimmy has brought them.

Now the two women become armed robbers. As they cruise across the Southwest, knocking over convenience stores and swilling bourbon, they are overtaken by an outlaw spirit. At one point Thelma says, "Something's crossed over in me. I can't go back. . . . I just couldn't live."[42] The ties they have cut and the danger they face bring something wild and elemental into their lives. They are capable and unafraid. They are even unwilling to put up with sexist behavior, so they lure the obscene truck driver into pulling over just so they can shoot up his rig. More than one critic has read feminist implications into this scene, seeing the exploding tanker truck as a phallic symbol.

In the end, after an off-road car chase through the desert, the women are trapped against the rim of the Grand Canyon. They cannot turn back, as Thelma says, "Let's not get caught. Let's keep going." As they join hands, Louise guns the engine and the car flies off the edge.

Thelma & Louise is a well-paced action movie, but the question remains: Is it a truly feminist film or is it just a female *Butch Cassidy and the Sundance Kid* in a boss convertible? Certainly Thelma and Louise's act of self-immolation is no less spectacular than Butch and Sundance's, even if, unlike those male outlaws, the women don't try to take anybody out with them. But seeing this film as just another Western does not explain the intense national discussion which surrounded it. All three of the major news magazines entered the debate; *Time* even devoted a cover story to it.

At one extreme was critic John Leo, who considered the film to be an example of "toxic feminism." Writing in *U.S. News & World Report*, Leo called the film fascistic, objecting to what he saw as the movie's radical feminist message that "'[t]here is no hope for women, or for any truce in the battle of the sexes, because the patriarchy will crush all women who resist or simply try to live their own lives.'"[43]

At the other extreme were critics who embraced *Thelma & Louise* as a dead-to-rights feminist film. This view was expressed by film critic Kathi Maio in *Ms.* Calling the film "an indictment against patriarchy," Maio perceived Thelma and Louise's reaction to violence as understandable: "*Thelma & Louise* portrayed male violence as an ordinary, everyday event. It's more than rape—it's a husband's verbal abuse of his wife; it's a stranger feeling he has the right to harass any woman. Thelma and Louise become outlaws not because they love violence, but because men won't leave them be."[44]

Other critics thought the film offered a mild, even escapist, feminism. Stuart Klawans noted that the film opened a day after the Supreme Court decision in *Rust v. Sullivan* which "restrict[ed] the medical advice a woman may receive if she's simultaneously pregnant and poor." For Klawans, under these real-world circumstances, *Thelma & Louise* could at best provide "a lite-feminist fizz . . . without seeming pretentious."[45] And a piece in *Newsweek* opined that even though "Thelma and Louise . . . employ some well-known male techniques of self-assertion . . . of course they're [still] feminists, but not because they have pistols tucked into their jeans. This is a movie about two women whose clasped hands are their most powerful weapon."[46]

Amid the controversy over whether the film simply bashed males or represented two women quite naturally establishing their freedom, some critics offered the opinion that *Thelma & Louise* was neither anti-male nor feminist. Star Geena Davis, for one, couldn't understand what all the fuss was about: Quoted in *Time*: "'Why,' she asked, 'because it stars women, is this suddenly a feminist treatise, given the burden of representing all women?'"[47] And *New Yorker* film critic Terrence Rafferty thought "that the feminist ideas [were] used opportunistically, just to keep the narrative moving—that every time Thelma and Louise have a chance to give themselves up, a man does something horrible and strengthens their conviction that that they're better off on the run."[48] Thus for Rafferty the film "seem[ed] less a feminist parable than an airy, lyrical joke about a couple of women who go off in search of a little personal space and discover that they have to keep going and going and going to find a space that's big enough."[49]

Still other critics saw the film as anti-feminist in that it dressed up in drag male plots and male resolutions to conflict. An article by Margaret Carlson entitled "Is This What Feminism Is All About?: By Playing Out a Male Fantasy, 'Thelma and Louise' Shows Hollywood Is Still a Man's World" takes this stance. For Carlson "Thelma and Louise act out a male fantasy of life on the road, avoiding intimacy with loud music, Wild Turkey, fast driving—and a gun in the pants." Further, Carlson objects to the implicit female stereotypes in the film: "The turning point of Thelma's character rests on one of the most enduring and infuriating male myths in the culture: the only thing an unhappy woman needs is good sex to make everything all right."[50]

Clearly, *Thelma & Louise* touched a chord with viewers. In the final analysis, however, the debate surrounding its merits as a feminist work says more about the difficulty of defining feminism than it does about the film itself, for in many ways *Thelma & Louise* is an old-fashioned Western. From its opening shot of a road stretching invitingly across a South-western plain to its final white out as the green convertible hits the sky over the Grand Canyon, the film speaks to the kind of vicarious, often reckless, freedom that Western movies have offered for one hundred years. Out West, many of these films whisper, is the chance to escape the mundane grind, to discover emotion unvarnished by societal nice-ties. That *Thelma & Louise* finally lets female characters embody this thrill could simply be a matter of: it's about time.

More generally, then, *Thelma & Louise* illustrates the continuing allure of the West. Had their story been set in an Eastern city, it would have been much different in form and in thematic content. Thelma and Louise running through New York City likely would have provoked discussion of the evils of urban violence. Instead, in part because it was set in the West, where time and space and cultural aspirations all meet, *Thelma & Louise* was often read as a tale of the identity and destiny, positive or not, of American women.

Whether storytellers set their tales in the old or the modern West, they will come into contact with the enduring popular appeal of the supposed virtues of Western experience. In American popular culture the West is still seen as inviting and special, as a place where people should be stronger and freer. Frederick Jackson Turner's 100-year-old idea that the West was America's moral crucible may be disputed by historians, but it certainly holds force in our contemporary fictions.[51] The myth of the West as a locus of America's developing national character in opposition to tainted Eastern values makes it attractive as a set-ting for stories that speak to our most cherished ideals. To the extent that the West is still seen as a place where our national character is formed and tested, it becomes an ideal setting for writers and filmmakers who wish to provoke an examination of issues that overlay the question of who Americans are and who they are becoming.

NOTES

Chapter 1

1. "Devoid alike of ethical and social meaning, the Western story could develop in no direction save that of a straining and exaggeration of its formulas. It abandoned all effort to be serious . . . [and eventually] sunk to the near-juvenile level it was to occupy with virtually no change down to our own day." Henry Nash Smith, *Virgin Land: The American West as Symbol and Myth*. (1950; reprint, Cambridge: Harvard Univ. Press, 1978), 119-20.

2. John G. Cawelti, *The Six-Gun Mystique* (Bowling Green: Bowling Green Univ. Popular Press, 1970); *Adventure, Mystery, and Romance: Formula Stories as Art and Popular Culture* (Chicago: Univ. of Chicago Press, 1976).

3. The critical praise for these two films is naturally in keeping with their both having won Academy Awards for Best Picture. Some reviewers of *Dances With Wolves*, however, were amused by the 1960's ethos of the film. Reviewer Caryn James, for example, chuckles at Kevin Costner's anachronistically enlightened "meditations." On one such meditation, she comments, "It's as if he and the Beatles have just visited the Maharishi Mahesh Yogi." See James, Caryn, "Frugging with Wolves." In *The New York Times Film Reviews, 1991-1992*, 13 January 1991. Times Books and Garland Publishing, Inc., 1993,4.

Reviews for *Unforgiven* are decidedly less mixed, the film being almost universally praised for its social critique. See reviews: Peter Biskind, *Premiere*, (August 1992); Richard Corliss, *Time*, (10 August 1992); Brian D. Johnson, *Maclean's*, (17 August 1992); Charles Leerhsen, *Newsweek*, (10 August 1992); and Michael Sragow *The New Yorker*, (10 August 1992). Furthermore, in a literate, thought-provoking essay, Stuart Klawans compares *Unforgiven* with Genesis, concluding his review with the comment, "Clint Eastwood's westerns are distinctive, and . . . *Unforgiven*, as the most fully realized, is the most distinctive of all." See "*Unforgiven*," *The Nation*, 14 September 1992, 260.

Writing on the 1990s resurgence of Hollywood Westerns, reporter Richard Zoglin, discovers in *Dances With Wolves* and *Unforgiven* a desire to make Westerns that reinterpret the past to shed light on contemporary social issues. Zoglin quotes historian Patricia Limerick, who seems to believe that a new era of socially conscious Westerns is about to unfold: "'We don't have to create an image and an ideology of ourselves as heroic expanders of the frontier and innocents who fight evil. All of that cold war fervor that drove the old westerns has lifted, so you can do more complex and interesting westerns.'" See Richard Zoglin, "Back from Boot Hill," *Time*, 15 November 1993, 93.

4. In *The Six-Gun Mystique*, for example, Cawelti argues that formula Westerns are predicated on the desire for order and "masculine supremacy" (6). Jane Tompkins argues that Westerns serve a patriarchal worldview in *West of Everything: The Inner Life of Westerns* (New York: Oxford Univ. Press, 1992).

5. In an interview, Paretsky stated that she deliberately set out to break old formulas in the detective novel because she perceived the role for women in such fiction to be decidedly limited. Moreover, she believes women can find in her works a vicarious "sense of courage and a sense of empowerment." See Norma Libman, "New Breed of Detective: V.I. Warshawski is tough, funny, feisty," *Chicago Tribune*, 11 August 1991, sec. 6, p. 12.

6. Richard Slotkin, *Gunfighter Nation: The Myth of the Frontier in Twentieth-Century America* (New York: HarperPerennial, 1993), 169-83.

7. Ibid., 364.

8. Coined by Fiedler and employed by Bold, the term anti-Western is used to refer to any Western that "exploit[s]" the conventions of the genre to make apparent the "illusoriness and the two-dimensionality of the

Western formula" (Bold, 157). Expanding on ideas first presented on the anti-Western by Leslie Fiedler in *The Return of the Vanishing American*, Christine Bold argues that *Midnight Cowboy* can be properly placed in a study of the genre because "Joe is a caricature of the Virginian, but one who agrees with the Virginian's author on the crucial requirements of the cowboy image." In addition to Joe in James Leo Herlihy's novel *Midnight Cowboy*, Bold singles out Hud Bannon in the Larry McMurtry novel *Horseman, Pass By* as examples of the kind of inverted Western hero, or anti-hero, that frequently appears in anti-Westerns. These characters are often exact opposites of the morally upright heroes found in formulaic Westerns, and their immorality belies the stereotype that life in the West inevitably builds character. Bold lists several other novels from the 1960s to 1970s that she categorizes as anti-Westerns. Among these are: Robert Flynn's *North to Yesterday*, Ishmael Reed's *Yellow Black Radio Broke-Down*, John Seelye's *The Kid*, H. Allen Smith's *The Return of the Virginian*, George L. Voss's *The Man who Believed in the Code of the West*, and Robert Day's *The Last Cattle Drive* (Bold, 157-58). See Christine Bold, *Selling the Wild West: Popular Western Fiction, 1860-1960* (Bloomington: Univ. of Indiana Press, 1987), 163.

9. Loren D. Estleman, a veteran author of Western and detective novels, has created two comparable protagonists who operate similarly in their respective genres. See his Page Murdock Westerns and his Amos Walker detective novels.

10. That my view of the Western as a genre is more iconographic than formulaic or thematic attests to the range of specific approaches authors and filmmakers have taken in creating "Westerns." Because of the wide variety of Westerns produced in this century, a more open view of the genre is necessary. Critic Jim Kitses argues, for example, that the Western cannot be easily fixed within a single form precisely because the forms are constantly changing: "Only a pluralist vision [of the Western] makes sense of our experience of the genre and begins to explain its amazing vigour and adaptability, the way it moves closer and further from our own world, brightening or darkening with each succeeding decade." See Jim Kitses, "The Western: Ideology and Archetype," in *Focus on the Western*, ed. Jack Nachbar (Englewood Cliffs, N.J.: Prentice-Hall, 1974), 68.

11. In *Adventure, Mystery, and Romance*, 249, Cawelti writes,

> [A] number of westerns of the classic period such as High
> Noon and The Ox-Bow Incident *were explicitly con-*
> *ceived as allegories with strong implications for the con-*
> *temporary scene. Critics, also, began to interpret west-*
> *erns in terms of contemporary situations and to point*
> *out analogies between the western film and such politi-*
> *cal events of the period as the Korean conflict and*
> *McCarthy's crusade against communism. Whatever one*
> *may think about the validity of such interpretations, the*
> *tendency to make them indicates the degree to which at*
> *least some of the more sophisticated members of the pub-*
> *lic responded explicitly to the classic western's expres-*
> *sion of American value conflicts.*

After this brief passage, Cawelti continues his discussion of "classic westerns" and their identifiable common characteristics. He is clearly more concerned with exploring the formula of the classic Western than he is with examining specific works for their social and political content.

12. Cawelti, *Adventure, Mystery, and Romance*, 16.

13. Daryl Jones, *The Dime Novel Western* (Bowling Green: Bowling Green Univ. Popular Press, 1978), 12.

14. Ibid., 14.

15. Ibid., 168.

16. Cawelti, *Six-Gun Mystique*, 32.

17. John G. Cawelti, "Prolegomena to the Western," in *Western Writing*, ed. Gerald W. Haslam (Albuquerque: Univ. of New Mexico Press, 1974), 124.

18. Ibid., 124.

19. Will Wright, *Six Guns and Society: A Structural Study of the Western* (Berkeley: Univ. of California Press, 1975), 12.

20. Ibid., 14.

21. Tompkins, *West of Everything*, 45.

22. Ibid., 6-7.

23. Ibid., 7. Tompkins writes that "when you read a Western novel or watch a Western movie on television, you are in the same world no matter what the medium: the hero is the same, the story line is the same, the setting, the values, the actions are the same."
This view of the relative merits of Western novels and films certainly serves Tompkins's purpose. However, such a view, if universally accepted, would preclude other critical purposes. For example, a study of the thematic differences between the novel *Little Big Man* and its film version could reveal much about the limits and possibilities of prose versus celluloid narrative.

24. John H. Lenihan, *Showdown: Confronting Modern America in the Western Film* (Urbana: Univ. of Illinois Press, 1980), 7.

25. Ibid., 9.

26. Slotkin, *Gunfighter Nation*, 4.

27. Ibid., 6.

28. Ibid., 645-48.

29. Ibid., 658.

30. Ibid., 659, Slotkin's emphasis.

31. Margaret Atwood, *Lady Oracle* (New York: Simon and Schuster, 1976), 246-47.

32. Richard White, "Frederick Jackson Turner and Buffalo Bill," in the *Frontier in American Culture*, ed. James R. Grossman (Berkeley: Univ. of California Press, 1994), 55.

33. Slotkin, "Gunsmoke and Mirrors," *Life* 15 April 1993, 68.

34. Obviously the television Western no longer dominates prime-time lineups as it did in the 1950s and 1960s, and cinematic Westerns are also increasingly rare. In addition, the *1996 Writer's Market* lists 33 publishers of Westerns, less than the number of publishers for Mystery, Romance, and Fantasy respectively. Operating on the assumption that television, film, and book producers know what sells, these facts could reflect a diminishing market for Westerns.

35. Quoted in "Westerns Harness New Audiences," *Library Journal* 15 February 1994, 124.

36. Denis E. Showalter, "Blazing a New Trail: The New 'Old West' Books Are Attracting a Wider Readership with Historically Accurate Plots Featuring Women and Ethnic Groups," *Publishers Weekly*, 11 January 1993, 37.

37. Ibid., 40.

38. Ibid., 42. Further, author Jack Curtis contends that if the genre is to remain attractive to readers, the subject matter of Westerns must constantly be made relevant to contemporary concerns. Thus, Curtis says, he "is able to examine contemporary problems such as political show biz, corruption in high places, law officers overriding constitutional rights, science-business versus humanism—all vital issues for this generation of readers—within the context of the Old West." Jack Curtis, "Resilient Western Writing," *The Writer*, December 1994, 16.

39. Jeff Strickler, "Why Are Westerns Popular?" *Minneapolis Star Tribune*, 4 September 1994, 5F.

Chapter 2
1. Glendon Swarthout, *The Shootist* (New York: Doubleday, 1975. Pap. ed. Signet, 1986.)

2. Politics, the showdown mentality, the Western's frequent insistence on clear-cut good versus evil, and popular culture all meet in some of Herbert Block's political cartoons. Examples include a cartoon from July 16, 1954, bearing the caption "High Noon in Washington" and featuring a sheriff labeled "Resolution to Curb McCarthy" trying to deputize a quaking Senator Knowland. In a similar vein, a work published April 6, 1954, has a gunman symbolizing the Soviet Union incredulously asking a sheriff with "Nato" on his star, "You Mean You Won't Swear Me In As A Deputy?" See Herbert Block, *Herblock's Here and Now* (New York: Simon and Schuster, 1955) 123, 185. This collection of Block's work as well as the later *Straight Herblock* (New York: Simon and Schuster, 1958) offer numerous cartoons in which the gunslinger and the showdown in the street are used as symbols in the portrayal of Cold War politics.

3. Richard Slotkin, *Regeneration Through Violence: The Mythology of the American Frontier, 1600-1860* (Middeltown, Conn.: Wesleyan Univ. Press, 1973), 5.

4. An explicit connection between the morals reflected in Westerns and the political beliefs found in contemporary America is made by Anthony Lejeune, who laments the increasing levels of violence found in Westerns, particularly of the spaghetti variety. He equates the moral heroism of the classic Western with the politics "on which Americans most pride themselves[:] . . . progress, democracy, and 'the people.'" To Lejeune, the "essence" of the classic Western—and *Shane* appears to be one of his favorites—is "youth recalled, hope undimmed, the land beginning again, morning in America; everything we loved in real Westerns and find totally missing in spaghetti Westerns." Echoed in Lejeune's rhetoric are many of the themes upon which 1980s Republicans campaigned for president including the message of "morning in America" and George Bush's "thousand points of light." Anthony Lejeune, "The Rise and Fall of the Western," *National Review*, (31 December 1989), 23-26.

5. Slotkin, *Regeneration Through Violence*, 563. The phrase "super-TVA-type development" refers to the Tennessee Valley Authority, a project

undertaken as part of Franklin Roosevelt's New Deal to provide electricity to seven Southern states.

6. Bernard DeVoto, "Birth of an Art," in *Western Writing*, ed. Gerald W. Haslam (Albuquerque: Univ. of New Mexico Press, 1974), 12.

7. Ibid., 11-12.

8. Ibid., 13.

9. Ibid., 13-14.

10. See *The New York Times* 24 July 1971, sec. 14, p. 1, in *The New York Times Film Reviews 1971-1972*, (New York: New York Times Press, 1973), 106.

Critic David Denby, however, while fully aware of *Little Big Man*'s political resonance, nonetheless argued that the political message interfered with the film's artistic integrity: "What starts out as an elegy for lost values winds up as an exercise in white self-hatred, and although it may seem incongruous to say so, I can't help feeling that Penn's movie is another victim of the war in Vietnam." See David Denby, "Americana" in *Film 70/71: An Anthology by the National Society of Film Critics*, ed. David Denby (New York: Simon and Schuster, 1971), 61.

11. Edward Buscombe, ed. *The BFI Companion to the Western* (New York: Atheneum, 1988), 300.

Further, a contemporary critic of *Soldier Blue* acknowledged the film's political dimension: "The mode of the Western is pastoral, not patriotism, and political content is therefore as natural to it as horses, pistols, or Monument Valley. Such content appears as significantly in the great John Ford conservative Westerns of the 1950s as it does in Ralph Nelson's not-so-great radical, or at least radicalized Western, very much of 1970."

See Roger Greenspun, "Candice Bergen Stars in Violent Western," *The New York Times*, 13 August 1970, sec. 29, p. 1, in *The New York Times Film Reviews 1969-1970*. New York: New York Times Press, 1971, 201.

12. Quoted in John Mack Faragher, "The Tale of Wyatt Earp," in *Past Imperfect: History According to the Movies*, ed. Mark C. Carnes (New York: Holt, 1995), 159.

13. Max Westbrook, "The Night John Wayne Danced With Shirley Temple," in *Old West-New West: Centennial Essays*, ed. Barbara Howard Meldrum (Moscow: Univ. of Idaho Press, 1993), 62.

14. Ibid., 63

15. *Man Who Shot Liberty Valance*, dir. John Ford, written by James Warner Bellah and Willis Goldbeck, starring John Wayne, James Stewart, and Vera Miles (Paramount, 1962).

16. Slotkin, *Regeneration Through Violence*, 4-5.

17. *Stagecoach*, dir. John Ford, written by Dudley Nichols, starring John Wayne, Claire Trevor, Thomas Mitchell, and Andy Devine (United Artists, 1939).

18. Peter Bogdanovich, for one, sees Ford not as a political film-maker but as "a poet" and "a comedian" who nonetheless delivered his every desired effect. Peter Bogdanovich, *John Ford* (Univ. of California Press, 1978), 30-31, 33. And it may be an oversimplification to label Ford a pure conservative. Joseph McBride and Michael Wilmington argue that Ford should not be labeled so conclusively because

> [h]is characters are typically refugees from constricting societies (Europe, urbanized America) in which vital traditions have hardened into inflexible dogmas, and they usually rebel against intolerant and unjust conditions in their own communities as well. As Philippe Haudiquet put it, Ford had "an obsession with justice", and it is his odd synthesis of anarchism and authoritarianism which makes his work equally attractive to those on both extremes of the political spectrum. (John Ford, London: Seeker & Warburg, 1974, 21).

Suggestive of Ford's elusive politics is the fact that the script—the production of which Ford supervised—for *Fort Apache* is based on a short story by James Warner Bellah—"a romantic chronicler of the cavalry during the Indian Wars" whose tales "are heavy on rape and racism"—as rewritten by Frank Nugent, an eastern intellectual who took a "liberal, outsider's view of America." Dan Ford, *Pappy: The Life of John Ford* (Englewood Cliffs, N.J.: Prentice Hall, 1979), 213-15.

19. Mark Schorer, *Sinclair Lewis: An American Life* (New York: McGraw Hill, 1961), 707.

Dore Schary confirms Schorer's belief that MGM was afraid to handle such a political theme in his introduction to the novelization of the screenplay. See Sinclair Lewis and Dore Schary, *Storm in the West* (New York: Stein and Day, 1963).

20. Schorer, *Sinclair Lewis*, 705.

21. David Robinson, *The History of World Cinema* (New York: Stein and Day, 1973), 253. Other critics, too, are convinced that *High Noon* is a political film. Edward Buscombe, for example, editor of *The BFI Companion to the Western*, notes the anti-McCarthy undertones of the film. If not noted for its political dimension, *High Noon* is at least considered by critics like Gerald Mast to be scathing commentary on "the American social climate of 1952." See Mast's *A Short History of the Movies*, 4th ed. (New York: Macmillan, 1986), 293.

22. Bosley Crowther, "'High Noon' a Western of Rare Achievement, Is New Bill at the Mayfair Theatre," *The New York Times*, 25 July, 1952, 14:2, in *The New York Times Film Reviews, 1913-1968*, vol. 4 (New York: New York Times and Arno Press, 1970), 2628.

23. Jon Tuska, *The Filming of the West* (Garden City: Doubleday, 1976), 539.

24. Terry Christian, *Reel Politics: American Political Movies from* Birth of a Nation *to* Platoon (New York: Basil Blackwell, Inc., 1987), 93.

25. Tuska, *Filming of the West,* 539.

26. It seems, however, that the studio was worried about public opinion over Foreman's trouble with the McCarthy committee. As Jay Hyams notes, "United Artists didn't even want to put [Foreman's] name on the credits—they were afraid of picketing." Jay Hyams, *The Life and Times of the Western Movie* (New York: Gallery Books, 1983), 115.

27. Buscombe, *BFI Companion*, 299.

28. Tuska, *Filming of the West*, 541-2; Peter Biskind *Seeing is Believing: How Hollywood Taught Us to Stop Worrying and Love the Fifties* (New York: Pantheon Books, 1983), 47.; Buscombe, *BFI Companion*, 269.

29. Biskind, *Seeing is Believing*, 47.

30. Ibid., 47-48.

31. Ibid., 49.

32. Walter Van Tilburg Clark, *The Ox-Bow Incident*, (New York: Signet Classics, 1940). Quoted in Walter Prescott Webb, Afterword to the Signet Classics edition, 1960, 222.

33. John R. Milton notes that Clark was familiar with Sinclair Lewis' *It Can't Happen Here*, and that he believed Nazism was a greater threat to the United States than Communism. See John Milton, *The Novel of the American West*, 201-11, for Milton's discussion of the psychological and symbolic aspects of *The Ox-Bow Incident*.

34. Clark, quoted in Webb's Afterword to *The Ox-Bow Incident*, 223-24.

35. Clark, *The Ox-Bow Incident*, 49.

36. Milton, *Novel of the American West*, 202.

37. Clark, *The Ox-Bow Incident*, 100-01.

38. Ibid., 105-6.

39. Ibid., 157.

40. Ibid., 210.

41. Clark, quoted in Webb's Afterword to *The Ox-Bow Incident*, 223-24.

Chapter 3

1. Richard Slotkin, *Regeneration Through Violence*, 22.

2. John G. Cawelti, *Six-Gun Mystique*, 53-54.

3. John G. Cawelti, *Adventure, Mystery and Romance*, 250.

4. *My Darling Clementine*, dir. John Ford, written by Samuel G. Engel and Winston Miller, starring Henry Fonda, Linda Darnell, and Victor Mature (Fox, 1946).

5. Examples include *A Fistful of Dollars* (1967) and *The Good, the Bad and the Ugly* (1968).

6. John G. Cawelti, "Reflections on the New Western Films," in *Focus on the Western*, ed. Jack Nachbar, (Englewood Cliffs, N.J.: Prentice-Hall, 1974), 115.

7. Thomas Hobbes describes man in a "natural" or uncivilized state "without a common power to keep" man in check: "no arts; no letters; no society; and which is worst of all, continual fear, and danger of violent death; and the life of man, solitary, poor, nasty, brutish, and short." Thomas Hobbes, *Leviathan: or the Matter, Forme and Power of a Commonwealth Ecclesiasticall and Civil*, ed. Michael Oakeshott, (1651; reprint, Oxford: Basil Blackwell, 1935), 82.

8. Two recent film versions of this story, *Tombstone* (1993) and *Wyatt Earp* (1994), still depict the Earps, particularly Wyatt, as moral icons worthy of imitation.

9. Loren D. Estleman, *Bloody Season* (New York: Bantam, 1987), 21. This passage reveals much about Estleman's method and themes. He will write as realistically as possible about the Earps and about violence. In the Postscript, Estleman notes that since much of the dialogue is invented, *Bloody Season* must be considered a work of fiction. However, he then insists that he has "attempted to tell the story of the Earp-Holliday-Clanton-McLaury feud with as much accuracy and objectivity as is possible after all this time."

10. Cawelti, *Six-Gun Mystique*, 14.

11. Ibid., 59-60.

12. I am inclined to read *Bloody Season* as a critique of violence. For one thing, the structure of the novel is too suggestive. As I've noted, the famous gunfight opens the novel, which runs counter to other fictional representations of this event. So in structuring his book, Estleman has chosen not to offer the fight as a culmination of a story. Once he describes the shooting, Estleman's chances for telling the prescriptive Western yarn are lost, and he is too experienced a writer not to know what he has done. Most of the novel, then, seeks to explain the motives for the gun battle, and to do this Estleman must examine the personalities of the Earps, Holliday, the Clantons, et al. What he finds, or what he recreates, is far from the good guys versus bad guys structure that Cawelti believes is usually a part of almost every Western.

Of the male characters, Estleman describes little that is good, unless one accepts their loyalty to their respective gangs as a virtue. Noting that "some experts have termed [the Fly's Boarding House massacre] the first true gang war in American history," (237) Estleman supplies his reading of the motives for this war: power and greed. As U.S. marshals, the Earps could better control their economic holdings in Tombstone; and as sheriff, Johnny Behan worked closely with the Clantons, et al., to protect them from having to suffer the consequences of their stage robbing and cattle rustling. Estleman sums up the Earps' method of operation this way: "Others had come into the region, among them the Earp brothers, blond giants who operated together like parts of the same animal to knock an apple off every tree in the county from prostitution and gambling to timber stands and mineral rights, and had got themselves badges to license their weapons to protect the harvest" (210). The two gangs, then, really clash over the control of "turf."

Ultimately, Estleman de-mythologizes the Earps, and by extension the Old West. While the Earps are shown to have been corrupt and vicious, Tombstone is described so much like a political cesspool that it is difficult not to think of the modern American cities depicted in crime fiction. Estleman's "story" dissolves into a plotless series of sketches and historical summary about the fates of his characters, though by the time a reader reaches these summaries it is difficult to care about these characters' lives. If there is any implicit solace in *Bloody Season* it is this: Corruption and violence have always been a part of American life, so since there is no utopia to look back to, it is incumbent upon Americans to look forward to find solutions for society's ills.

13. Brian Garfield notes this division of critical opinion in *Western Films: A Complete Guide* (New York: Rawson Associates, 1982). Furthermore, he writes that the film "especially seems to inspire critical divisiveness between men and women (I have met very few women who liked it, and can recall no female critics who approved of it)." 348

14. Ibid., 55.

15. Ibid., 55.

16. Stanley J. Solomon, *Beyond Formula: American Film Genres* (San Diego: Harcourt Brace Jovanovich, 1976), 55.

17. Garfield, *Western Films*, 56.

18. Peter Biskind singles out the character of Matt as an example of the "feminization" of male characters in certain 1950s Western movies. Because Matt eschews violence, rules by consensus, and desires the spread of civilization—settling down—instead of the building of an empire in a hostile environment, Biskind sees him as "softer" than Dunson. In this film and others that Biskind notes, the traditional symbolic role of the female

characters in Westerns—that is the role as nesters and peacemakers—is usurped by male characters. See Biskind, *Seeing is Believing*, 278-84.

19. William K. Everson, *The Hollywood Western* (New York: Citadel Press, 1992), 240.

20. Despite director Ralph Nelson's contention that his was an anti-war film, critic Edward Buscombe does not accept *Soldier Blue* as anti-violent because the film "lacks any real *explanation* for the final massacre, which it turns into a *mere* exercise in bloodletting of the kind it purports to condemn." Edward Buscombe *BFI Companion*, 300.

21. Richard Slotkin praises both films for "call[ing] our attention to . . . the dark side of American cultural myth." See Slotkin, "Gunsmoke and Mirrors," 68.

22. Compare these films to the Westerns *Young Guns* (1988) and *Young Guns II* (1990).

23. John Ford's last Western *Cheyenne Autumn*, (1964) which is based on a narrative history by Mari Sandoz, depicts a Cavalry troop ordered to massacre Indians. And both the novel *Little Big Man* and its film adaptation (1971) characterize the Indians as noble human beings oppressed by vicious whites, although the novel treats its Indian characters more realistically. For sympathetic portrayals of Native Americans in Western fiction one may turn to Dorothy M. Johnson's *A Man Called Horse*; A. B. Guthrie's *The Way West* and Douglas C. Jones' *Season of Yellow Leaf*. In addition, the films *Broken Arrow* (1950), *The Scalphunters* (1968), *A Man Called Horse* (1970), *Soldier Blue* (1970), *Jeremiah Johnson* (1972), and *Ulzana's Raid* (1972) explicitly attempted to reverse the simplistic pattern of previous Westerns in which Indians represented an evil force.

Without slighting the merits of the film, William K. Everson is also quick to point out the precedents for *Dances With Wolves*: "Critical reception [for Costner's Academy-Award-winning film] especially from reviewers with conveniently short memories, was rhapsodic. It is of course no discredit to the film that it was covering ground that *had* been covered before, in Delmer Daves's *Broken Arrow*, and far more specifically in Samuel Fuller's *Run of the Arrow*, which managed to tell exactly the same story (historically and personally) in less than ninety minutes." Everson, *The Hollywood Western*, 278.

24. *Dances With Wolves*, dir. Kevin Costner, written by Michael Blake, starring Kevin Costner, Mary McDonnell, Graham Greene, and Rodney A. Grant (Orion, 1990).

25. See chapter five for a critical discussion of the portrayal of Native Americans in films which proclaim to offer anti-racist messages.

26. *Unforgiven*, dir. Clint Eastwood, written by David Webb Peoples, starring Clint Eastwood, Gene Hackman, and Morgan Freeman (Warner Bros., 1992).

27. Anecdotically, I can offer partial evidence for this claim. I first saw *Unforgiven* on an American Air Base in Japan. The audience was made up principally of service members in the Air Force and Navy. As the movie ended and I left the theater, I heard one young serviceman remark, "He took long enough getting to it." Apparently, for this young man the film was not paced quickly enough, and I surmised that he had expected to see the kind of Western Eastwood once appeared in regularly: An *Outlaw Josie Wales* (1976) type of film in which Eastwood's character kills often and with apparent justification.

Chapter 4

1. A partial explanation for the scarcity of women in so many Westerns can be found in the fact that there were precious few women in the real West. Author Jenni Calder notes that "[i]t was often easier to import pianos and champagne than to bring out suitable mates for frontiersmen." However, Calder recognizes that this explanation is not complete when she argues that Westerns which either do not portray women at all or which romanticize their few female characters "[consigned] to oblivion the women who were there." See Jenni Calder, *There Must Be a Lone Ranger* (London: Hamish Hamilton, 1974), 157-58.

Indeed, recent historical scholarship has sought to document more fully the lives and contributions of western women. *The Women's West*, edited by Susan Armitage and Elizabeth Jameson, is a collection of essays designed to demonstrate not only that there were women on the frontier of the Trans-Mississippi West, but also to "free [scholarship and the popular conception] from the all-pervasive masculinity of the popular image of the American West." See Armitage and Jameson, *The Women's West* (Norman: Univ. of Oklahoma Press, 1987), 5.

2. John G. Cawelti, *Six-Gun Mystique*, 48-49.

3. Henry Nash Smith, *Virgin Land*, 118.

4. Cawelti, *Six-Gun,* 49.

5. Ibid., 58.

6. Ibid., 58.

7. Tompkins, *West of Everything*, 45. See also Geoffrey O'Brien, "Killing Time," *The New York Review of Books*, 5 March 1992, 40.

8. *These Thousand Hills*, dir. Richard Fleischer, written by Alfred Hayes, starring Don Murray, Lee Remick, and Richard Eagan (Twentieth Century Fox, 1959). It should be noted, for what it's worth, that this character who so disparages women is clearly the villain of the film.

9. Sandra Kay Schackel, "Women in Western Films: The Civilizer, The Saloon Singer, and Their Modern Sister," in *Shooting Stars: Heroes and Heroines of Western Film*, ed. Archie P. McDonald (Bloomington: Indiana Univ. Press, 1987), 197.

10. Ibid., 215.

11. Ibid., 200. Historian Cheryl J. Foote also discovers that women's roles in Westerns have changed over time. She notes that during World

War II, as more women entered the work force and as they became the majority of movie-goers, female characters in Westerns grew more forceful. She cites Barbara Stanwyck's roles in *The Great Man's Lady* (1942) and *The Furies* (1950) as examples. However, when the war ended and American men came home, this brief period of strong females in Westerns ended. See Cheryl Foote, "Changing Images of Women in the Western Film," *Journal of the West* 22 (October 1983), 67.

12. Schackel, "Women in Western Films," 215. Foote seems to disagree with Schackel's contention that recent portrayals of strong women in Westerns form a stereotype all their own. While both Foote and Schackel praise the film *Heartland*, unlike Schackel, Foote does not believe that the main female character becomes a stereotype. On the contrary, of *Heartland*, which depicts a strong pioneer woman who comes to share a deep love for a man without sacrificing her sense of independence, Foote writes: "[P]erhaps more than any other film [this one] demonstrates that roles for women in the Western need not fall victim to stereotypes." See Foote, "Changing Images," 70-71.

13. Molly Haskell, *From Reverence to Rape: The Treatment of Women in the Movies* (New York: Holt, Rinehart and Winston, 1973), 24.

14. While Haskell was specifically referring to men in the early 1970s, her comments on the transformations men must undergo to accept the changing role of women hold force today. If nothing else, a suggestive, symbolic representation of male escape into an uncomplicated male camaraderie can be found in two recent Westerns, *Tombstone* (1993) and *Wyatt Earp* (1994). In both films, the most compelling relationship occurs between Wyatt Earp and Doc Holliday, and not between Wyatt and the women in his life.

15. Haskell, *Reverence to Rape*, 24.

16. Ibid., 25.

17. Charles Portis, *True Grit* (New York: Simon and Schuster, 1968), 223-24. Portis's novel formed the basis for the popular movie version starring John Wayne.

18. Brian Garfield, *Western Films*, 203.

19. Stanley J. Solomon, *Beyond Formula*, 43.

20. Ibid., 41.

21. *Johnny Guitar*, dir. Nicholas Ray, written by Philip Yordan, starring Joan Crawford, Mercedes McCambridge, and Sterling Hayden (Republic, 1953).

22. An alternative reading of this conflict has been suggested to me by a colleague. Evelyn Baldwin Miranda interprets the name Vienna as connotative of Old World culture. In this context, the name Emma refers nicely to Emma Lazarus, the author of the poem which appears on the Statue of Liberty. If the symbolism of the names is accepted, then it may be possible to read the Vienna/Emma conflict in cultural terms.

23. Richard White, *"It's Your Misfortune and None of My Own": A History of the American West* (Norman: Univ. of Oklahoma Press, 1991), 628.

24. Norris Yates, *Gender and Genre: An Introduction to Women Writers of Formula Westerns, 1900-1950* (Albuquerque: Univ. of New Mexico Press, 1995), 4.

25. Ibid., 5.

26. Vicki Piekarski, ed. *Westward the Women: An Anthology of Western Stories by Women* (Garden City, N.Y.: Doubleday, 1984), 1-12.

27. Ibid., 10-11. Not only can Western novels and stories by women elicit a re-thinking of the Old West experience, but, in keeping with the talent of their authors, they can also be highly entertaining. Among the many fine examples Piekarski lists, I will single out two as especially enjoyable: Dorothy M. Johnson's *A Man Called Horse* and Marilyn Durham's *The Man Who Loved Cat Dancing*.
Not on Piekarski's list is a more recent Western by a woman: *Heart of the West* by Penelope Williamson. A novel about an Eastern woman who

elopes with a cowboy and comes to live in Montana, *Heart of the West* seeks "to change [the] simplistic frontier picture" that Western women were limited to being "schoolmarms, dance-hall girls or somebody's mom." See Joyce R. Slater, "Heart of the West," *Minneapolis Star Tribune*, May 1995, Books & Games section, 7.

28. Mari Sandoz, *Miss Morissa: Doctor of the Gold Trail* (New York: Hastings House, 1955), 16.

29. Morissa is, among her other pursuits, a skillful gardener. As such she follows the concern Annette Kolodny discovers in real pioneer women. Kolodny believes that part of a particularly female response to the West was the cultivation of the land as opposed to the extraction of natural resources, which she argues was the male response. See Kolodny, *The Land Before Her: Fantasy and Experience of the American Frontiers, 1630-1860.* (Chapel Hill: Univ. of North Carolina Press, 1984).

30. Sandoz, *Miss Morissa*, 176.

31. Ibid., 248.

32. *Thousand Pieces of Gold*, dir. Nancy Kelly, written by Nunnally Johnson, starring Rosalind Chao, Dennis Dun, Chris Cooper, and Michael Paul Chan (Greycat, 1991).

33. *The Ballad of Little Jo*, dir. Maggie Greenwald, written by Maggie Greenwald, starring Suzy Amis, Bo Hopkins, Ian McKellan, and David Chung (Fine Line Features, 1993).

34. Too, Westerns may be considered feminist if in addition to depicting complex female characters they are able to re-fashion the tired formulas of so much Western fiction. Perhaps the most recognizable Western plot device is the final shoot-out, and such an ending could be considered by feminist critics to be a particularly male construction. Critic Josephine Donovan argues that one aspect of a "women's poetics" is a

non-linear plot line, one that is "grounded in an idea of temporal order more appropriate to the cyclic experience of women's lives." Further, both she and critic Marcia Holly contend that a feminist aesthetic must be based on women's experiences. Holly locates such an aesthetic in works that arise from an understanding of truly human impulses and experiences, and not from a gender-biased view of life which is arbitrarily applied to both sexes. For Holly, "[A] feminist literary aesthetic [is] one that is fundamentally at odds with masculinist value standards." Because the cathartic resolution of action through violence is most often associated with fiction about men created by men, a truly feminist Western would likely eschew such a resolution. See Josephine Donovan, "Toward a Women's Poetics," in *Feminist Issues in Literary Scholarship*, ed. Shari Benstock (Bloomington: Indiana Univ. Press, 1987),101; and Marcia Holly, "Consciousness and Authenticity: Toward a Feminist Aesthetic," in *Feminist Literary Criticism: Explorations in Theory*, 2d ed., ed. Josephine Donovan (Lexington: Univ. Press of Kentucky, 1989), 46.

This is just one reason why I cannot accept the film *Bad Girls* (1994) as a feminist Western. Originally conceived as a feminist work starring an African-American actress ("Riding into the Sunrise," 79), *Bad Girls* instead became a transparent attempt to reverse standard plots by having female characters fulfill the rough-and-tumble roles served by men in so many oaters. Unfortunately, the result becomes, in the words of film critic Roger Ebert, "like *Young Guns* in drag." Ebert pans the film for offering "cowgirls instead of cowboys" and nothing more. Not only are the worst Western clichés here, but the film objectifies its female stars, placing them in a semi-nude "Swimmin' Hole scene" and making them up "like models in a Calvin Klein ad." See Roger Ebert, "Bad Girls," *Roger Ebert's Reviews and Features*, CompuServ, GO-EBERT (The Ebert Co., Ltd., 1994).

Chapter 5

1. David Daly and Joel Persky, "The West and the Western," *Journal of the West* 29 (April 1990): 33.

2. Ibid., 30.

3. Robert F. Berkhofer, *The White Man's Indian: Images of the American Indian from Columbus to the Present* (New York: Knopf, 1978), 111.

4. Ralph E. Friar and Natasha A. Friar, *The Only Good Indian . . . The Hollywood Gospel* (New York: Drama Book Specialists, 1972). Geoffrey O'Brien also dismisses Western films' ability to correctly depict Indians: "[N]ot even the most liberal and well-intentioned of Westerns bothered to attempt even minimal accuracy in the presentation of Native American cultures and artifacts." See Geoffrey O'Brien, "Killing Time," 40.

5. Raymond William Stedman, *Shadows of the Indians: Stereotypes in American Culture* (Norman: Univ. of Oklahoma Press, 1982).

6. David Rich Lewis, "Still Native: The Significance of Native Americans in the History of the Twentieth-Century American West," *The Western Historical Quarterly* 24 (May 1993): 221. Robert F. Berkhofer agrees with Lewis:

> In the more extreme countercultural films of the 1970s, the Indian hero becomes a mere substitute for the oppressed Black or hippie White youth alienated from modern mainstream American society. Although the action and locale purport to be laid in the past, the dialogue and thrust of the plot speak more to the recent conflict in Vietnam than to the battle over the American plains and mountains. As before, the latest countercultural use of the Indian reflects some Whites' disquietude with their own society and indicates that even today's sympathetic artists chiefly understand Native Americans according to their own artistic needs and moral values rather than in terms of the outlook and desires of the people they profess to know and depict.

See Robert Berkhofer, *The White Man's Indian*, 103.

In a specific application of these views, film critic David Denby contends that Arthur Penn's *Little Big Man* is more about contemporary white concerns that it is about the lives of nineteenth-century Native Americans. Denby writes, "What starts out as an elegy for lost values winds up as an exercise in white self-hatred, and although it may seem incongruous to say so, I can't help feeling that Penn's movie is another victim of the war in Vietnam." See Denby, "Americana," 61.

A more positive view of the movie *Little Big Man* is offered by Edward Buscombe who believes the film "contribut[ed] mightily to the belated popular recognition of America's guilty history of genocide towards its original inhabitants." See Buscombe, *The BFI Companion*, 281.

Other countercultural, revisionist Western films worth a look include *Tell Them Willie Boy Is Here* (1970), *A Man Called Horse* (1970), and *Jeremiah Johnson* (1972).

7. Ward Churchill, Mary Anne Hill, and Norbert S. Hill, Jr., "Examination of Stereotyping: An Analytical Survey of Twentieth-Century Indian Entertainers," in *The Pretend Indians: Images of Native Americans in the Movies*, eds. Gretchen M. Bataille and Charles L. P. Silet (Ames: Iowa State Univ. Press, 1980), 46.

8. John E. O'Connor, *The Hollywood Indian* (Trenton: New Jersey State Museum, 1980), 3-4, 68.

9. James Welch with Paul Stekler, *Killing Custer: The Battle of the Little Bighorn and the Fate of the Plains Indians* (New York: W. W. Norton, 1994), 98.

10. Ibid., 99.

11. George N. Fenin and William K. Everson. *The Western: From Silents to the Seventies* (New York: Grossman Publishers, 1973), 371.

12. Charles R. Larson, *American Indian Fiction* (Albuquerque: Univ. of New Mexico Press, 1978), 14.

13. Ibid., 125.

14. James Welch, *Fools Crow* (New York: Viking Penguin 1986), 339-40.

15. Douglas C. Jones, *Season of Yellow Leaf*, (New York: Holt, Rinehart and Winston, 1983) 69.

16. Douglas C. Jones, *Gone the Dreams and Dancing* (New York: Holt, Rinehart and Winston, 1984), 2.

17. Ibid., 4.

18. Ibid., 12.

19. Ibid., 241-42.

20. John E. O'Connor, for one, credits *Little Big Man* the novel for characterizing members of the Cheyenne and Sioux tribes as individuals, a credit he does not extend to the film version. See O'Connor, *Hollywood Indian*, 68. Indeed, a comparison of the novel *Little Big Man* to its film adaptation shows that the latter is much less subtle in its satire; the film's humor is not only more farcical, but it also simplifies the novel's characterizations.

21. Thomas Berger, *Little Big Man* (New York: Dial Press, 1964. Paper ed. New York: Delta/Seymour Lawrence, 1989), 435.

22. Harold Mantell, "Counteracting the Stereotype," *American Indian* 5 (Fall 1950), 16-20, in *Western Films 2: An Annotated Critical Bibliography from 1974 to 1987*, eds. Jack Nachbar, Jackie R. Donath, and Chris Foran (New York: Garland Publishing, 1988), 50.

23. John H. Lenihan, *Showdown*, 57.

24. Ibid., 61.

25. Ibid., 70-71.

26. Ibid., 78.

27. Ibid., 79.

28. Ibid., 81. While Lenihan's work shows that Western films began to treat Indians sympathetically, such a liberal view of Native Americans

sometimes even found its way into television Westerns. The short-lived series *Hondo* (1967), for example, features a title character, Hondo Lane, who was married to an Apache chief's daughter. After his wife is killed in a cavalry massacre, Hondo roams the West as a peacekeeper between Indians and whites. One episode has him giving lessons on the Winchester rifle to Apache men to help them become better hunters. A cavalry officer objects to such training on the grounds that the Apaches "'managed to get along for centuries without firearms.'" To this Hondo replies, "'But they weren't competing with the white man for living space during those centuries, and they weren't pinned down on the reservation.'" See Noel Holston, "Western flop 'Hondo' rides on as early-morn hit for Ted Turner," *Minneapolis Star Tribune*, 26 May 1995, E14.

29. Daly and Persky list *Indian Justice* (1911), *A Squaw's Love* (1911), and *Hiawatha* (1910) as among the earliest films to offer serious treatment of Native Americans. See "The West and the Western," 32.

30. William Everson, *The Hollywood Western*, 238.

31. Ibid., 238. Lenihan praises the film, too, seeing it "as an advance in society's grappling with its prejudices." See Lenihan *Showdown*, 62.

32. Peter Biskind argues that in *Broken Arrow* the character of Cochise is made palatable to white audiences because he works for peace. Biskind sees in this as an implicit acceptance of a white, albeit moderate, view of civilization. In this and other Westerns which offer an integrationist message, Biskind perceives the idea of racial integration as a matter of the dominant white society imposing upon the Native one its values and worldview. Biskind links this integrationist message to the Black Civil Rights Movement of the 1950s, a movement which many sought to control, at least in Biskind's opinion, by preaching togetherness and acceptance of white values, however tolerant some of those values were. See *Seeing is Believing: How Hollywood Taught Us to Stop Worrying and Love the Fifties* (New York: Pantheon Books, 1983), 238-40.

While many praise *Broken Arrow* for at least offering some kind of breakthrough in the depiction of Native Americans on film, other critics dismiss it as not significant, Friar and Friar, for example, view *Broken Arrow* as patronizing toward real Native Americans, in part because they object to the white Jeff Chandler playing Cochise and because they argue that *Broken Arrow* began a series of Westerns that purported to be sympathetic to Native Americans but that showed Indian "customs, culture, and traditions . . . [that] remained the creations of the writer's [*sic*] imaginations." See Friar and Friar, *The Only Good Indian*, 202.

33. *Broken Arrow*, dir. Delmer Daves, written by Michael Blankfort (based on the novel *Blood Brothers* by Elliott Arnold), starring James Stewart, Jeff Chandler, and Debra Paget (Twentieth Century Fox, 1950).

34. Everson, *The Hollywood Western*, 238.

35. Biskind, *Seeing is Believing*, 239, footnote.

36. Ibid., 238-39.

37. *Apache*, dir. Robert Aldrich, written by James R. Webb, starring Burt Lancaster and Jean Peters (United Artists, 1954).

38. Biskind, *Seeing is Believing*, 245.

39. Geoffrey O'Brien "Killing Time," 42.

40. *Ulzana's Raid*, dir. Robert Aldrich, written by Alan Sharp, starring Burt Lancaster and Bruce Davison (Universal, 1972).

41. Richard Zoglin, "Back from Boot Hill," 92.

42. *Geronimo: An American Legend*, dir. Walter Hill, written by John Milius and Larry Gross, starring Jason Patric, Robert Duvall, Gene Hackman, and Wes Studi (Columbia, 1993).

43. Richard O'Connor, *Bret Harte: A Biography* (Boston: Little, Brown and Company, 1966), 122.

44. Ibid., 121.

45. Slotkin, "Gunsmoke and Mirrors," 66.

46. *The Ballad of Gregorio Cortez*, dir. Robert M. Young, written by Victor Villasenor, starring Edward James Olmos, James Gammon, and Tom Bower (Embassy Pictures, 1982).

47. Daly and Persky, "The West and the Western," 49.

48. Rosalind Bentley, "Show Studies Segregated Early Cinema," *Minneapolis Star Tribune*, 26 October 1994, 11E.

49. Daly and Persky, "The West and the Western," 50.

50. Ibid., 51.

51. Lenihan, *Showdown*, 56.

52. Strode appeared in numerous Westerns in the 1950s, 60s and 70s. Among these were: *The Gambler from Natchez* (1954), *Two Rode Together* (1961), *The Man Who Shot Liberty Valance* (1962), *Shalako* (1968), *Once Upon a Time in the West* (1969), *The Last Rebel* (1971), and *The Revengers* (1972). See Donald Bogle, *Blacks in American Film and Television: An Encyclopedia* (New York: Garland Publishing, 1988), 467-68.

Elsewhere, Bogle claims that early in his career Strode was used largely as "one more elegant period piece provided by an imaginative set designer." However, in *Sergeant Rutledge*, Bogle argues that Strode gave his best performance. Bogle cites a *New York Times* review which found Strode's acting to be superior to the merits of the film as a whole. See Bogle, *Toms, coons, mulattoes, mammies, and bucks: An Interpretive History of Blacks in American Films* (New York: Viking Press, 1973), 185-86.

53. Bogle notes that some audience members in the mid-1960s had difficulty accepting the historical validity of a black cowboy, the part Poitier played. But Poitier proudly acted the role, well aware that there

had indeed been African-American cowhands. See Bogle, *Blacks in American Film and Television: An Encyclopedia*, 76.

54. Sammy Davis, Jr., also appeared in episodes of television Westerns, including *Zane Grey Theatre* (1959), *Rifleman* (1961), and *Wild, Wild West* (1966). See Bogle, *Blacks in American Film and Television*, 381.

55. Ibid., 40.

56. Ibid., 41.

57. Daly and Persky, "The West and the Western," 51.

58. Ibid., 51.

59. Bogle, *Blacks in American Film and Television*, 5-6.

60. Ibid., 131-32.

61. Ibid., 146.

62. Peter Travers, "'Posse' Leader Mario Van Peebles Shoots from the Lip," *Rolling Stone* (June 10, 1993), 76.
Years before the Van Peebles film, noted playwright August Wilson produced a musical satire on the Old West which also attempted to raise an awareness of racial issues in an entertaining fashion. When it was staged in St. Paul, Minnesota, in 1981, one reviewer of the unpublished *Black Bart and the Sacred Hills* called the play a "half spoof, half satire" which included "a bit of raging black anger." See David Hawley, "'Black Bart' is too much, too soon," *St. Paul Pioneer Press*, 12 July 1981, Metro/Region sec., p. 8.

63. See Travers, "Shoots from the Lip," as well as the accompanying article in the same issue of *Rolling Stone*, Peter Travers, "New Jack Cowboys," 73-74. See also Brian D. Johnson, "Black in the Sad-

dle: A Master Has the Last Word on Westerns," *Maclean's* (May 17, 1993), 50.

64. *Posse*, dir. Mario Van Peebles, written by Sy Richardson and Dario Scardapane, starring Mario Van Peebles, Tone Loc, Billy Zane, and Blair Underwood (Polygram, 1993).

65. Travers, "Shoots from the Lip," 76.

66. Brian Johnson, "Black in the Saddle," 50.

67. This sheriff is named Bates, a deliberate echo of Daryl Gates, the Los Angeles police chief during the Rodney King beating and the subsequent riots. See Johnson, "Black in the Saddle," 50.

68. There is also a series of Western novels with a Jewish hero. Three novels by W. T. Ballard—*Give a Man a Gun* (1971), *Go West, Ben Gold* (1974), and *Gold Goes to the Mountains* (1974)—features "Ben Gold . . . a Jewish storekeeper, Indian fighter, horseman and expert with gun and dice." See Bernard A. Drew, et al., *Western Series and Sequels: A Reference Guide* (New York: Garland Publishing, 1986), 53.

69. Dee Brown, Foreward to *The Wild West* (New York: Time-Life Books, 1993), 25.

70. James K. Folsom, *The American Western Novel* (New Haven, Conn.: College and University Press, 1966), 29.

Chapter 6

1. James K. Folsom, "Westerns as Social and Political Alternatives," in *Focus on the Western*, ed. Jack Nachbar (Englewood Cliffs, N.J.: Prentice Hall, 1974), 81-82.

2. Cawelti, *Six-Gun Mystique*, 74.

3. Bold, *Selling the Wild West*, 166.

4. Ibid., 75.

5. Folsom, "Political Alternatives," 81-82.

6. Slotkin, "Gunsmoke and Mirrors," 65.

7. *Invitation to a Gunfighter*, dir. Richard Wilson, written by Elizabeth Wilson and Richard Wilson, starring Yul Brynner, Janice Rule, and George Segal (United Artists, 1964).

8. Portis, *True Grit*, 9.

9. Ibid., 18.

10. Ibid., 14-15.

11. Ibid., 86.

12. Ibid., 82.

13. Ibid., 142.

14. Ibid., 194, original emphasis.

15. Ibid., 222.

16. Ibid., 220.

17. Ibid., 222.

18. Douglas C. Jones, *Roman* (New York: Henry Holt, 1986), 307.

19. Ibid., 308.

20. *Silent Tongue*, dir. Sam Shepard, written by Sam Shepard, starring Richard Harris, River Phoenix, and Alan Bates (Le Studio Canal +, 1992).

Chapter 7

1. Alex Gordon, et al., eds. *Your Movie Guide to Western Video Tapes and Discs*. (n. p.: Signet, 1985), 9.

2. At least of unflattering racial stereotypes: More than one gag is made about Bart's penis size.

3. *Blazing Saddles* , dir. Mel Brooks, written by Mel Brooks, Norman Steinberg, Andrew Bergman, Richard Pryor, and Alan Unger, starring Cleavon Little, Gene Wilder, Madeline Kahn, and Slim Pickens (Warner Bros., 1974).

4. Patricia Waugh, *Metafiction: The Theory and Practice of self-conscious Fiction*, (London: Routledge, 1984), 64.

5. Ibid., 64.

6. Ibid., 66-67.

7. Waugh erroneously refers to him as "Calvetti."

8. Waugh, *Metafiction*, 81-82.

9. Bold, *Selling the Wild West*, 159.

10. Ibid., 159-61.

11. E. L. Doctorow, *Welcome to Hard Times* (New York: Random House, 1960), 212.

12. Ibid., 210.

13. Blue's last words, "And I have to allow, with great shame, I keep thinking someone will come by sometime who will want to use the wood," seem to suggest hopefulness. He will not burn the town because it may have a use. But even as he decides this, he recognizes the monstrous senselessness in still harboring hope, 212.

14. Ibid., 184.

15. Ibid., 4.

16. Ibid., 28.

17. Ibid., 184.

18. Ibid., 192.

19. Ibid., 72.

20. Ibid., 65.

21. See the back page of the dust jacket for Robert Ward, *Cattle Annie and Little Britches* (New York: William Morrow, 1977).

22. Historian Richard White reveals that among Oklahomans at the time, the connection between Bill Doolin and Robin Hood was explicit, one made, for example, in the press. See White, *"It's Your Misfortune and None of My Own,"* 336-37.

23. Ward, *Cattle Annie*, 179.

24. Ibid., 196.

25. Ibid., 198.

26. Ibid., 213.

27. Ibid., 205.

28. Ibid., 205.

29. Ward, *Cattle Annie*, 216.

30. In this Ward leaves behind historical accuracy: Though he states that the year of the novel's setting is 1895, the World's Columbian Exposition in Chicago took place in 1893. Still, Ward can certainly be excused this license, for by finishing the gang members in the fantastic and garish surroundings of a World's Fair, Ward underlines the suspect status of popular criminal "heroes" and the unreal nature of the popular fictions which perpetuate their dubious fame.

31. Richard Brautigan, *The Hawkline Monster: A Gothic Western* (New York: Simon and Schuster, 1974), 10.

32. Ibid., 27-28.

33. Ibid., 46.

34. See, for example, Charles J. Stewart, Craig Allen Smith, and Robert E. Denton, Jr., *Persuasion and Social Movements,* 2nd ed. (Prospect Heights, Il.: Waveland Press, 1989), 193-96.

Chapter 8

1. *The Misfits*, dir. John Huston, written by Arthur Miller, starring Clark Gable, Marilyn Monroe, and Montgomery Clift (Seven Arts Productions, 1961).

2. *The Last Picture Show*, dir. Peter Bogdanovich, written by Larry McMurtry and Peter Bogdanovich, starring Timothy Bottoms, Jeff Bridges, and Cybil Shepard (Columbia, 1971).

3. Wallace Stegner, *The Big Rock Candy Mountain* (1943; reprint, Lincoln: Univ. of Nebraska Press, 1983), 83.

4. Ibid., 460.

5. *Delusion*, dir. Carl Colpaert, written by, Ca-l Colpaert and Kurt Voss starring Jim Metzler, Jennifer Rubin, and Kyle Secor (Cineville, 1990).

6. *City Slickers*, dir. Ron Underwood, written by Lowell Ganz and Babaloo Mandel, starring Billy Crystal, Daniel Stern, Bruno Kirby, and Jack Palance (Castle Rock, 1991).

7. *Hud*, dir. Martin Ritt, written by Irving Ravetch and Harriet Frank, Jr., Paul Newman, Melvyn Douglas, and Patricia Neal (Paramount, 1962).

8. Bosley Crowther, "Hud," *The New York Times* 29 May 1963, 36:1, in *The New York Times Film Reviews, 1959-1968* vol 5, (New York: Times Books and Garland Publishing, Inc., 1990), 3390.

9. Cormac McCarthy, *All the Pretty Horses* (New York: Vintage International, 1992), 21.

10. Ibid., 5.

11. Ibid., 7.

12. Ibid., 239.

13. Gail Moore Morrison, "All the Pretty Horses: John Grady Cole's Expulsion from Paradise," in *Perspectives on Cormac McCarthy*, eds. Edwin T. Arnold and Dianne C. Luce (Jackson: Univ. Press of Mississippi, 1993), 173-93.

14. Edwin T. Arnold, "Blood and Grace: The Fiction of Cormac McCarthy," *Commonweal*, 4 November 1994, 14.

15. Denis Donoghue, "Dream Work," *The New York Review of Books*, 24 June 1993, 10.

16. Richard D. Woodward, "Cormac McCarthy's Venomous Fiction," *The New York Times Magazine*, 19 April 1992, 36.

17. *Lonely Are the Brave*, dir. David Miller, written by Dalton Trumbo, starring Kirk Douglas, Gena Rowlands, and Walter Matthau (Universal-

International, 1962). The film is based on the novel *The Brave Cowboy* by Edward Abbey.

18. *Giant,* dir. George Stevens, written by Fred Guiol and Ivan Moffat, starring Elizabeth Taylor, Rock Hudson, and James Dean (Warner Bros., 1956).

19. *Bad Day at Black Rock*, dir. John Sturges, written by Millard Kaufman and Don McGuire, starring Spencer Tracy, Robert Ryan, and Walter Brennan (MGM, 1954).

20. N. Scott Momaday, *House Made of Dawn* (New York: Harper & Row, 1968), 104.

21. Charles R. Larson, *American Indian Fiction*, 90.

22. Ibid., 95.

23. Ibid., 93.

24. Susan Scarberry-Garcia, *Landmarks of Healing: A Study of* House Made of Dawn (Albuquerque: Univ. of New Mexico Press, 1990).

25. Momaday, *House Made of Dawn*, 114.

26. Larson, *American Indian Fiction*, 87.

27. Leonard Maltin, ed., *Leonard Maltin's Movie Encyclopedia* (New York: Dutton, 1994), 504.

28. *Billy Jack*, dir. T. C. Frank (pseud. Tom Laughlin), written by Frank Christina and Teresa Christina, starring Tom Laughlin and Delores Taylor (Warner Bros., 1971).

29. Tom Robbins, *Even Cowgirls Get the Blues* (New York: Houghton Mifflin, 1976; reprint New York: Bantam, 1993), 400.

30. Ibid., 389-90.

31. Ibid., 238-39.

32. Robert Nadeau, *Readings from the New Book on Nature: Physics and Metaphysics in the Modern Novel* (Amherst: Univ. of Massachusetts Press, 1981), 150.

33. Ibid., 157.

34. Ibid., 158.

35. Peter Wild, "Into the Heart's Wild Places," *Sierra*, May/June 1989, 100.

36. Susan M. Trosky, ed., *Contemporary Authors: New Revision Series*, vol. 41 (Detroit: Gale Research Inc., 1994), 2.

37. *Time*, 27 March, 1989, 85.

38. Gregory McNamee, "Scarlet 'A' on a Field of Black," in *Resist Much, Obey Little: Some Notes on Edward Abbey*, eds. James Hepworth and Gregory McNamee (Salt Lake City: Dream Garden Press, 1985), 25.

39. Edward Abbey, *The Monkey Wrench Gang* (Philadelphia: Lippincott, 1975), 153.

40. Ibid., 203.

41. A. Carl Bredahl, Jr., *New Ground: Western American Narrative and the Literary Canon* (Chapel Hill: Univ. of North Carolina Press, 1989), 30.

42. *Thelma & Louise*, dir. Ridley Scott, written by Callie Khouri, starring Susan Sarandon, Geena Davis, and Harvey Keitel (MGM, 1991).

43. John Leo, "Toxic Feminism on the Big Screen," *U.S. News & World Report*, 10 June 1991, 20.

44. Kathi Maio, "Women Who Murder for the Man," *Ms.*, November/December 1991, 83.

45. Stuart Klawans, "Thelma & Louise," *The Nation*, 24 June 1991, 863.

46. Laura Shapiro, et al., "Women Who Kill Too Much: Is 'Thelma & Louise' Feminism, or Fascism?" *Newsweek*, 17 June 1991, 63.

47. Richard Schickel, "Gender Bender," *Time*, 24 June 1991, 56.

48. Terrence Rafferty, "Outlaw Princesses," *The New Yorker*, 3 June 1991, 86.

49. Ibid., 87.

50. Margaret Carlson, "Is This What Feminism Is All About?: By Playing Out a Male Fantasy, Thelma and Louise Shows Hollywood Is Still a Man's World," *Time*, 24 June 1991, 57.

51. The on-going role of Old West myths in twentieth-century literature is evidenced by two recent studies: Barbara Meldrum, ed., *Under the Sun: Myth and Realism in Western American Literature* (Troy, N.Y.: Whitson Publishing Company, 1985) and J. Bakker, *The Role of the Mythic West in Some Representative Examples of Classic and Modern American Literature: The Shaping Force of the American Frontier* (Lewiston, N.Y.: Edwin Mellen Press, 1991).

BIBLIOGRAPHY

Books and Articles

Abbey, Edward. *The Brave Cowboy: An Old Tale in a New Time*. 1956. Reprint, Albuquerque: Univ. of New Mexico Press, 1977.

————. *Desert Solitaire*. New York: McGraw, 1968.

————. *The Monkey Wrench Gang*. Philadelphia: Lippincott, 1975.

Adams, Les and Buck Rainey. *Shoot-Em-Ups: The Complete Reference Guide to Westerns of the Sound Era*. New Rochelle, NY: Arlington House, 1978.

Armitage, Susan and Elizabeth Jameson, eds. *The Women's West*. Norman: Univ. of Oklahoma Press, 1987.

Arnold, Edwin T. "Blood and Grace: The Fiction of Cormac McCarthy." *Commonweal,* 4 November 1994, 11-12, 14, 16.

Atwood, Margaret. *Lady Oracle*. New York: Simon and Schuster, 1976.

Bakker, J. *The Role of the Mythic West in Some Representative Examples of Classic and Modern American Literature: The Shaping Force of the American Frontier*. Lewiston, N.Y.: Edwin Mellen Press, 1991.

Bedford, Denton R. *Tsali*. San Francisco: Indian Historian Press, 1972.

Bentley, Rosalind. "Show Studies Segregated Early Cinema." *Minneapolis Star Tribune* 26 October 1994, 1E, 11E.

Berger, Thomas. *Little Big Man*. New York: Dial Press, 1964. Pap. ed. Delta/Seymour Lawrence, 1989.

Berkhofer, Robert F. *The White Man's Indian: Images of the American Indian from Columbus to The Present*. New York: Knopf, 1978.

Biskind, Peter. "Back in the Saddle: Eastwood Returns with a Western in the Revisionist Tradition of 'The Wild Bunch.'" *Premiere*, August 1992, 35-6.

————. *Seeing is Believing: How Hollywood Taught Us to Stop Worrying and Love the Fifties*. New York: Pantheon Books, 1983.

Block, Herbert. *Herblock's Here and Now*. New York: Simon and Schuster, 1955.

——. *Straight Herblock*. New York: Simon and Schuster, 1958.

Bogdanovich, Peter. *John Ford*. Berkeley: Univ. of California Press, 1978.

Bogle, Donald. *Blacks in American Films and Television: An Encyclopedia*. New York: Garland Publishing, 1988.

——. *Toms, coons, mulattoes, mammies, and bucks: An Interpretive History of Blacks in American Films*. New York: Viking Press, 1973.

Bold, Christine. *Selling the Wild West: Popular Western Fiction, 1860 to 1960*. Bloomington: Univ. of Indiana Press, 1987.

Brautigan, Richard. *The Hawkline Monster: A Gothic Western*. New York: Simon and Schuster, 1974.

Bredahl, A. Carl, Jr. *New Ground: Western American Narrative and the Literary Canon*. Chapel Hill: Univ. of North Carolina Press, 1989.

Brown, Dee. Foreword to *The Wild West*. New York: Time-Life Books, 1993.

Buscombe, Edward, ed. *The BFI Companion to the Western*. New York: Atheneum, 1988.

Calder, Jenni. *There Must Be a Lone Ranger*. London: Hamish Hamilton, 1974.

Carlson, Margaret. "Is This What Feminism Is All About?: By Playing Out a Male Fantasy, 'Thelma & Louise' Shows Hollywood Is Still a Man's World." *Time*, 24 June 1991, 57.

Cawelti, John G. *Adventure, Mystery, and Romance: Formula Stories as Art and Popular Culture*. Chicago: Univ. of Chicago Press, 1976.

——. "Prolegomena to the Western." In *Western Writing*, ed. Gerald W. Haslam. Albuquerque: Univ. of New Mexico Press, 1974.

——. "Reflections on the New Western Films." In *Focus on the Western*, ed. John G. Nachbar, 113-7. Englewood Cliffs, N.J.: Prentice-Hall, 1974.

——. *The Six-Gun Mystique*. Bowling Green: Bowling Green Univ. Popular Press, 1970.

Chief Eagle, Dallas. *Winter Count*. Colorado Springs: Denton-Berkeland Printing Co., 1967.

Christian, Terry. *Reel Politics: American Political Movies from* Birth of a Nation *to* Platoon. New York: Basil Blackwell, Inc., 1987.

Churchill, Ward et al. "Examination of Stereotyping: An Analytical Survey of Twentieth-Century Indian Entertainers." In *The Pretend Indians: Images of Native Americans in the Movies*, eds. Gretchen M. Bataille and Charles L. P. Silet. Ames: Iowa State Univ. Press, 1980.

Clark, Walter Van Tilburg. *The Ox-Bow Incident*. New York: Signet Classics, 1940.

Corliss, Richard. "The Last Roundup." *Time*, 10 August 1992, 66.

Crowther, Bosley. "*High Noon*: a Western of Rare Achievement, is New Bill at the Mayfair Theatre," *The New York Times Film Reviews, 1913-1968*, vol 4. New York: New York Times and Arno Press, 1970, 2627-28.

————. "Hud." In *The New York Times Film Reviews, 1959-1968*, vol 5. New York: Times Books and Garland Press, Inc., 1990, 3390.

Curtis, Jack. "Resilient Western Writing." *The Writer*, December 1994, 16-17, 40.

Daly, David and Joel Persky. "The West and the Western." *Journal of the West* 29 (April 1990), 3-64.

Day, Robert. *The Last Cattle Drive*. 1977. Reprint. New York: Avon, 1978.

Denby, David. "Americana." In *Film 70/71: An Anthology by the National Society of Film Critics*, ed. David Denby. New York: Simon and Schuster, 1971.

DeVoto, Bernard. "Birth of an Art." In *Western Writing*, ed. Gerald W. Haslam. Albuquerque: Univ. of New Mexico Press, 1974.

Doctorow, E. L. *Welcome to Hard Times*. New York: Random House, 1960.

Donoghue, Denis. "Dream Work." *The New York Review of Books*, 24 June 1993, 5-6, 8-10.

Donovan, Josephine. "Toward a Women's Poetics." In *Feminist Issues in Literary Scholarship*, ed. Shari Benstock. Bloomington: Indiana Univ. Press, 1987.

Drew, Bernard A. et al. *Western Series and Sequels: A Reference Guide*. New York: Garland Publishing, 1986.

Durham, Marilyn. *The Man Who Loved Cat Dancing*. New York: Harcourt Brace Jovanovich, 1972.

Ebert, Roger. "Bad Girls." Roger Ebert's Reviews and Features, CompuServ, GO-EBERT. The Ebert Company, Limited, 1994.

Estleman, Loren D. *Bloody Season*. New York: Bantam, 1987.

————. *The Wister Trace: Classic Novels of the American Frontier*. Ottawa, Il.: Jameson Books, 1987.

Everson, William K. *The Hollywood Western: 90 Years of Cowboys and Indians, Train Robbers, Sheriffs and Gunslingers, and Assorted Heroes and Desperados*. New York: Citadel Press, 1992.

Faragher, John Mack. "The Tale of Wyatt Earp." In *Past Imperfect: History According to the Movies*, ed. Mark C. Carnes. New York: Holt, 1995.

Fenin, George N. and William K. Everson. *The Western: from Silents to the Seventies*. New York: Grossman Publishers, 1973.

Ferber, Edna. *Giant*. Garden City, N.Y.: Doubleday, 1952.

Fiedler, Leslie. *The Return of the Vanishing American*. New York: Stein and Day, 1968.

Flynn, Robert. *North To Yesterday*. 1967. Reprint. Fort Worth: Texas Christian Univ. Press, 1985.

Folsom, James K. *The American Western Novel*. New Haven, Conn.: College and University Press, 1966.

————. "Westerns as Social and Political Alternatives." In *Focus on the Western*, ed. Jack Nachbar. Englewood Cliffs, N.J.: Prentice-Hall, 1974.

Foote, Cheryl J. "Changing Images of Women in the Western Film." *Journal of the West* 22 (October 1983), 64-71.

Ford, Dan. *Pappy: The Life of John Ford*. Englewood Cliffs, N. J.: Prentice Hall, 1979.

Friar, Ralph E. and Natasha A. Friar. *The Only Good Indian . . . The Hollywood Gospel*. New York: Drama Book Specialists, 1972.

Garfield, Brian. *Western Films: A Complete Guide*. New York: Rawson Associates, 1982.

Garvey, Mark, ed. *1996 Writer's Market*. Cincinnati, Ohio: Writers Digest Books, 1995.

Greenspun, Roger. "Candice Bergen Stars in Violent Western." *New York Times*, 13 August 1970, p. 29, col. 1. In *The New York Times Film Reviews 1969-1970*. New York: New York Times Press, 1971, 201-2.

Guthrie, A. B. Jr., *The Way West*. New York: Bantam, 1949.

Gordon, Alex et al., eds. *Your Movie Guide to Western Video Tapes and Discs*. n. p.: Signet, 1985.

Hamilton, Cynthia S. *Western and Hard-Boiled Detective Fiction in America: From High Noon to Midnight.* Iowa City: Univ. of Iowa Press, 1987.

Haskell, Molly. *From Reverence to Rape: The Treatment of Women in the Movies.* New York: Holt, Rinehart and Winston, 1973.

Haslam, Gerald W. "Introduction: Western Writers and the National Fantasy." In *Western Writing*, ed. Gerald W. Haslam. Albuquerque: Univ. of New Mexico Press, 1974.

Hawley, David "'Black Bart' is too much, too soon." *St. Paul Pioneer Press*, 12 July 1981, Metro/Region, sec 8.

Herlihy, James Leo. *Midnight Cowboy.* New York: Simon and Schuster, 1965.

Holly, Marcia. "Consciousness and Authenticity: Toward a Feminist Aesthetic." In *Feminist Literary Criticism: Explorations in Theory.* 2d ed. Edited by Josephine Donovan. Lexington: Univ. Press of Kentucky, 1989.

Holston, Noel. "Western flop 'Hondo' rides on as early-morn hit for Ted Turner." *Minneapolis Star Tribune*, 26 May 1995, E14.

Hyams, Jay. *The Life and Times of the Western Movie.* New York: Gallery Books, 1983.

James, Caryn. "Frugging with Wolves." 13 January 1991. In *The New York Times Film Reviews, 1991-1992.* New York: Times Books and Garland Publishing, Inc., 1993, 4.

Johnson, Brian D. "Back in the Saddle: A Master Has the Last Word on Westerns." *Maclean's*, 17 August 1992, 50.

————. "Black in the Saddle." *Maclean's*, 17 May 1993, 50.

Johnson, Dorothy M. *A Man Called Horse.* (Originally published as *Indian Country.*) New York: Ballantine, 1953.

Jones, Daryl. *The Dime Novel Western.* Bowling Green: Bowling Green Univ. Popular Press, 1978.

Jones, Douglas C. *Season of Yellow Leaf.* New York: Holt, Rinehart, and Winston, 1983.

————. *Gone the Dreams and Dancing.* New York: Holt, Rinehart and Winston, 1984.

————. *Roman.* New York: Henry Holt, 1986.

Kitses, Jim. "The Western: Ideology and Archetype." In *Focus on the Western*, ed. John G. Nachbar. Englewood Cliffs, N.J.: Prentice-Hall, 1974.

Klawans, Stuart. "Thelma & Louise." *The Nation*, 24 June 1991, 862-63.

————. "Unforgiven." *The Nation*, 14 September 1992, 258-60.

Kolodny, Annette. *The Land Before Her: Fantasy and Experience of the American Frontiers, 1630-1860*. Chapel Hill: Univ. of North Carolina Press, 1984.

Larson, Charles R. *American Indian Fiction*. Albuquerque: Univ. of New Mexico Press, 1978.

Leerhsen, Charles. *Newsweek*, 10 August 1992, 52.

Lejeune, Anthony. "The Rise and Fall of the Western." *National Review*, 31 December 1989, 23-26.

Lenihan, John H. *Showdown: Confronting Modern America in the Western Film*. Urbana: Univ. of Illinois Press, 1980.

Leo, John. "Toxic Feminism on the Big Screen." *U.S. News & World Report*, 10 June 1991, 20.

Lewis, David Rich. "Still Native: The Significance of Native Americans in the History of the Twentieth-Century American West." *The Western Historical Quarterly* 24 (May 1993): 203-27.

Lewis, Sinclair. *It Can't Happen Here*. Garden City, N.Y.: Doubleday, Doran, and Company, 1936.

Lewis, Sinclair and Dore Schary. *Storm in the West*. New York: Stein and Day, 1963.

Libman, Norma. "New Breed of Detective: V.I. Warshawski is tough, funny, feisty." *Chicago Tribune*, 11 August 1991, sec. 6, 12.

Maio, Kathi. "Women Who Murder for the Man." *Ms.*, November/December 1991, 82-84.

Manchel, Frank. *Film Study: An Analytical Bibliography*. Vol. 1. London: Associated University Presses, 1990.

Mast, Gerald. *A Short History of the Movies*, 4th ed. New York: Macmillan, 1986.

McBride, Joseph and Michael Wilmington. *John Ford*. London: Secker & Warburg, 1974.

McCarthy, Cormac. *All the Pretty Horses*. New York: Vintage International, 1992.

McCunn, Ruthanne Lum. *Thousand Pieces of Gold: A Biographical Novel*. San Francisco: Design Enterprises of San Francisco, 1981.

McMurtry, Larry. *Horseman, Pass By*. 1961. Reprint, College Station: Texas A & M Univ. Press, 1985.

————. *The Last Picture Show*. 1966. Reprint, New York: Simon and Schuster, 1989.

McNamee, Gregory. "Scarlet 'A' on a Field of Black." In *Resist Much, Obey Little: Some Notes On Edward Abbey*, eds. James Hepworth and Gregory McNamee. Salt Lake City: Dream Garden Press, 1985.

Meldrum, Barbara, ed. *Under the Sun: Myth and Realism in Western American Literature*. Troy, N.Y.: Whitson Publishing Company, 1985.

Milton, John R. *The Novel of the American West*. Lincoln: Univ. of Nebraska Press, 1980.

Momaday, N. Scott. *House Made of Dawn*. New York: Harper & Row, 1968.

Morrison, Gail Moore. "All The Pretty Horses: John Grady Cole's Expulsion from Paradise." In *Perspectives on Cormac McCarthy*, eds. Edwin T. Arnold and Dianne C. Luce. Jackson: Univ. Press of Mississippi, 1993.

Nachbar, Jack et al. *Western Films 2: An Annotated Critical Bibliography from 1974 to 1987*. New York: Garland Publishing, 1988.

Nadeau, Robert. *Readings from the New Book on Nature: Physics and Metaphysics in the Modern Novel*. Amherst: Univ. of Massachusetts Press, 1981.

O'Brien, Geoffrey. "Killing Time." *The New York Review of Books*, 5 March 1992, 38-42.

O'Connor, John E. *The Hollywood Indian*. Trenton: New Jersey State Museum, 1980.

Piekarski, Vicki, ed. *Westward the Women: An Anthology of Western Stories by Women*. Garden City, N.Y.: Doubleday, 1984.

Pitts, Michael R. *Western Movies: A TV and Video Guide to 4200 Genre Films*. Jefferson, N. C.: McFarland & Company, 1986.

Portis, Charles. *True Grit*. New York: Simon and Schuster, 1968.

"Pravda Finds 'Little Big Man' Exposes 'Crimes of Capitalism.'" *New York Times*, 24 July 1971, sec. 14, 1. In *The New York Times Film Reviews 1971-1972*. New York: New York Times Press, 1973, 106.

Rafferty, Terrence. "Artist of Death." *The New Yorker*, 6 March 1995, 127-29.

————. "Outlaw Princesses." *The New Yorker*, 3 June 1991, 86-87.

Reed, Ishmael. *Yellow Black Radio Broke-Down*. Garden City, N.Y.: Doubleday, 1969.

"Riding into the Sunrise." *The Economist*, 16 July 1994, 79-80.

Robbins, Tom. *Even Cowgirls Get the Blues*. New York: Bantam, 1976.

Robinson, David. *The History of World Cinema*. New York: Stein and Day, 1973.

Robinson, Forrest G. *Having It Both Ways: Self-Subversion in Western Popular Classics*. Albuquerque: Univ. of New Mexico Press, 1993.

Sandoz, Mari. *Cheyenne Autumn*. New York: McGraw Hill, 1953.

————. *Miss Morissa: Doctor of the Gold Trail*. New York: Hastings House, 1955.

Scarberry-Garcia, Susan. *Landmarks of Healing: A Study of* House Made of Dawn. Albuquerque: Univ. of New Mexico Press, 1990.

Schackel, Sandra Kay. "Women in Western Films: The Civilizer, the Saloon Singer, and Their Modern Sister." In *Shooting Stars: Heroes and Heroines of Western Film,* ed. Archie P. McDonald. Bloomington: Indiana Univ. Press, 1987.

Schaefer, Jack. *Shane*. Boston: Houghton Mifflin Company, 1949.

Schickel, Richard. "Gender Bender." *Time*, 24 June 1991, 52-56.

Schorer, Mark. *Sinclair Lewis: An American Life*. New York: McGraw Hill, 1961.

Seelye, John. *The Kid*. New York: Viking Press, 1972.

Shapiro, Laura, et al. "Women Who Kill Too Much: Is 'Thelma & Louise' Feminism, or Fascism?" *Newsweek*, 17 June 1991, 63.

Showalter, Dennis E. "Blazing a New Trail: The New 'Old West' Books Are Attracting a Wider Readership with Historically Accurate Plots Featuring Women and Ethnic Groups." *Publishers Weekly*, 11 January 1993, 37, 40-42.

Slater, Joyce R. "Heart of the West." *Minneapolis Star Tribune*, May 1995, Books & Games section, 7.

Slotkin, Richard. *Gunfighter Nation: The Myth of the Frontier in Twentieth-Century America*. New York: Atheneum, 1992; paperback ed. New York: HarperPerennial, 1993.

————. "Gunsmoke and Mirrors." *Life*, 15 April 1993, 60-68.

————. *Regeneration Through Violence: The Mythology of the American Frontier, 1600-1860*. Middeltown, Conn.: Wesleyan Univ. Press, 1973.

Smith, H. Allen. *The Return of the Virginian*. Garden City, N.Y.: Doubleday, 1974.

Smith, Henry Nash. *Virgin Land: The American West as Symbol and Myth*. 1950. Reprint, Cambridge: Harvard Univ. Press, 1978.

Solomon, Stanley J. *Beyond Formula: American Film Genres*. San Diego: Harcourt, Brace, Jovanovich, 1976.

Sragow, Michael. "Outlaws." *The New Yorker*, 10 August 1992, 70-71.

Stedman, Raymond Williams. *Shadows of the Indians: Stereotypes in American Culture*. Norman: Univ. of Oklahoma Press, 1982.

Stegner, Wallace. *The Big Rock Candy Mountain*. 1943. Reprint, Lincoln: Univ. of Nebraska Press, 1983.

Storm, Hyemeyohsts. *Seven Arrows*. New York: Harper & Row, 1972.

Strickler, Jeff. "Why Are Westerns Popular?" *Minneapolis Star Tribune*, 4 September 1994, 5F.

Swarthout, Glendon. *The Shootist*. Reprint 1986. New York: Doubleday, 1975. Pap. ed. Signet, 1986.

Tompkins, Jane. *West of Everything: The Inner Life of Westerns*. New York: Oxford Univ. Press, 1992.

Travers, Peter. "New Jack Cowboys." *Rolling Stone*, 10 June 1993, 73-74.

———. "'Posse' Leader Mario Van Peebles Shoots from the Lip." *Rolling Stone*, 10 June 1993, 76.

Tuska, Jon. *The American West in Film: Critical Approaches to the Western*. Lincoln: Univ. of Nebraska Press, 1985.

———. *The Filming of the West*. Garden City: Doubleday, 1976.

Voss, George L. *The Man who Believed in the Code of the West*. New York: St. Martin's, 1975.

Ward, Robert. *Cattle Annie and Little Britches*. New York: William Morrow and Company, 1978.

Waugh, Patricia. *Metafiction: The Theory and Practice of Self-Conscious Fiction*. London: Routledge, 1984.

Welch, James. *Fools Crow*. New York: Viking Penguin, 1986.

———. *Killing Custer: The Battle of the Little Bighorn and the Fate of the Plains Indians*. New York: W. W. Norton, 1994.

Westbrook, Max. "The Night John Wayne Danced With Shirley Temple." In *Old West-New West: Centennial Essays*, ed. Barbara Howard Meldrum. Moscow: Univ. of Idaho Press, 1993.

"Westerns Harness New Audiences." *Library Journal*, 15 February 1994, 124.

White, Richard. "Frederick Jackson Turner and Buffalo Bill." In *The Frontier in American Culture*, ed. James R. Grossman. Berkeley: Univ. of California Press, 1994.

————. *"It's Your Misfortune and None of My Own": A History of the American West*. Norman: Univ. of Oklahoma Press, 1991.

Wild, Peter. "Into the Heart's Wild Places." *Sierra*, May/June 1989, 100-01.

The Wild West. New York: Time-Life Books, 1993.

Williamson, Penelope. *Heart of the West*. New York: Simon and Schuster, 1995.

Woodward, Richard B. "Cormac McCarthy's Venomous Fiction." *The New York Times Magazine,* 19 April 1992, 28-31, 36, 40.

Wright, Will. *Six Guns and Society: A Structural Study of the Western*. Berkeley: Univ. of California Press, 1975.

Yates, Norris. *Gender and Genre: An Introduction to Women Writers of Formula Westerns, 1900-1950*. Albuquerque: Univ. of New Mexico Press, 1995.

Zoglin, Richard. "Back from Boot Hill." *Time*, 15 November 1993, 90-93.

Films

100 Rifles. Dir. Tom Gries. Written by Clair Huffaker and Tom Gries. Starring Jim Brown, Raquel Welch, and Burt Reynolds. Fox, 1968.

A Fistful of Dollars. Dir. Sergio Leone. Written by Sergio Leone, Duccio Tessari, Victor A. Catena, and Jaime Comas. Starring Clint Eastwood, Marianne Koch, and John Wells. United Artists, 1967.

A Man Called Horse. Dir. Elliot Silverstein. Written by Jack DeWitt. Starring Richard Harris, Dame Judith Anderson, and Jean Gascon. National General, 1970.

Apache. Dir. Robert Aldrich. Written by James R. Webb. Starring Burt Lancaster and Jean Peters. United Artists, 1954.

Bad Day at Black Rock. Dir. John Sturges. Written by Millard Kaufman and Don McGuire. Starring Spencer Tracy, Robert Ryan, and Walter Brennan. MGM, 1954.

Bad Girls. Dir. Jonathan Kaplan. Written by Ken Friedman and Yolande Finch. Starring Madeleine Stowe, Mary Stuart Masterson, and Andie MacDowell. Twentieth Century Fox, 1994.

Big Jake. Dir. George Sherman. Written by Harry Julian Fink and R. M. Fink. Starring John Wayne, Richard Boone, and Maureen O'Hara. National General, 1971.

Billy Jack. Dir. T. C. Frank, (pseud. Tom Laughlin). Written by Frank Christina and Teresa Christina. Starring Tom Laughlin and Delores Taylor. Warner Bros., 1971.

Blazing Saddles. Dir. Mel Brooks. Written by Mel Brooks, Norman Steinberg, Andrew Bergman, Richard Pryor, and Alan Unger. Starring Cleavon Little, Gene Wilder, Madeleine Kahn, and Slim Pickens. Warner Bros., 1974.

Boss Nigger. Dir. Jack Arnold. Written by Fred Williamson. Starring Fred Williamson, D'Urville Martin, and William Smith. Dimension Productions, 1974.

Broken Arrow. Dir. Delmer Daves. Written by Michael Blankfort. Starring James Stewart, Jeff Chandler, and Debra Paget. Twentieth Century Fox, 1950.

Buck and the Preacher. Dir. Sidney Poitier. Written by Ernest Kinoy. Starring Sidney Poitier, Harry Belafonte, and Ruby Dee. Columbia, 1972.

Cat Ballou. Dir. Elliot Silverstein. Written by Walter Newman and Frank R. Pierson. Starring Lee Marvin and Jane Fonda. Harold Hecht, 1965.

Cheyenne Autumn. Dir. John Ford. Written by Joseph R. Webb. Starring Richard Widmark, Carroll Baker, Dolores Del Rio, and Ricardo Montalban. Warner Bros., 1964.

City Slickers. Dir. Ron Underwood. Written by Lowell Ganz and Babaloo Mandel. Starring Billy Crystal, Daniel Stern, Bruno Kirby, and Jack Palance. Castle Rock, 1991.

Dances With Wolves. Dir. Kevin Costner. Written by Michael Blake. Starring Kevin Costner, Mary McDonnell, Graham Greene, and Rodney A. Grant. Orion, 1990.

Destry Rides Again. Dir. George Marshall. Written by Felix Jackson, Gertrude Purcell, and Harry Myers. Starring Marlene Dietrich and James Stewart. Universal, 1939.

Doc. Dir. Frank Perry. Written by Pete Hamill. Starring Harris Yulin and Stacy Keach. United Artists, 1971.

Duel at Diablo. Dir. Ralph Nelson. Written by Marvin H. Albert and Michel M. Grilikhes. Starring Sidney Poitier, James Garner, and Bibi Andersson. United Artists, 1966.

Fort Apache. Dir. John Ford. Written by Frank S. Nugent. Starring John Wayne, Henry Fonda, and Shirley Temple. RKO, 1948.

Geronimo: An American Legend. Dir. Walter Hill. Written by John Milius and Larry Gross. Starring Wes Studi, Jason Patric, Gene Hackman, and Robert Duvall. Columbia, 1993.

Giant. Dir. George Stevens. Written by Fred Guiol and Ivan Moffat. Starring Elizabeth Taylor, Rock Hudson, and James Dean. Warner Bros., 1956.

The Gunfighter. Dir. Henry King. Written by William Bowers, William Sellers. Starring Gregory Peck and Helen Westcott. Twentieth Century Fox, 1950.

Heartland. Dir. Richard Pearce. Written by Beth Ferris. Starring Conchata Ferrell and Rip Torn. Wilderness Women / Filmhaus, 1979.

High Noon. Dir. Fred Zinnemann. Written by Carl Foreman. Starring Gary Cooper and Grace Kelly. United Artists, 1952.

High Plains Drifter. Dir. Clint Eastwood. Written by Ernest Tidyman. Starring Clint Eastwood, Verna Bloom, and Marianna Hill. Universal, 1972.

Hour of the Gun. Dir. John Sturges. Written by Edward Anhalt. Starring James Garner, Jason Robards Jr., and Robert Ryan. United Artists, 1967.

Hud. Dir. Martin Ritt. Written by Irving Ravetch and Harriet Frank, Jr. Starring Paul Newman, Melvyn Douglas, and Patricia Neal. Paramount, 1962.

Invitation to a Gunfighter. Dir. Richard Wilson. Written by Elizabeth Wilson and Richard Wilson. Starring Yul Brynner, Janice Rule, and George Segal. United Artists, 1964.

Jeremiah Johnson. Dir. Sidney Pollack. Written by John Milius and Edward Anhalt. Starring Robert Redford, Will Geer, and Stefan Gierasch. Warner Bros., 1972.

Jesse James. Dir. Henry King. Written by Nunnally Johnson. Starring Tyrone Power, Henry Fonda, and Nancy Kelly. Fox, 1939.

Johnny Guitar. Dir. Nicholas Ray. Written by Philip Yordan. Starring Joan Crawford, Mercedes McCambridge, and Sterling Hayden. Republic, 1953.

Little Big Man. Dir. Arthur Penn. Written by Calder Willingham. Starring Dustin Hoffman, Faye Dunaway, and Martin Balsam. National General, 1971.

Little Moon and Jud McGraw. Dir. Bernard Girard. Screenwriter unknown. Starring Sammy Davis, Jr. and James Caan. American National, uncertain.

Lonely Are the Brave. Dir. David Miller. Written by Dalton Trumbo. Starring Kirk Douglas, Gena Rowlands, and Walter Matthau. Universal-International, 1962.

Man and Boy. Dir. E. W. Swackhamer. Written by Harry Essex and Oscar Saul. Starring Bill Cosby, Gloria Foster, and Leif Erickson. Levitt-Pickman, 1971.

McCabe and Mrs. Miller. Dir. Robert Altman. Written by Robert Altman and Brian McKay. Starring Warren Beatty and Julie Christie. Warner Bros., 1971.

Midnight Cowboy. Dir. John Schlesinger. Written by Waldo Salt. Starring Dustin Hoffman and Jon Voight. United Artists, 1969.

My Darling Clementine. Dir. John Ford. Written by Samuel G. Engel. Starring Henry Fonda, Linda Darnell, and Victor Mature. Fox, 1946.

Posse. Dir. Mario Van Peebles. Written by Sy Richardson and Dario Scardapane. Starring Mario Van Peebles, Billy Zane, and Blair Underwood. Polygram, 1993.

Red River. Dir. Howard Hawks. Written by Borden Chase and Charles Schnee. Starring John Wayne and Montgomery Clift. United Artists. 1948.

Rio Bravo. Dir. Howard Hawks. Written by Leigh Brackett and Jules Furthman. Starring John Wayne and Dean Martin. Warner Bros., 1959.

Rio Grande. Dir. John Ford. Written by James Kevin McGuinness. Starring John Wayne, Maureen O'Hara, and Ben Johnson. Republic, 1950.

Sergeant Rutledge. Dir. John Ford. Written by James Warner Bellah and Willis Goldbeck. Starring Jeffrey Hunter and Woody Strode. Warner Bros., 1960.

Shane. Dir. George Stevens. Written by A. B. Guthrie, Jr. and Jack Sher. Starring Alan Ladd, Jean Arthur, and Van Heflin. Paramount, 1953.

She Wore a Yellow Ribbon. Dir. John Ford. Written by Frank S. Nugent and Laurence Stallings. Starring John Wayne, Joanne Dru, and John Agar. RKO, 1949.

Silent Tongue. Dir. Sam Shepard. Written by Sam Shepard. Starring Richard Harris, River Phoenix, and Alan Bates. Le Studio Canal +, 1992.

Silver Lode. Dir. Allan Dwan. Written by Karen DeWolf. Starring John Payne and Dan Duryea. RKO, 1954.

Soldier Blue. Dir. Ralph Nelson. Written by John Gay. Starring Candice Bergen, Peter Strauss, and Donald Pleasance. Avco Embassy, 1970.

Stagecoach. Dir. John Ford. Written by Dudley Nichols. Starring John Wayne, Claire Trevor, Thomas Mitchell, and Andy Devine. United Artists, 1939.

Tell Them Willie Boy Is Here. Dir. Abraham Polonsky. Written by Abraham Polonsky. Starring Robert Redford, Katherine Ross, and Robert Blake. Universal, 1970.

The Ballad of Gregorio Cortez. Dir. Robert M. Young. Written by Victor Villasenor. Starring Edward James Olmos, James Gammon, and Tom Bower. Embassy Pictures, 1982.

The Ballad of Little Jo. Dir. Maggie Greenwald. Written by Maggie Greenwald. Starring Suzy Amis, Bo Hopkins, Ian McKellan, and David Chung. Fine Line Features, 1993.

The Cheyenne Social Club. Dir. Gene Kelly. Written by James Lee Barrett. Starring James Stewart, Henry Fonda and Shirley Jones. National General, 1970.

The Furies. Dir. Anthony Mann. Written by Charles Schnee. Starring Barbara Stanwyck and Walter Huston. Paramount, 1950.

The Good, the Bad and the Ugly. Dir. Sergio Leone. Written by Age Scarpelli, Luciano Vincenzoni, and Sergio Leone. Starring Clint Eastwood, Eli Wallach, and Lee Van Cleef. United Artists, 1968.

The Great Man's Lady. Dir. Willian A. Wellman. Written by W. L. River. Starring Barbara Stanwyck, Joel McCrea, and Brian Donleavy. Paramount, 1942.

The Last Picture Show. Dir. Peter Bogdanovich. Written by Larry McMurtry and Peter Bogdanovich. Starring Timothy Bottoms, Jeff Bridges, and Cybil Shepard. Columbia, 1971.

The Legend of Nigger Charley. Dir. Martin Goldman. Written by Martin Goldman and Larry G. Spangler. Starring Fred Williamson, D'Urville Martin, and Don Pedro Colley. Paramount, 1972.

The Magnificent Seven. Dir. John Sturges. Written by William Roberts. Starring Yul Brynner, Eli Wallach, and Steve McQueen. MGM, 1960.

The Man Who Shot Liberty Valance. Dir. John Ford. Written by James Warner Bellah and Willis Goldbeck. Starring John Wayne, James Stewart, and Vera Miles. Paramount, 1962.

The Misfits. Dir. John Huston. Written by Arthur Miller. Starring Clark Gable, Marilyn Monroe, and Montgomery Clift. United Artists/ Seven Arts Productions, 1961.

The Missouri Breaks. Dir. Arthur Penn. Written by Thomas McGuane. Starring Marlon Brando, Jack Nicholson, and Kathleen Lloyd. United Artists, 1976.

The Outlaw Josey Wales. Dir. Clint Eastwood. Written by Phil Kaufman and Sonia Chernus. Starring Clint Eastwood, Chief Dan George, and Sondra Locke. Warner Bros., 1976.

The Ox-Bow Incident. Dir. William A. Wellman. Written by Lamar Trotti. Starring Henry Fonda, Dana Andrews, and Anthony Quinn. Twentieth Century Fox, 1943.

The Scalphunters. Dir. Sidney Pollack. Written by William Norton. Starring Burt Lancaster, Shelley Winters, and Ossie Davis. United Artists, 1968.

The Searchers. Dir. John Ford. Written by Frank S. Nugent. Starring John Wayne, Jeffrey Hunter, and Natalie Wood. Warner Bro., 1956.

The Shootist. Dir. Don Siegel. Written by Miles Hood Swarthout and Scott Hale. Starring John Wayne, Lauren Bacall, Ron Howard, and James Stewart. Paramount, 1976.

The Wild Bunch. Dir. Sam Peckinpah. Written by Walton Green and Sam Peckinpah. Starring William Holden, Ernest Borgnine, and Robert Ryan. Warner Bros., 1969.

Thelma & Louise. Dir. Ridley Scott. Written by Callie Khouri. Starring Susan Sarandon, Geena Davis, and Harvey Keitel. MGM, 1991.

These Thousand Hills. Dir. Richard Fleischer. Written by Alfred Hayes. Starring Don Murray, Richard Eagan, and Lee Remick. Twentieth Century Fox, 1959.

Thousand Pieces of Gold. Dir. Nancy Kelly. Written by Anne Makepeace. Starring Rosalind Chao, Dennis Dun, Chris Cooper, and Michael Paul Chan. Greycat, 1991.

Tombstone. Dir. George P. Cosmatos. Written by Kevin Jarre. Starring Kurt Russell, Val Kilmer, Sam Elliott, and Dana Delany. Buena Vista Pictures, 1993.

True Grit. Dir. Henry Hathaway. Written by Marguerite Roberts. Starring John Wayne, Glen Campbell, and Kim Darby. Paramount, 1969.

Ulzana's Raid. Dir. Robert Aldrich. Written by Alan Sharp. Starring Burt Lancaster, Bruce Davison, and Richard Jaeckel. Universal, 1972.

Unforgiven. Dir. Clint Eastwood. Written by David Webb Peoples. Starring Clint Eastwood, Gene Hackman, and Morgan Freeman. Warner Bros., 1992.

Valdez Is Coming. Dir. Edwin Sherin. Written by Roland Kibbee and David Rayfield. Starring Burt Lancaster. United Artists, 1971.

Wyatt Earp. Dir. Lawrence Kasdan. Written by Dan Gordon and Lawrence Kasdan. Starring Kevin Costner, Dennis Quaid, and Gene Hackman. Warner Bros., 1994.

Young Guns. Dir. Christopher Cain. Written by John Fusco. Starring Emilio Estevez, Kiefer Sutherland, and Lou Diamond Phillips. Twentieth Century Fox, 1988.

Young Guns II. Dir. Geoff Murphy. Written by John Fusco. Starring Emilio Estevez, Kiefer Sutherland, and Lou Diamond Phillips. Twentieth Century Fox, 1990.

Television Programs

Hondo. Produced by Andrew J. Fenady. Starring Ralph Taeger. ABC, 1967.

Maverick. Created by Roy Huggins. Starring James Garner and Jack Kelly. Warner Brothers Television, 1957-62.

Kung Fu. Created by Richard Rawlings. Starring David Carradine. Warner Brothers Television, 1972-5.

Novels and Non-fiction Books Adapted into Films

Abbey, Edward. *The Brave Cowboy: An Old Tale in a New Time*. (1956. Reprint, Albuquerque: Univ. of New Mexico Press, 1977). *Lonely Are the Brave*.

Albert, Marvin H. *Apache Rising*. (New York: Fawcett, 1957). *Duel at Diablo*.

Arnold, Elliott. *Blood Brother*. (New York: Duell, Sloan and Pearce, 1950). *Broken Arrow*.

Berger, Thomas. *Little Big Man*. (New York: Dial Press, 1964). *Little Big Man*.

Blake, Michael. *Dances with Wolves*. (New York: Fawcett Gold Medal, 1988). *Dances with Wolves*.

Brand, Max. *Destry Rides Again*. (1930. Reprint, Boston: Gregg Press, 1979). *Destry Rides Again*.

Busch, Niven. *The Furies*. (New York: Dial Press, 1948). *The Furies*.

Carter, Forrest. *The Rebel Outlaw, Josey Wales*. (Gantt, Alabama: Whipporwill, 1973) or *Gone to Texas*. (New York: Delacorte Press, 1975). *The Outlaw Josey Wales*.

Chanslor, Roy. *The Ballad of Cat Ballou*. (Boston: Little Brown, 1956). *Cat Ballou*.

————. *Johnny Guitar*. (New York: Simon and Schuster, 1953). *Johnny Guitar*.

Chase, Borden. *Blazing Guns on the Chisholm Trail*. (New York: Random House, 1948). *Red River*.

Clark, Walter Van Tilburg. *The Ox-Bow Incident*. (New York: Signet Classics, 1940). *The Ox-Bow Incident*.

Ferber, Edna. *Giant*. (Garden City, N.Y.: Doubleday, 1952). *Giant*.

Fisher, Vardis. *Mountain Man: A Novel of Male and Female in the Early American West*. (New York: Morrow, 1965); Thorp, Raymond W. and Robert Bunker. *Crow Killer: The Saga of Liver-Eating Johnson*. [non-fiction] (Bloomington: Indiana Univ. Press, 1958). *Jeremiah Johnson*.

Guthrie, A.B., Jr. *These Thousand Hills*. (Boston: Houghton Mifflin, 1956). *These Thousand Hills*.

Herlihy, James Leo. *Midnight Cowboy*. (New York: Simon and Schuster, 1965). *Midnight Cowboy*.

Lake, Stuart N. *Wyatt Earp, Frontier Marshal*. [non-fiction] (1931. Reprint, New York: Pocket Books, 1994). *My Darling Clementine*.

Lawton, Harry W. *Willie Boy, a Desert Manhunt*. [non-fiction] (Balboa Island, Calif.: Paisano Press, 1960). *Tell Them Willie Boy Is Here*.

Le May, Alan. *The Searchers*. (New York: Harper and Brothers Publishers, 1954). *The Searchers*.

McCunn, Ruthanne Lum. *Thousand Pieces of Gold: A Biographical Novel*. (San Francisco: Design Enterprises of San Francisco, 1981). *Thousand Pieces of Gold*.

McMurtry, Larry. *Horseman, Pass By*. (1961. Reprint, College Station: Texas A&M Univ. Press, 1985). *Hud*.

————. *The Last Picture Show*. (1966. Reprint, New York: Simon and Schuster, 1989). *The Last Picture Show*.

Naughton, Edmund. *McCabe*. (New York: Macmillan, 1959). *McCabe and Mrs. Miller*.

Olsen, Theodore V. *Arrow in the Sun*. (New York: Doubleday, 1969). *Soldier Blue*.

Portis, Charles. *True Grit*. (New York: Simon and Schuster, 1968). *True Grit*.

Sandoz, Mari. *Cheyenne Autumn*. [non-fiction] (New York: McGraw Hill, 1953). *Cheyenne Autumn*.

Schaefer, Jack. *Shane*. (Boston: Houghton Mifflin, 1949). *Shane*.

Swarthout, Glendon. *The Shootist*. (New York: Doubleday, 1975). *The Shootist*.

Wellman, Paul I. *Broncho Apache*. (New York: Macmillan, 1936). *Apache*.

INDEX